What Was Jesus
Hoping to Achieve?

What Was Jesus
Hoping to Achieve?

ROGER AMOS

Foreword by Stephen I. Wright

WIPF & STOCK · Eugene, Oregon

WHAT WAS JESUS HOPING TO ACHIEVE?

Wipf & Stock
An Imprint of Wipf and Stock Publishers
199 W. 8th Ave., Suite 3
Eugene, OR 97401

www.wipfandstock.com

PAPERBACK ISBN: 978-1-6667-3437-9
HARDCOVER ISBN: 978-1-6667-9015-3
EBOOK ISBN: 978-1-6667-9016-0

DECEMBER 20, 2021 2:29 PM

History is reconstruction through hypothesis and verification
BEN F. MEYER (*AIMS*, 19)

CONTENTS

Foreword

Since the investigations of Hermann Samuel Reimarus in the eighteenth century, questions about the historical background and motivations of Jesus of Nazareth have never been far from the surface in the world of scholarship. In his posthumously published work, Reimarus voiced the suspicion that the Gospel records of Jesus' life were in essence a cover-up, masking the historical reality of a failed Messianic takeover through rewriting the history of Jesus in the terms of later theology. The Jesus who, in Reimarus's view, had mounted a *coup d'état* which ended in disaster had become the Jesus who died to atone for the sins of the world.

Subsequent historians have occupied a range of positions on this question, from Reimarus's radical scepticism at one end to an acceptance of the Gospel records as essentially veracious, within the canons of the historiography of the time, at the other. Those who approach the matter from a Christian standpoint have been required to wrestle with the question of whether and how the Gospels' witness to theological truth is dependent on, or at least connected to, their witness to historical events. Once the era of modern historical enquiry had opened over two centuries ago, there was no escaping this question. The Gospels need to be seen as evidence to be weighed as well as testimony to be received.

In this book Roger Amos offers a clear, thoughtful and well-researched contribution to the debate. Fundamental to his approach, as to that of many others today, is the conviction that Jesus must be located within the Judaism of his era. Also in common with others, Amos draws on important contemporary studies of the social, economic and political conditions of the Galilee in which Jesus grew up. He advances a case for Jesus' initially being a social activist, motivated by concern for the hardships and injustices being suffered by his fellow-Galileans.

Of particular interest to readers will be Amos's research on the background of John the Baptizer and the influence exercised by John on Jesus. Whereas much study of the historical Jesus has understandably focused on the evidence for his public ministry and the events leading up to his death, Amos invites us to consider what circumstances and events may have propelled Jesus to prominence in the first place. The significance of Jesus growing up as a carpenter's son plays a part in this story.

This leads on to a useful summary of the distinctive elements of Jesus' earthly ministry: what exactly set his activity and teaching apart from others within contemporary Judaism? There follows a reconstruction of the sequence of events within this ministry, proposing historical reasons for the hostility of the Jewish establishment, which started early and grew steadily worse, in turn affecting Jesus' aims and tactics. From hoping to reform institutional Judaism as a whole, Jesus turned to those traditionally excluded from it.

The book deliberately focuses on the historical questions rather than the theological ones. Amos takes a trusting but also questioning attitude to the Gospels' witness, probing behind the texts to imagine the unwritten phenomena behind them. There is ample justification for this focus, as stated in the epilogue: "it is surely the epic growth of the global community worshipping the transcendent Christ that inspires researchers to discover more of the historical person who founded it." Amos shows that this approach is not inimical to our reception of the Gospels as theological testimony to the nature of Jesus, but enriching of it.

With its appendices summarizing the contributions of key figures in the "quest of the historical Jesus," and criteria used in that quest, this book forms a very helpful introduction for those who may not have encountered the debate before, as well as plenty of fresh insights and suggestions for those who have.

Stephen I. Wright
Spurgeon's College, London
October 2021

PREFACE

One Question Leads to Another

"WHAT WAS JESUS HOPING TO achieve?" is the latest in a series of questions that has occupied my attention in recent years. The first was "Who were the 'sinners' who figure so prominently in Jesus' ministry as recorded in the gospels?" That question led me to undertake the excellent MA course in Aspects of Biblical Interpretation (by Distance Learning) from the London School of Theology. Research for my MA thesis on that topic raised the next question: "Was Jesus a Pharisee?" The findings of my privately conducted research into that question were published in 2015 as the monograph *Hypocrites or Heroes? The Paradoxical Portrayal of the Pharisees in the New Testament.*

The latest question arose during the writing of that monograph: I noticed that at times in his ministry Jesus appears to have been on friendly terms with the Pharisees, while at other times they were at loggerheads. This inconsistency sparked a desire to investigate the underlying purpose of his ministry—"What was Jesus hoping to achieve?"—and, in particular, the extent to which John the Baptist was involved in the formulation of that purpose. After my experiences as an independent researcher, however, I was determined that this time I should have proper access to academic resources, such as a well stocked library, the latest scholarly journals, and, not least, the guidance of one or more learned supervisors. The outcome was a PhD project, conducted at Spurgeon's College, London, where I had trained for the Baptist ministry fifty years previously, and the University of Chester, giving me access to the extensive resources of both institutions.

After three years of research my thesis was largely finished: the main arguments were in place and most of what remained to be done was "tidying." At this point the University decided that my subject was too broad for a PhD and urged me to start again with a more tightly defined one. But this happened in April 2020 when the coronavirus pandemic had closed all academic libraries, making it arguably the most inauspicious moment in history in which to begin a new research project. As there was no way in which I could have undertaken the research necessary to create a new thesis before the closing date for submission, I had no option but to withdraw, reluctantly, from the program. My bid for a PhD had failed, but my research had already yielded some interesting findings and I was determined that these should not be filed away and forgotten. What you have before you is essentially that thesis edited into conventional book format.

I acknowledge my heartfelt gratitude to my supervisors at Spurgeon's College, Stephen Wright and Tony Rich, who were always on hand to answer my questions, to point me in the appropriate direction and to guide me back to earth when I took off on my wilder flights of fancy. Stephen has been kind enough to supply the foreword for this book despite his heavy commitments as Vice-Principal. Many other people and institutions have contributed to this project through their encouragement and willingness to comment on ideas. These include Robert Letham of the Union School of Theology in Bridgend, John King, leader of the New Testament Greek group at the Percival Guildhouse in Rugby, whose weekly gatherings provide a valuable sounding board for theological and historical hypotheses, and Alastair Wehbeh, a fellow research student at Chester whose project overlapped with mine inasmuch as both featured John the Baptist; we exchanged ideas on several occasions. Lastly Pat Took, a fellow research student at Spurgeon's College, whom I had met previously while serving in the Baptist ministry; her encouragement fortified me when my research findings challenged my faith.

In a true research project we do not know at the outset what we shall discover; we may have suspicions, but must remain sufficiently open-minded to accept the findings of the research, whether it confirms those suspicions or refutes them. When I began this project, I believed that John the Baptist was the most significant factor shaping Jesus' mission. When my research indicated that the socio-economic circumstances of Galilean Jews provided the initial stimulus for Jesus' ministry and were arguably a more potent factor than the Baptist, I had to make many adjustments. My evangelical background made it uncomfortable for me to accept that Jesus had begun his ministry as what westerners today would regard as a purely political activist; I drew some encouragement from the Jewish lack of distinction between politics and religion. The Baptist now became an advisor rather than a prime mover, although it is surely significant that Jesus shared most of his distinctive features. This project has both broadened and deepened my understanding of Jesus and his mission. I hope that it may do the same for you too.

Roger Amos,
Rugby, England,
October, 2021

ABBREVIATIONS

ABD	Freedman, David Noel (Editor in Chief), *Anchor Bible Dictionary*
BAGD	Arndt, William F. and F. Wilbur Gingrich, *A Greek-English Lexicon of the New Testament and Other Early Christian Literature*
CD	Damascus Document
DSS	Dead Sea Scrolls
KJV	King James Version
LXX	Septuagint
NET	New English Translation Bible
NIV	New International Version
NRSV	New Revised Standard Version
NT	New Testament
OT	Old Testament
RSV	Revised Standard Version

1

INTRODUCTION
What Was Jesus Hoping to Achieve?

ASK MANY CHRISTIANS—including even some ministers—precisely what outcome Jesus was hoping to achieve from his earthly ministry and you are more likely to provoke gasps of astonishment than a considered answer. Even though the matter could be hardly be more central to the Christian faith, it seems that Christians are reluctant to think about it. Perhaps this is out of reverence or fear that the matter is so sacred that dire consequences might devolve upon ordinary mortals who dare to pry into it. Nevertheless, it is the subject of the present study whose intention is surely worthy: a better appreciation of what Jesus was hoping to achieve should illuminate our understanding of the gospel narratives and, ultimately, of what Jesus accomplished on our behalf.

In fact our question is one of four that have been identified as central to the scholarly study of the historical Jesus: (i) What were his aims? (ii) What was his relationship with his contemporaries in Judaism? (iii) Why did he die? And (iv) how can we explain the rapid rise of the early Christian movement? Three scholars who (with some variations of wording and order) have identified these questions as critical issues are E. P. Sanders at the start of his 1985 book *Jesus and Judaism*,[1] N. T. Wright in *Jesus and the Victory of God* (1996),[2] and Helen Bond, whose specialist study of the

---

1. Sanders, *Jesus and Judaism*, 1.
2. Wright, *Victory*, 90f.

development of Jesus research was published in 2012 as *The Historical Jesus: A Guide for the Perplexed*.[3]

While accepting that these questions are inextricably interlinked, this study is concerned principally with the first of them, which was the first in Sanders's and Bond's lists and the second in Wright's, namely that concerning Jesus' aims or purpose. Arguably this is the most important of them because his aims surely determined the nature of his ministry. The primary research question of this study is, "Precisely what outcome was Jesus hoping to achieve from his earthly ministry?" That such a fundamental matter is still being debated nearly 2000 years after his earthly ministry indicates that finding the answer is not straightforward.

In the past scholars attempted to discover Jesus' agenda by analyzing his teaching and actions as recorded in the gospels. Their efforts, however, identified a remarkable diversity of aims. Wright lists some of these as: (i) to die as a sacrifice for the sins of the world; (ii) to liberate Jews from their Roman overlords; (iii) to change individuals, society, the world, or all of these; and (iv) to found the church.[4] It is not altogether surprising that extrapolation from the gospel accounts of his ministry yielded conflicting results, for those accounts contain contradictory elements. For example, sometimes Jesus appears to be attempting to reform Judaism—the Sermon on the Mount is classic reforming material. And sometimes he appears to be inaugurating a new religion—as in his statement to Peter that he is the rock on which he will establish his church (Matt 16:18).

Because of these contradictions, this study will adopt a different approach. It will attempt to deduce Jesus' aims by identifying the factors impacting him that led him to undertake his ministry. It is surely reasonable to assume that Jesus undertook his ministry in response to one or more needs within his society. The rationale is summarized in a secondary research question: "What motivated a thirty-year-old[5] carpenter/builder[6]

---

3. Bond, *Historical*, 21.

4. Wright, *Victory*, 99.

5. According to Luke 3:23, Jesus was "about thirty years old" at the start of his ministry. Luke's language emphasizes approximation, but if Matthew's tradition that the infant Jesus fled persecution by Herod the Great is true, he must have been born before Herod's death in 4 BCE. His crucifixion must have happened between 28 and 32 CE, that being the period of overlap of Pontius Pilate's procuratorship and Caiaphas's high priesthood. So if Jesus' ministry lasted between three and five years, it is indeed plausible that Jesus was "about thirty" at the start of his ministry.

6. According to Mark 6:1–3, the congregation in the synagogue at Nazareth

from an obscure village in Galilee to abandon his trade and become the itinerant preacher, teacher, and healer described in the gospels?" In first-century Jewish society such drastic career changes were most unusual. If we can identify in Jesus' circumstances a stimulus sufficiently acute to lead him to make such a radical change, surely that will provide clues concerning the purpose of the ministry that followed. Answering this question, then, should provide a fresh insight into Jesus' aims. And that insight should enable a clearer understanding of his ministry and mission.

TRIGGERS FOR JESUS' MINISTRY

The secondary research question identified above—"What motivated a thirty-year-old carpenter/builder from an obscure village in Galilee to abandon his trade and become the itinerant preacher, teacher, and healer described in the gospels?"—defines the process by which we shall seek an answer to the first question. While many Christians may be content to state that Jesus' ministry was a response to a divine calling, surely if God is rational his calling is never arbitrary, but issued for practical reasons. If so, Jesus' ministry was intended to satisfy one or more specific needs in his society. An investigation of the circumstances of that society—and especially those aspects of it that needed some kind of improvement—should therefore reveal factors that might have triggered Jesus' ministry; these should be potent clues to its intended purpose.

Jesus' Baptism

Even a cursory search of the gospels for possible trigger events inevitably highlights Jesus' baptism. The evidence that this was a major turning point in his career is that prior to it little is recorded about him, suggesting that until then his life had been unremarkable for a Jew at that time. Soon afterwards, however, his momentous ministry begins. Interestingly, even the most skeptical scholars acknowledge the historicity of the baptism:[7] an

---

recognized Jesus as their former carpenter/builder (*tektōn*). See fn 46 on page 33.

   7. Rudolf Bultmann, for example, does not dispute Mark's account of Jesus' baptism (*Synoptic Tradition*, 247). E. P. Sanders includes Jesus' baptism in his list of "indisputable facts" about Jesus (*Jesus and Judaism*, 11).

episode which caused the early Christian communities such difficulty[8] is unlikely to have been invented.

Nevertheless, the baptism itself cannot have been the trigger of Jesus' career change. As Joan Taylor observes, many people were baptized by John without being led to a mission like that of Jesus, so something else must have led to Jesus' ministry.[9] Indeed, there must have been a prior factor that led Jesus to approach John in the first instance. We need to identify that.

Galilee

Let us take a step backwards and view the wider scene. Despite the above suggestion that prior to his baptism Jesus' life had been "unremarkable for a Jew at that time," the *place* in which Jesus lived subjected him to an auspicious combination of circumstances. Firstly, he lived in Galilee at the height of Herod Antipas's development schemes which caused considerable suffering for many of Galilee's indigenous Jews. Secondly, he lived in Nazareth, a small Jewish village that was predominantly agricultural; it was the agricultural community that was most severely affected by Antipas's land-grabbing tendencies, its members being liable to lose their land or their livelihood, or both. Thirdly, he lived so close to Sepphoris, Galilee's largest city, that he probably acquired some familiarity with its Hellenistic culture. He might even have worked on Antipas's reconstruction of that city; if so, it is likely that he received hostility from his neighbors in Nazareth who would have regarded that as collaboration with Antipas's pro-Roman regime. Fourthly, his closest friends, fishermen from Capernaum, probably faced circumstances similar to his own, prospering from trade with Hellenistic Jews while their neighbors suffered. If they discussed these matters—and it is hard to imagine that they did not—this might have fostered in Jesus and his companions a desire to demonstrate their solidarity with their Jewish community by some kind of action on behalf of its beleaguered members. So Galilee provided Jesus with both a need requiring satisfaction and the encouragement of others to achieve that satisfaction.

---

8. As J. D. Crossan observes, the embarrassment is because John's baptizing Jesus makes John seem superior and Jesus sinful (*Historical Jesus*, 232).

9. Taylor, *John the Baptist*, 268.

Judaism

But perhaps we need to take a further step backwards. Galilee was historically a part of Israel, the Promised Land to which God had led his people,
the Jews, in the Exodus which provides the root metaphor of Judaism. For
the Jews their religion, Judaism, dominated every aspect of life; the present-
day western world's sharp distinction between sacred and secular—a consequence of the Protestant Reformation—would have been unimaginable
for first-century Jews. Since the evidence suggests that Jesus was raised in
a pious home within the Jewish community, Judaism must be included in
any consideration of the forces acting upon him at the start of his ministry.

PROCEDURE

Our quest, then, is to discover the purpose of Jesus' ministry by analyzing
the pressures acting upon him that led him to undertake it. We have already
identified Judaism, Galilee—and especially the socio-economic upheav-
als taking place there—and his baptism by John the Baptist as potential
contributory factors. Chapters 2 and 3 will examine Judaism and Galilee
respectively. Chapter 4 will consider the person and work of John the Baptist and Chapter 5 the impact of John on Jesus' career and, especially, his
teaching. Chapter 6 will attempt to reconstruct Jesus' ministry taking into
account the findings of previous chapters; the aim is to see whether those
findings fit together to form a coherent picture. Chapter 7 will draw conclusions from these findings. Appendices provide additional background
information on the quest for the historical Jesus, criteria of authenticity,
and literature on John the Baptist.

2

Judaism in the First Century

ANY STUDY OF THE FACTORS that led Jesus to undertake his ministry is bound to consider Judaism. The gospels portray Jesus as an observant Jew: they record him teaching in the synagogue on the Sabbath[1] and journeying to Jerusalem for the Passover.[2] They also mention that some Jews regarded him as a prophet.[3]

This chapter examines the characteristics of first-century Judaism and Jewish society that seem most likely to have impacted Jesus. But first it is necessary to define "Judaism." The principal sources are secondary literature, which often refer to the primary literature, generally the NT or the OT.

DEFINING JUDAISM

It is notoriously difficult to define what constituted "normal" or "normative" Judaism in Second Temple times. Apart from the three contrasting "ideologies"—the Essenes, the Sadducees, and the Pharisees—that Josephus compares on three occasions,[4] there were many groups and individuals who, although undeniably Jewish, fell outside those three "ideologies." For example, the "tax collectors and sinners" mentioned frequently in the

---

1. For example, Mark 1:21 etc.; 3:1 etc.; 6:2 etc; John 6:59.
2. For example, Mark 10:32 etc.; John 2:13; 5:1; 11:55–12:12.
3. For example, Matt 21:11, 46; John 6:14; 7:40; 9:17.
4. Josephus, *War* 2:8:2–14; *Antiquities* 13:5:9; 18:1:2–6.

gospels and discussed later in this chapter would have been disowned by members of those "ideologies." Some scholars[5] bracket such "unaffiliated" Jews under the term 'amme ha'arez, the "people of the land," but arguably this designation is confusing as the expression occurs frequently in the OT, where it generally denotes simply "the inhabitants of the land" without any connotations of religious adherence; moreover, most of the OT canon, with the probable exception of Daniel, had been written by the time of the Maccabean Rebellion, during which the three "ideologies" emerged.

E. P. Sanders defines "normal" or "common" Judaism as what the priests and the people agreed on. "Normal" Judaism was to some degree "normative" in that it established a standard by which loyalty to Israel and her God was measured. Jews in general believed that their sacred books were truly Holy Scripture. Throughout the empire Jews gathered on the sabbath to learn God's way. They worshipped him with prayers and offerings; and they observed holy days.[6] Indeed Sanders devotes ten chapters of *Judaism: Practice and Belief* to "common Judaism," that is, those elements that supposedly united all Jews and made Judaism one religion rather than a collection of several. The ten chapters cover the temple, priests and Levites, sacrifices, the common people, festivals, tithes and taxes, worship and Sabbath, purity, food, charity, theology, and future hopes.[7]

Although those elements were theoretically shared by all Jews, Judaism nevertheless exhibited considerable diversity. As Sanders explains, whatever was regarded as "normal" was based on assent and was "normative" only in so far as common opinion has considerable coercive power, but nevertheless allows dissenters to break away.[8] For example, as will be seen later, John the Baptist repudiated the priesthood and set up a process for the remission of sins in competition with the temple cultus, but the populace still recognized him not only as a fellow Jew, but also as a prophet, a genuine messenger from God.

JUDAISM AT THE TIME OF JESUS

Josephus's frequent mentions of the three 'ideologies' suggest that they were an important feature of Jewish society in the first century CE. Emerging

5. Such as Morton Smith in "The Dead Sea Sect," 356.

6. Sanders, *Judaism: Practice and Belief*, 47f.

7. Sanders, *Judaism: Practice and Belief*, 45–314.

8. Sanders, *Judaism: Practice and Belief*, 47.

from the Maccabean Revolt of 167 to 164 BCE, each of these claimed to represent authentic Judaism. The Essenes insisted that the Jewish hierarchy was corrupt and that the holiness and ritual purity demanded by Torah could be achieved only by total separation from worldly society; for this reason they established their communities in isolated locations. In view of this reclusive lifestyle it is hardly surprising that they are not mentioned in the NT. The Pharisees, in contrast, are mentioned frequently.[9] They too emphasized holiness and ritual purity, but believed that this must be maintained whilst participating in mainstream society in order to exert a beneficial influence upon it; this indeed was their mission. They argued for a more liberal interpretation of scripture, their interpretations (the *paradosis* or oral law) retaining the authority of the original. Moreover, they accepted the Prophets and the Writings as authoritative scripture on a par with the Torah, establishing the OT canon still recognized today by most Jews and protestant Christian traditions. The Sadducees, a smaller grouping consisting mainly of high priestly and other aristocratic families, are mentioned occasionally in the NT.[10] They claimed to continue the priestly tradition of pre-Maccabean times.

Of the three, Pharisaism emerged as dominant; Ellis Rivkin claims that the Gospels, Acts, and the Epistles of Paul all reveal the prominence of the Pharisees; the whole culture was so solidly Pharisaic that when Jesus, Paul, and the earliest disciples confronted the Pharisees, they could do so using only tools the Pharisees themselves had devised.[11] Indeed, some scholars insist that Pharisaism was the normative Judaism of NT times.[12] As

9. Not only does the Greek word *Pharisaios* occur 98 times, but it is supplemented by alternative terms such as *grammateus*, "scribe, teacher of the law," (63 times), *nomikos*, "lawyer," (9 times), and *nomodidaskalos*, "teacher of the law" (3 times), all of which are often used synonymously or nearly so with *Pharisaios*. Moreover, in John's Gospel many of the 67 occurrences of *hoi Ioudaioi*, "the Jews," refer in fact to the Pharisees, giving a potential total of 240 mentions. Even though this must be reduced to allow for terms in apposition and some occurrences of *grammateus, nomikos* and *hoi Ioudaioi* that do not refer to the Pharisees, the total number of mentions still exceeds 200 (Amos, *Hypocrites*, 1, 105).

10. *Saddoukaios* occurs 14 times in the NT.

11. Rivkin, *Revolution*, 275.

12. For example, Roland Deines describes Pharisaism as a separate movement *within* the nation *for* the nation, whose legitimacy was indeed *accepted* by large parts of the people, even though its requirements were not *observed* to an equal extent. Pharisaism was normative Judaism because the majority acknowledged it as the legitimate and authentic interpretation of the divine will ("Pharisees," 501). Hyam Maccoby has stated that a new trend asserts the existence of a normative Judaism in the first century, and

Jesus spent most of his life in Galilee, it is unlikely that he had much contact with Sadducees and there is no evidence that he ever encountered Essenes. His teaching, however, reveals that he accepted such Pharisaic norms as the broad canon of scripture,[13] the resurrection of the dead,[14] the future coming of God's judgment upon humanity,[15] and the existence of angels,[16] all these being subsequently accepted by the Christian movement. So, although he and his family might not have called themselves or even thought of themselves as Pharisees,[17] they certainly belonged within the broader Pharisaic tradition. This study accepts not only the dominance of the Pharisees at the time of Jesus, but also that Pharisaism was the "normative" Judaism, the branch of Judaism to which ordinary Jews belonged by default.

Disillusionment with the Jewish Authorities

Although the Essenes openly demonstrated their disaffection with conventional Jewish society, including the Temple cultus, by establishing their communities in the wilderness, there is evidence that disillusionment was widespread, many Jews believing that their hierarchy, especially the upper echelons of the priesthood, was corrupt. The readiness with which the high priests co-operated with the Romans, for example, was widely regarded as treachery—they were prioritizing their own prestige and security over loyalty to Israel and her God. Josephus claims that "the behavior of the Sadducees [to which the principal high priestly families belonged] one towards another is in some degree wild, and their conversation with those that are of their own party is as barbarous as if they were strangers to them" (Josephus, *War*, 2:8:14).

---

identifies this with Pharisaism; he claims that there is plenty of ancient testimony to support this (*Jesus*, 76).

13. For example, he reads Isa 61:1f in Luke 4:17–20 and in Mark 12:35–37 he cites Ps 110.

14. For example, in Mark 12:18–27 he refutes the Saddusaic view that there is no resurrection.

15. In the Q tradition Jesus makes numerous references to the coming judgment, *for example,* Matt 10:15; 11:22, 24; 12:41f; Luke 10:14; 11:31f.

16. For example, Mark 8:38; 12:25; 13:27, 32.

17. In the NT the only person who ever claimed to be a Pharisee is the apostle Paul (Acts 23:6; 26:5; Php 3:5). The term seems mainly to have been used as a (perhaps derogatory) nickname applied by others.

The gospels do not refer to this disillusionment explicitly, but arguably some passages imply it. John the Baptist's administration of "a baptism of repentance for the forgiveness of sins" was, as will be seen, an implicit criticism of the official process for the remission of sins provided by the temple cultus. Jesus' cleansing of the temple and his predictions of its destruction are implicit judgments upon it and, therefore, upon those in charge of it. Matthew's portrayal of the chief priests' treatment of Judas in Matt 27:3f corroborates Josephus' description of them cited above. Other examples are the chief priests' sending of temple police to arrest Jesus not because he had committed any offence, but because of what the crowds were saying about him (John 7:32) and, not least, in their plotting to kill him: "The chief priests and the scribes were looking for a way to arrest Jesus by stealth and kill him" (Mark 14:1). The words "by stealth" (*en dolō*) suggest a fundamental lack of principle.

Although most Jews were surely aware that such attitudes were prevalent amongst the high priests, there was little or no action that they could take to alleviate the situation; Israel was not a democracy and they were effectively powerless. Even the Sanhedrin probably considered itself under threat from all sides: on the one hand was the constant pressure of the Roman yoke—Sanders speaks of the precarious *status quo* with Rome[18]—while on the other was the ever-present desire for insurrection by radical Jews, who besides ousting the Roman presence increasingly sought also the removal of the Jewish hierarchy which had kowtowed to them.

Jewish Society

As mentioned earlier, mainstream Jewish society at the time of Jesus was dominated by the Pharisees. Although Jesus was critical of some aspects of their lifestyle, his sayings acknowledge their popularity with the Jewish populace: "They love to have the place of honor at banquets and the best seats in the synagogues, and to be greeted with respect in the marketplaces, and to have people call them rabbi" (Matt 23:6f). The people's admiration for them was probably for two reasons. Firstly, the Pharisees were ordinary Jews who worked strenuously to improve the lot of the Jews as a whole; in this regard they stood in striking contrast with the Sadducees and, to some extent, the Essenes. Secondly, their system of oral laws did make life easier for scrupulous Jews, especially in regard to Sabbath observance.

18. Sanders, *Jesus and Judaism*, 288.

It may seem remarkable that the NT never refers explicitly to the Pharisaic system of oral law; presumably the writers were so familiar with it that it did not occur to them that some readers might need an explanation. Several passages, however, reflect the influence and the consequences of the *paradosis*. One "Q" passage shows Jesus as concerned that the multifarious oral commandments intended to show Jews how Torah principles applied in specific circumstances conflicted with one another; observance of one law infringed another, so that it became impossible to please God: "They tie up heavy burdens, hard to bear, and lay them on the shoulders of others; but they themselves are unwilling to lift a finger to move them" (Matt 23:4 paralleled in Luke 11:46). Similarly in Peter's speech in Acts 15:10 surely it is the oral law that is described as the "yoke that neither our ancestors nor we have been able to bear" and which Pharisee converts had been trying to impose upon the whole Christian community. Jesus' gracious invitation in Matt 11:28, "Come to me, all you that are weary and are carrying heavy burdens, and I will give you rest," sounds as though it too might have been addressed to Jews who found themselves overwhelmed by the demands of the oral law; R. T. France insists that other interpretations are possible, but his failure to suggest any may leave readers unconvinced.[19] Specific examples of the oral law may underlie the gospel passages in which Pharisees criticize Jesus for dining with tax collectors and "sinners" (Matt 9:11 and parallels) and for allowing his disciples to eat without first washing their hands (Matt 15:1f and parallels); neither action infringed any commandment in the written Torah.

Purity

There is evidence that at the time of Jesus a ritual purity[20] movement was influential in Judaism. For example, the Fourth Gospel's passing mentions of "a discussion about purification" (John 3:25) and of "stone water jars for the Jewish rites of purification, each holding twenty or thirty gallons" (John 2:5) seem to expect readers to be conversant with these. It is also surely significant that in one archaeological excavation in Sepphoris every house

---

19. France, *Matthew*, 448.

20. Cecilia Wassén provides an excellent summary of the principles of purity in "Jewishness," 20–22.

examined was reported to have been equipped with underfloor ritual baths for purity rites.[21]

As James Charlesworth reveals, many Jerusalem priests and Saddu-cees were insistent that all Jews should observe the holiness regulations that at one time applied only to priests. Moreover, these were regarded as bind-ing whether Jews resided in Jerusalem or Galilee.[22] He claims that Herod the Great's massive expansion of the Jerusalem Temple was an expression of this movement.[23] But he is surely overstepping the mark in his claim that the high priests sent officials out from Jerusalem to other regions of Palestine to ensure that all Jews were complying with these new ritual pu-rity regulations.[24] He finds support for this in Mark 7:1, in which scribes who have come to Galilee from Jerusalem reprimand Jesus for allowing his disciples to eat with their hands unwashed (Mark 7:1). Most scholars, however, recognize that Pharisees and scribes rarely visited Galilee[25] and this study will seek to demonstrate that the scribes mentioned in Mark 7:1 had a different reason for their visit to Galilee.[26]

Furthermore, Charlesworth sees ritual purity concerns as underlying the Jewish establishment's persecution of Jesus; the priests were disturbed by Jesus' apparently cavalier treatment of their understanding of purity and his refusal to acknowledge themselves as the only people qualified to in-terpret Torah and purity.[27] It is surely significant that Charlesworth admits that other factors besides purity motivated the priests' actions.

Morten Jensen observes that some scholars regard this ritual purity movement as a form of resistance against the pressure to conform to Ro-man norms, while others regard it as part of a deepening religious fervor, although these two explanations are not mutually exclusive.[28] That Jesus critiqued the movement as distracting Jews from their primary obligations to God (Mark 7:1–23) indicates that he was aware of the movement, but skeptical regarding its value.

---

21. See fn 20 on page 26.
22. Charlesworth, "Temple," 395f.
23. Charlesworth, "Temple," 402–406.
24. Charlesworth, "Temple," 407.
25. See fn 66 on page 42.
26. See *Under Surveillance* on page 123.
27. Charlesworth, "Temple," 408.
28. Jensen, "Purity," 33.

The "Sinners"

Although "sinners" are mentioned frequently[29] in the NT, the precise nuance of the word *hamartōlos*[30] is a subject of debate among scholars. Most insist that it denotes the "wicked," that is, those who in various ways deliberately turned traitor and denied God's covenant with Israel,[31] while others accord a broader meaning to the word. Joachim Jeremias, for example, points out that in the world of Jesus, the term "sinner" was not only a general designation for those who notoriously failed to observe the commandments of God, but also a specific term for those engaged in certain despised trades. These included those thought to lead to immorality and dishonesty, such as gamblers with dice, usurers, tax collectors, publicans and even herdsmen, because it was suspected that they led their herds on to other people's land

29. The 47 occurrences of *hamartōlos* are distributed as follows: 5 in Matthew, 6 in Mark, 18 in Luke, 4 in John, 8 in the Pauline corpus, 2 in Hebrews, 2 in James, 1 in 1 Peter and 1 in Jude.

30. The noun is derived from the verb *hamartanō*, whose primary meanings according to the Liddell and Scott lexicon are "to miss, miss the mark," hence "to fail of doing, fail of one's purpose" and ultimately "fail, do wrong, err, sin." The implication, then, is that "sinners" are not necessarily violent criminals, but people who have failed to achieve some target. Nevertheless Liddell and Scott's definition of *hamartōlos*, originally an adjective, as "sinful, hardened in sin" appears to reflect a tendency to blacken "sinners"—"hardened," in particular, implies deliberate rebellion against accepted standards rather than an unsuccessful attempt to attain them.

31. Sanders devotes a chapter of *Jesus and Judaism* to the sinners and includes in it sections seeking to distinguish the sinners from the wicked, the poor, and the *'amme ha-arets* (176f). Like Keener and France (see below) he identifies the sinners with the *resha'im*, the "wicked." He concludes that while it is easy to understand why "tax collectors" and "sinners" go together frequently in the Gospels—they were all traitors, guilty of collaborating with Rome—the wicked were also guilty of betraying God who redeemed Israel and gave them his law. There was no distinction between "religious" and "political" betrayal in first-century Judaism (*Jesus and Judaism*, 178).

Keener's 1999 commentary on Matthew contains an excursus, "Who Were the 'Sinners'?", surveying Jewish literature from New Testament times, but this leaves the title question largely unanswered. He concentrates on the relationship between "sinners" and the *'am ha'arets*—the "people of the land"—the common people whom the Pharisees despised for failing to observe food laws. Keener regards the term *'am ha'arets* as denoting all Jews who were not members of such sects as the Pharisees or the Essenes. He concludes that the term "sinners" probably specifies deliberate violators of the law (Keener, *Matthew*, 294–296). France's commentary on Matthew agrees broadly with Keener (France, *Matthew*, 353). Davies and Allison in their commentary on Matthew concur, identifying the "sinners" with the *resha'im*, Jews who have abandoned the law (Davies *et al, Matthew*, 1:100). Thus many recent scholars agree that the sinners not only neglected scribal tithing and purity laws, but also were guilty of more serious violations of Torah.

and pilfered the produce of the herd. So when the gospels refer to "sinners," they may denote those in despised trades as well as those whose way of life was disreputable.[32]

On this basis, then, "sinners" included folk who may themselves have been honest and respectable, but whose reputations were tarnished by popular conceptions concerning the trade that they plied. This could explain the "many sinners" who attended Levi's feast (Mark 2:15). How likely is it that even a tax collector would invite "sinners" (as distinct from other tax collectors) if they were the "wicked" types that most scholars suggest? But if Jeremias is correct, they could have been the tradesmen who supplied Levi's household provisions—a tax collector and his family would not have been welcome in the regular markets, so would of necessity have resorted to a trader who was none too scrupulous. Moreover, the purity movement (see above) caused an intensification of Torah's demands—or at least of their interpretation according to the general consensus. This was exacerbated by Roman rule and Hellenisation which placed new pressures upon ordinary Jews to compromise their faith by complying with the comparatively lax standards of the Gentile world. Consequently there were many more ways of becoming a "sinner" than before and ever more Jews were finding themselves assigned to this category.

This picture is supported broadly by the synoptic gospels' accounts of the way in which in Jesus frequently engaged with "sinners"; indeed, they form his principal target during most of his ministry. James Dunn points out that the very fact that the gospel traditions have preserved so many episodes concerning this subject indicates that his ministry to "sinners" must have been an important feature of his mission.[33] For example, Jesus pronounces what appears to be a mission statement: "I have come to call not the righteous but sinners,"[34] Luke appending the words "to repentance," as though an explanation were needed. Sanders, although critical of such declarations of purpose, nevertheless concedes that this saying has apparently "expanded an authentic motif."[35]

The statement presupposes a binary division of the populace, the "righteous" and the "sinners" forming the alternative categories. The context suggests that the righteous consists of the Pharisees and those who

32. Jeremias, *Theology*, 109f.
33. Dunn, *Discipleship*, 63.
34. Matt 9:13; Mark 2:17; Luke 5:32.
35. Sanders, *Jesus and Judaism*, 174.

identified themselves with them. The "sinners" must therefore be those outside the righteous/Pharisee category and despised by its members. Jesus was criticized by the Pharisees for dining with tax-collectors and sinners; indeed the gospels portray Jesus as acquiring a reputation as a "friend of tax collectors and sinners,"[36] this being the antithesis of what would be expected of a respectable Jew, especially one regarded by some as an authoritative teacher. His attitude to "sinners" suggests that—to some extent at least—he regarded them as the victims of injustice rather than the perpetrators of it.

James Dunn's view of the "sinners" resonates with this analysis: he points out that the Pharisees and the Essenes regarded anyone outside their group as effectively apostate. So those outside the group were "sinners." But these "sinners" are not just those who break the law in ways that any Jew would recognize; rather, they are Jews who disagree with the group's sectarian interpretation of the law. For those who considered that their understanding of righteousness was the only valid one, people who were unacceptable to them, "sinners," they assumed were also unacceptable to God.[37]

According to Dunn, then, in a Pharisaic environment a "sinner" could be any Jew who failed to follow the Pharisaic lifestyle and was therefore considered to be outside the Pharisee movement. A difficulty with Dunn's interpretation is that it assumes that the Pharisees were a sect like the Essenes which had a tightly defined membership. If, however, as suggested earlier, Pharisaism *was* normative Judaism, Dunn's interpretation takes on new dimensions. Now we are dealing with a Pharisaism that had no formal membership: all Jews were Pharisees by default, unless they opted out by joining the Essenes or the Sadducees.

Excommunication: a Hypothesis

At this point we are obliged to enter the realm of hypothesis. The hypothesis proposed here is that since under Roman rule the death penalty was unavailable to the Jews (according to John 18:31), excommunication—exclusion from the community—was used as a substitute and "sinner" (*hamartōlos*) became a technical term designating a person who had been excommunicated. Although Pharisaism kept no list of members, presumably the Jewish hierarchy, which was dominated by the Pharisees, did keep some kind of

---

36. Matt 11:19; Luke 7:34; *c.f.* Luke 15:2; 19:7.

37. Dunn, *Discipleship*, 69f.

record of those whom it expelled. It used excommunication as a penalty for many offences, which included becoming a tax collector or a prostitute. Indeed excommunication was a symbolic death sentence inasmuch as victims forfeited the benefits of living in the Jewish community. "Respectable" Jews were encouraged to shun "sinners," which had severe consequences: the victim's family was compelled to disown him or her, bringing disgrace on them as well. Not only was the victim's property forfeit, but victims were denied access to the synagogue, respectable employment, and probably the regular markets. Perhaps this is reflected in the use of the terms "the lost" or "the perished" (*ta apolōta* or *to apolōlos*) as alternative designations for the "sinners."[38] The Jewish authorities may have seen a precedent in the use made of excommunication by the reformers Ezra and Nehemiah:

> Anyone who failed to appear within three days would forfeit all his property, in accordance with the decision of the officials and elders, and would himself be expelled from the assembly of the exiles. (Ezra 10:8)

> When the people heard this law, they excluded from Israel all who were of foreign descent. (Neh 13:3)

Since it was impossible to observe the whole of the Pharisaic oral law, especially the exacting requirements of the ritual purity movement (see above), there was a high offending rate and excommunications were common. The Fourth Gospel refers twice—presumably to those thus sentenced—as having been "put out of the synagogue" (*aposunagōgos genetai*) in John 9:22 and 12:42.[39] There is evidence in the Babylonian Talmud that any Rabbi had the authority to perform an excommunication or a reinstatement.[40]

38. For example in such passages as Mt 10:6; 15:24; Lk 15:4 and 19:10. In Lk 19:10 the context is the conversion of Zacchaeus, a chief tax collector.

39. Some scholars, such as C. K. Barrett (*John*, 362) and Craig Keener (*John*, 1:789), reject the authenticity of John's references to excommunication, claiming that they reflect conditions prevailing at the time the author wrote rather than the time of Jesus. In contrast, Beasley-Murray argues cogently that followers of Jesus suffered much from the time of Jesus onwards and that the decision of the Pharisees in John 9:22 should be viewed as typical (*John*, 154).

40. Peter Schäfer describes an incident recorded in the Babylonian Talmud in which Rabbi Yehoshua b. Perahya excommunicated his disciple for being frivolous and subsequently would have reinstated him, if the disciple had not misunderstood what he was doing. The excommunication procedure was apparently quite simple, except that it involved 400 *shofar* blasts (Schäfer, *Talmud*, 34–40). It is of course possible that the

The inevitable consequence of this was the formation of a whole Jewish underclass. This is not explicitly mentioned in the NT, probably because the authors assumed that their readers would be familiar with it. Every Jewish town and city acquired a population of excommunicated folk, who formed an alternative society whose structures in some degree mirrored those of regular society. Although banned from synagogues, some religious participation was still available to "sinners": they could visit the outermost court of the Temple ("the court of the Gentiles") and they could—and the gospels testify that they did (see below)—attend open-air rallies led by such preachers such as John the Baptist and Jesus. If they were banned from the regular markets, they would surely have set up their own. Moreover, some employment was available to them. Certain tradesmen inevitably found themselves excommunicated and classified as "sinners"; these included herdsmen, whose duties prevented them from meeting all Judaism's religious obligations, and tanners, who routinely worked with substances Judaism considered unclean. Tax collectors, who worked ultimately for the Romans, were automatically excommunicated and consigned amongst the "sinners." Often tax collectors could afford to employ other "sinners" as security guards,[41] domestic servants or in business ventures that they set up; this would have made them effectively leaders in the alternative society. The term "tax collectors and sinners," which occurs frequently in the gospels,[42] was surely a technical term denoting the alternative society of the "sinners" amongst whom the tax collectors were not only the most prominent, but also those with whom "respectable" Jews were most likely to have dealings. Occasionally, for example, in Matt 5:46 and Luke 7:29, the term "tax collectors" used on its own may carry the same technical meaning.

As noted earlier, supposedly respectable Jews such as the Pharisees refused to have any dealings with "sinners" or, at least, any more than were strictly necessary. There is some evidence that they believed the "sinners" to be under God's curse (John 7:49). Moreover, it appears that there was little or no prospect of restoration for those consigned amongst the "sinners."

---

practices described in the Babylonian Talmud reflect procedures current at the time of its compilation (the sixth century) and these may differ from those in use at the time of Jesus. For example, the authority to excommunicate and reinstate may have been restricted to certain individuals then.

41. There is evidence that the "soldiers" mentioned in Luke 3:14 were working for tax collectors; see fn 80 on page 72.

42. Nine times (Matt 9:10, 11; 11:19; Mark 2:15, 16 twice; Luke 5:30; 7:34; 15:1). In the first instance in Mark 2:16 the two terms are transposed.

The gospels mention that under the ministry of John the Baptist many of these folk repented and were baptized.[43] The Jewish authorities, however, had not endorsed John's ministry[44] and refused to reinstate to mainstream Jewish society the repentant "sinners" whom he had baptized.[45]

Thus this study hypothesizes that a binary division characterized Jewish society at the time of Jesus: on the one hand were the "respectable" Jews who believed themselves to be observing the Pharisaic twofold law; on the other were the "sinners" who on account of their failure to observe it had been excluded—to all intents and purposes permanently—from the "respectable" community, while continuing to live within sight and sound of it.[46] This division, as will be seen, was a significant factor in the ministries of both John the Baptist and Jesus.

Messianic Expectations

Although, on the whole, the Romans were enlightened rulers, making many concessions to their Jewish subjects,[47] at the time of Jesus many Jews

43. Matt 21:32 mentions tax collectors and prostitutes responding to John's ministry; Luke 3:12 describes tax collectors approaching John for baptism; Luke 7:29 refers to tax collectors who had been baptized by John.

44. Matt 21:23–27 and its parallels claim that the Jewish hierarchy had failed to recognize the hand of God in John's ministry; moreover they imply that it was about to do the same with Jesus.

45. This surely is the implication of Jesus' accusation against the scribes and Pharisees: "For you lock people out of the kingdom of heaven. For you do not go in yourselves, *and when others are going in, you stop them*" (Matt 23:13). It is also clearly the message of the Parable of the Prodigal Son (Luke 15:11–32). Nolland explicitly identifies the two brothers with the tax collectors and sinners on one hand and the Pharisees and scribes on the other hand (*Luke*, 2:780). Concerning the story's meaning George Caird insists that it was addressed to "respectable" Jews to urge them to rejoice with God over the restoration of sinners and to warn them of the dire peril that awaited if they refused to do this (*Saint Luke*, 184). Jesus' telling of this story demonstrates his concern for repentant sinners denied reinstatement to regular Jewish society.

46. Is there a hint of this agonizing situation in some of the parables of Jesus? For example, in the Ten Bridesmaids (Matt 25:1–13) the five foolish ones could presumably hear the festivities proceeding indoors while they were denied access and in the Rich Man and Lazarus (Luke 16:19–31) the rich man could see Lazarus in Abraham's company, but was prohibited from crossing the "great chasm" between them.

47. For example, Jews were exempt from conscription into the Roman army and, when Caesar worship was introduced as a test of loyalty to Rome, from the requirement to affirm Caesar as Lord. The Saddusaic ruling class collaborated with the Romans in exchange for certain privileges.

had a strong sense of national identity and divine election. Following the lead of the Pharisees, they resented the Roman regime, especially its crippling taxes,[48] cruel punishments (such as crucifixion) and the presence of Roman soldiers as a reminder of Jewish subjection. Indeed it was this subjection to which they objected most of all: as God's chosen people they wished to pursue their destiny without interference by a pagan power. This led to a significant "underground" movement determined to remove the Roman presence—by violent means if necessary—and restore national sovereignty. Josephus mentions a group "marked by an all-consuming passion for freedom," which in other respects followed the teaching of the Pharisees (*Antiquities* 18:1:6); this movement is presumably the one which in the uprising of 66 CE became known as the Zealots.

Jewish zeal to remove the Romans fuelled Messianic expectations, although, as Sanders points out, not all Jews shared such belief.[49] Even among those who did cherish Messianic hopes there was little consensus concerning the kind of Messiah who was expected or even the number.[50] Originally the term *Messiah* denoted kings—especially of the Davidic dynasty—and high priests who were anointed with oil upon taking office. It was, however, not only a kingly or priestly Messiah who was expected: John 1:19–21, for example, appears to distinguish three figures whom pious Jews were expecting. Perhaps it would be safest to say that a generic "expectancy" characterized the Jewish *zeitgeist*; the expectation was of imminent divine intervention in human history and, especially, in Jewish history.[51] Various Hebrew scriptures were considered to predict the sending of servants of God. One widely held belief—perhaps partly an instance of "wishful thinking"—was that a military leader, another Judas Maccabeus perhaps, would arise who would rally the people and lead them to expel the Romans by force so that Jewish self-rule could be re-established.[52] Some identified this military leader with the Messiah; others, influenced perhaps by the

48. For further see later under *Galilee's Socio-economic Conditions* on page 27.

49. Sanders, *Judaism Practice and Belief*, 295.

50. According to several of the DSS the Qumran community was expecting two Messiahs (K. G. Kuhn, "The Two Messiahs," 54; Sanders, *Judaism Practice and Belief*, 296).

51. For example, "they supposed that the kingdom of God was to appear immediately" (Luke 19:11).

52. For example, some thought that John the Baptist was the Messiah (Luke 3:15; John 1:20; 3:28). The disciples' question in Acts 1:6 suggests that even after Jesus' passion and resurrection the early Christian community regarded him as such a military Messiah.

"suffering servant" prophecies, insisted that the Messiah would use only peaceful methods and might even suffer vicariously for the people.[53]

The Messiah's coming was one of the "last things." Many Jews believed themselves to be living in the end times. This heightened interest in OT prophecy, especially the apocalyptic[54] genre which was concerned mainly with the eschata. The early Christian communities inherited this interest, their own use of apocalyptic being evident in the NT, most notably in the Book of Revelation.

According to Mark 8:27–30 Jesus claimed to be the Messiah[55]—or at least he did not deny it when Peter pronounced him such. Nevertheless, he ordered his disciples not to make his Messiahship known. In contrast, Sanders claims that Jesus was an eschatological prophet who proclaimed the coming of a personage called the Son of Man, although sometimes he used the phrase 'Son of Man' of himself.[56] This Semitic phrase occurs frequently in the OT (94 times in the Book of Ezekiel alone) where it generally means "human being" without any supernatural connotations; indeed, the NRSV usually renders it "human being." One OT occurrence, however, carries special significance:

> In my vision at night I looked, and there before me was one like a son of man, coming with the clouds of heaven. He approached the Ancient of Days and was led into his presence. He was given authority, glory and sovereign power; all peoples, nations and men of every language worshiped him. His dominion is an everlasting dominion that will not pass away, and his kingdom is one that will never be destroyed. (Dan 7:13f NIV)

On account of its use in Daniel, by NT times the term "Son of Man" had acquired Messianic connotations. In the NT the expression occurs in all four gospels, mostly on the lips of Jesus. Although some scholars believe that Jesus always used the phrase as a self-designation, it is possible to divide the occurrences in the gospels into two categories, although some could belong in either. One category refers unambiguously to Jesus himself, generally underscoring his human vulnerability, while the other alludes to

---

53. Such as Isa 52:13–53:12. Ps 22 also reflects a suffering servant of God.

54. Giorgio Jossa, describing the diversity in Judaism at the time of Jesus, claims that the apocalyptic currents were significant (*Jews*, 46f).

55. There are other passages in which Jesus explicitly identified himself as the Messiah, such as John 4:25f.

56. Sanders, *Historical Figure*, 247f.

the end times using apocalyptic imagery similar to that in Dan 7:13f. The two categories are harmonized if Jesus identified himself with the heavenly figure of Daniel's prophecy; Daniel's mention of the figure's indestructible *kingdom* would surely have resonated with Jesus.

Hellenistic Influences

Despite the Jews' monotheism and their belief that they alone were God's chosen people, they did not isolate themselves from the other peoples of the ancient world. The *pax romana* facilitated trade and travel: Jews traded with other nations and they traveled: a legacy of the Babylonian exile was a considerable Jewish diaspora, whose members sometimes journeyed to Jerusalem for the Passover. Moreover, successive foreign invasions had impacted Jewish culture. An inevitable consequence of these was that ideas from other religions and cultures had permeated Jewish thought and later, through it, Christian thought.

This interchange of ideas was eased by the universal presence of koiné Greek as *lingua franca*. In the fourth century BCE Alexander the Great's conquests had spread the Greek language throughout much of the then-known world. This, together with subsequent Hellenizing regimes such as those of the Ptolemies and Seleucids had left a lasting legacy in Palestine, not even Jerusalem being immune. Daniel Johansson, summarizing the work of Martin Hengel, describes Palestine at the time of Jesus as largely bilingual. Even the Maccabean revolt, itself a reaction against Hellenism, could not reverse the onward march of the Greek language. Alexander Janneus (103–76 BCE) issued bilingual coins and forty years later Herod the Great used only Greek inscriptions on Jewish coins. About forty percent of ossuaries in Jerusalem and its surroundings bore Greek inscriptions. Ten to twenty percent of the inhabitants of Jerusalem in this period had Greek as their mother tongue. Prominent Diaspora Jews returning to Jerusalem founded the Greek-speaking synagogues mentioned in Acts 6. Evidence from inscriptions suggests that many of the aristocracy spoke Greek, not only in Jerusalem but throughout the region. Two of Jesus' disciples, Andrew and Philip, had Greek names. Hengel concludes that during his lif··· ne the message of Jesus reached Diaspora Jews, who mostly spoke and formed the core of the Hellenist movement in Jerusalem. Jesus' ʒ was presumably translated into Greek well before he was crucified;

indeed, Jesus himself may have taught in Greek, at least in part.[57] In this latter regard Johansson sees significance in John 12:20f where "some Greeks" request to see Jesus.[58] But Keener points out that although John might have intended Diaspora Jews in this passage, it is more likely that he had Gentile Greeks in view.[59] Since it is unlikely that Gentiles or Diaspora Jews were conversant in Aramaic, it is certainly possible that their interest was aroused because Jesus had been teaching in Greek. Or had Philip, whom these "Greeks" approached, been providing a simultaneous translation? Hengel himself observes that even the Essenes, who were highly critical regarding the Greek world, made use of the Greek language, as evidenced by the Greek papyrus fragments found in Qumran.[60]

Johansson goes on to survey the extent to which Greek education flourished in Palestine and not only in the Hellenistic cities; there was a Greek secondary school in Jerusalem itself.[61] Hengel notes that according to the *Letter of Aristeas*, the high priest selected 72 scholars who were learned in both Jewish literature and in Greek for the translation of the Torah into Greek.[62] So three centuries before Jesus it was possible to find in Jerusalem 72 Jewish scholars sufficiently accomplished in Greek to create the Septuagint. Gerald Downing claims that it was through Greek education that Greek philosophy, especially Cynicism, penetrated Jewish thought.[63]

Indeed, with the revival of interest in the historical Jesus towards the end of the twentieth century some scholars[64] became convinced that Jesus himself had been introduced to Cynicism[65] and had embraced some of its

57. Johansson, "Judaism and Hellenism," 106f.

58. Johansson, "Judaism and Hellenism," 107, fn 15.

59. Keener, *John*, 2:871f.

60. Hengel, *Judaism and Hellenism*, 60f.

61. Johansson, "Judaism and Hellenism," 107.

62. Hengel, *Judaism and Hellenism*, 60.

63. Downing, "Deeper Reflections," 102.

64. N. T. Wright discusses this possibility at length and mentions that besides J. D. Crossan its advocates include B. L. Mack, L. E. Vaage, A. J. Malherbe and F. G. Downing (*Jesus*, 66–74).

65. It is generally accepted that the name *Cynic* is derived from the Greek *kuōn*, "dog," but scholars are divided concerning the nature of this derivation. Some consider that it was because they were regarded as barking at regular society, others because their lifestyle was unclean—dogs at that time were considered wild creatures rather than domestic pets. Still others believe that the term is derived from the name of the place where Cynicism was first taught. First formulated by Antisthenes, a pupil of Socrates in the fifth century BCE, Cynicism spread with the rise of the Roman Empire in the first century, but

teachings. Crossan, for example, seemed to think that living as close to Sepphoris as he did was likely to give Jesus some knowledge of Cynicism.[66] Parallels between the Cynics and Jesus have long been noted.[67] Two papers published in 1996 and 1998 provide useful overviews of the argument: Paul Rhodes Eddy contends persuasively that Jesus was *not* a Cynic,[68] while F. Gerald Downing critiques Eddy's paper and argues cogently that he *was* one.[69] Although both authors make valid points, Downing's demonstration of the pervasiveness of Cynicism and related ideas in the first century is particularly useful. Undoubtedly Jesus *was* influenced by Cynicism, as was everyone in the Graeco-Roman world. If some scholars choose to label Jesus a Cynic, this does not mean that he had renounced his Jewish heritage nor that he had consciously joined some Hellenistic philosophical cult, but rather that he had embraced some of its ideas. Perhaps some of Hellenism's syncretism had permeated Judaism facilitating its adoption of elements from diverse ideologies.

In the light of this it is not surprising that Johansson comments that the concept of primitive Christianity untouched by Greek ideas is impossible. Many supposedly Hellenistic elements in the Gospels may have originated with Jesus himself. Hengel noted parallels between Jesus' preaching and Stoicism, which led him to suggest a direct contact between Jesus and philosophers of that school.[70] As an example of Hellenistic ideas adopted into Christian thought Johansson refers to Wilhelm Heitmüller's studies of the sacraments in Paul. In his discussion of 1 Corinthians 10, for example, he argued that the concept of eating the very body and blood of Christ, and thereby coming into the closest imaginable, completely secret communion with him could not have originated in Judaism, but could have done so in the syncretistic oriental religion of the Hellenistic world.[71]

---

disappeared in the late fifth century. It taught that happiness could be achieved by living virtuously in harmony with Nature. Rejecting conventional desires for wealth, power, luxury and fame, the Cynics advocated a rigorously ascetic lifestyle free from all possessions. In practice its followers often pursued a nomadic lifestyle, dressed in ragged clothing, and begging for their daily needs.

66. Crossan, *Historical Jesus*, 421.

67. Eddy, "Jesus as Diogenes," 452.

68. Eddy, "Jesus as Diogenes," 449–469.

Downing, "Deeper Reflections," 97–104.

hansson, "Judaism and Hellenism," 109f.

ansson, "Judaism and Hellenism," 104, citing Wilhelm Heitmüller, *Taufe und bei Paulus*, 32; English translation in Baird, *History*, 2:242.

Undoubtedly its incorporation of aspects of Hellenistic thought facilitated the rapid spread of the Christian faith throughout the Hellenized world. Ilaria Ramelli claims that it is better to speak of the Christianization of Hellenism than of the 'Hellenization' of Christianity, which was already Hellenized at its very origin; the New Testament itself originates from a deeply Hellenized Judaism. The earliest Christians lived and studied within Hellenistic culture.[72]

CONCLUSION: HOW DID JUDAISM AFFECT JESUS?

Our quest is discover how Judaism might have affected Jesus' mission. The NT depicts Jesus as a practicing Jew, brought up by pious parents, familiar with the Hebrew scriptures, attending synagogue on the Sabbath and journeying to Jerusalem each year for the Passover. So what was his relationship with the religion that was his heritage?

As we have seen, at the time of Jesus Judaism was at a crossroads. It had served its adherents well when they were a nomadic or an agricultural people having only limited contact with the outside world. But when exposed to the urbanized, multi-cultural *milieu* of the Graeco-Roman world the cracks had begun to show. Ellis Rivkin eloquently explains how urbanisation so changed the experience of ordinary people that the Pentateuch, intended for an agricultural-priestly society, no longer catered for the needs and aspirations of an urban-agricultural society embedded within a world of *poleis* in which each individual was stirred by conflicting feelings—loneliness, alienation, and insignificance wrestling intimations of personhood, self-worth, and immortality.[73] Moreover, Judaism's senior leadership was corrupt, more intent upon appeasing the Romans than pleasing Yahweh and determined to silence rather than heed the voices demanding reform.

Nevertheless reform was happening. In the Maccabean crisis Judaism had had to reinvent itself in order to survive. Of the three "ideologies" that emerged from that crisis the Pharisees were the first to *internalize* the written and oral law; that is to say, they taught that what God demands of humanity is not just outward observance of the commandments, but conformity in the individual's inner life as well.[74] It had become universal,

72. Ramelli, "Origen," 251f.

73. Rivkin, *Revolution*, 206f.

74. It may seem that there is a conflict between Jesus' statement that Pharisaism was a religion of outward observance and his call for inward obedience to God's demands

applying wherever and in whatever cultural milieu a Jew might be. This more philosophical approach to piety enabled it to survive (as "rabbinical Judaism") to the present day, while the Essenes and the Sadducees had disappeared by the end of the first century CE. Rivkin reckons that this internalization of the law was the grand achievement of the Scribes and Pharisees. And this provided a foundation for emergent Christianity.[75]

It was noted earlier that Judaism was characterized by a sense of *expectancy*. Whether the one expected was the Messiah or someone else was almost immaterial; if Yahweh was real, he must intervene. Perhaps it was the dissatisfaction engendered by the urbanization of society; perhaps it was more fundamental, akin to the well-worn saying in today's western society: "There must be something more than this." And it was at this critical moment that first John the Baptist and then Jesus appeared. As will be seen, the Baptist filled a void left by the long silence of prophecy and the inadequacy of the temple cultus. He welcomed and baptized repentant "sinners," who had been excluded from regular Jewish society, although the Jewish establishment continued to exclude them. Jesus would build upon foundations laid by both the Pharisees and the Baptist to create an alternative faith community that would accept repentant "sinners."

(*for example,* in Matt 23:23–28). But, as N. T. Wright points out, that conflict is a misunderstanding. Jesus never spoke against the law and his teaching generally accorded with that of the Pharisees" (*Jesus,* 372). As to the misrepresentation of the Pharisees that this implies, "It is no exaggeration to say that the New Testament's depiction of the Pharisees is biased. Each individual reference can be justified, but nevertheless their combined effect blackens the Pharisees. Like all the best stories, the New Testament needs villains to counterbalance its heroes and polemics has forced the Pharisees undeservedly into the former role" (Amos, *Hypocrites,* 213).

75. Rivkin, *Revolution,* 302f.

3

GALILEE

THE SYNOPTIC GOSPELS SUGGEST THAT Jesus spent most of his life in the predominantly agricultural province of Galilee. Continuing our quest for the factors that led him to undertake his earthly ministry, this chapter examines the circumstances of the province at that time which might have affected him.

Morten Jensen draws attention to three distinct phases through which Jesus research has passed in its assessment of Galilee's importance in determining his aims. (i) At first scholars argued that Galilee was a hotbed of revolutionary activity, Jesus becoming one of many leaders opposing Roman oppression. (ii) Later scholars emphasized the extent to which the area had been Hellenized, suggesting that Jesus should be understood as a Greek philosopher. (iii) More recent debate, having largely discarded (i) and (ii), focuses on the socio-economic development of Galilee and especially the debt spiral that resulted from Herod Antipas's building program; Jesus rallied a protest movement against this.[1]

This study accepts Jensen's summary and also agrees with him that Jesus' ministry was more than simply a protest movement. If so, other factors must have shaped Jesus' career. Jensen argues cogently that the missing factor is the ritual purity movement which was prevalent in Judaism at that time.[2] Jesus' teaching, however, is contemptuous of the emphasis on ritual

---

1. Jensen, "Purity," 5f, *Herod Antipas in Galilee*, 16–30.
2. Jensen, "Purity," 35. For further on this movement see under *Purity* on page 6.

purity,[3] perhaps because of its exacerbation of Jewish antipathy towards all things foreign and therefore "unclean"; indeed this may have contributed to the impetus that led him to undertake his ministry. This chapter will begin with a detailed evaluation of the three phases in Jesus research that Jensen identified; it will then consider the individual ways in which conditions in Galilee impacted Jesus.

GALILEE AS A HOTBED OF REVOLUTIONARY ACTIVITY

During Herod the Great's reign, intensive resettlement in Galilee began to affect the indigenous Jewish population adversely. John Harrison claims that this was because Herod acquired land by executing large estate owners or forcing them into arrears by heavy taxation. He sold this land to pay for his extreme building programs. At the same time Rome's appetite for produce from further afield resulted in the indigenous agricultural community, which until then had consisted mostly of subsistence farmers, being compelled to use its land to produce "cash-crops," such as wine and olive products, for export. Romans and Jewish collaborators created larger estates, acquiring more land as owners of smaller farms fell behind on loan payments and defaulted. Many farmers who had once owned land became tenants on land formerly their own or on other estates. As tenants, they were required to pay rent and meet the production targets set by the landowners. If production fell below that demanded, they had to borrow money to pay their rent.[4] Consequently debt became a widespread problem in Galilee.

Not surprisingly, when Herod died in 4 BCE there was considerable unrest amongst Galilean Jews. Most significant was the insurrection led by the Messianic claimant Judas son of Ezekias, whom Josephus describes as follows:

> There was also Judas, the son of that Ezekias who had been head of the robbers; which Ezekias was a very strong man, and had with great difficulty been caught by Herod. This Judas, having gotten together a multitude of men of a profligate character about Sepphoris in Galilee, made an assault upon the palace [there,] and seized upon all the weapons that were laid up in it, and with them

---

3. Perhaps this is clearest in the episode when Pharisees and scribes complained to Jesus about his disciples eating without washing their hands (Mark 7:1–23 and parallels).

4. Harrison, "Weeds," 85.

armed every one of those that were with him, and carried away what money was left there; and he became terrible to all men, by tearing and rending those that came near him; and all this in order to raise himself, and out of an ambitious desire of the royal dignity; and he hoped to obtain that as the reward not of his virtuous skill in war, but of his extravagance in doing injuries (*Antiquities*, 17:10:5).

His gathering of the "multitude of men of a profligate character" suggests that, despite the alarming personality traits that Josephus ascribes to him, Judas attracted considerable support from the local peasantry, who were doubtless eager to free themselves from the thralls of the Herod dynasty. Josephus's contemptuous description of Judas's followers probably reflects his aristocratic background: like his peers among the Jewish nobility and their Roman overlords, he viewed the peasantry as a commodity to be exploited.

This uprising was one of several quelled by Varus, the Roman Governor of Syria, who, according to Josephus (*Antiquities* 17:10:9), committed his forces to his son and a friend of his and sent them to Galilee, where they attacked Judas's men, causing them to flee. They recaptured Sepphoris, enslaving its inhabitants and setting the city on fire, although archaeology has not found any evidence of the fire. The Galileans' bid for freedom from the Herod dynasty failed, Rome installing Herod's son Antipas as tetrarch of Galilee and Perea. His reign lasted until 39 CE, embracing the careers of John the Baptist and Jesus.

Having been brought up in Caesar's household, Antipas's outlook was cosmopolitan and Hellenistic, although not aggressively so. His ambition was to "modernize" Galilee, making it what he regarded as a thriving heartland of the Roman empire. He rebuilt Sepphoris and he built a new city, Tiberias, on the western shore of the Sea of Galilee, intending these Hellenistic centers to attract settlers from elsewhere in the Empire. Although Galilee had long had a reputation for being cosmopolitan, as Isaiah's pejorative reference to "Galilee of the Gentiles" (Isa 9:1) implies, many—if not most—of those whom Antipas encouraged to settle were in fact Jews,[5] probably Hellenistic Jews from the Diaspora.

Scholarship is divided as to whether Antipas's long reign benefited or damaged the indigenous Jewish population of Galilee[6] and whether or not

5. All of the houses excavated in Sepphoris had been occupied by observant Jews—see fn 20 on page 26.

6. Jensen provides an excellent summary of both sides of the argument in "Herod Antipas," 7–11.

it predisposed it to insurrection. Certainly one might expect the combination of suffering and the lack of effective Jewish hierarchical supervision in Galilee[7] to foster extremism; indeed similar circumstances had provoked Judas's failed rebellion in 4 BCE. Geza Vermes described Galilee as a hotbed of the Zealots, by which presumably he means those who later became known as the Zealots; indeed he claims that Jesus was executed as such, although he was not one, simply because he came from Galilee.[8] The same trait may underlie the curious episode mentioned in Luke 13:1 which refers to some "Galileans whose blood Pilate had mingled with their sacrifices." In this incident, which is not documented elsewhere, it appears that some Galileans had come to offer sacrifices and Pilate had had them executed, possibly in the temple itself, perhaps for no other reason than that Galileans were habitually presumed to be terrorists.

Seán Freyne and Jensen agree that Antipas's long reign was not disrupted by strife and internal dissension.[9] That, however, need not indicate that Antipas's subjects were contented. As James Crossley points out, peasant revolts are rare for the simple reason that peasants spend much of their lives so close to starvation that they would be imperiled by any departure from their normal routine.[10] This study will seek to show that discontent simmering beneath the surface was a significant factor in Jesus' ministry.

As to Jesus himself being a terrorist, it is true that some scholars have claimed the appearance of the name Simon the Zealot in some lists of the twelve disciples (for example, in Acts 1:13) as evidence that Jesus attracted followers who had military ambitions. T. L. Donaldson points out that from Reimarus to the work of Brandon scholars have attempted to demonstrate that Jesus was in sympathy with anti-Roman rebels. The principal reasons for this conclusion are: (i) Jesus' execution by Rome on a charge of political sedition ("the King of the Jews"); (ii) Jesus' triumphal entry into Jerusalem, with its royal overtones, followed by an assault on the temple; (iii) Jesus' identification with the common people, criticism of the wealthy and conflict with the powerful; and (iv) the presence within Jesus' band of disciples of at least one "Zealot." Some also appeal to Jesus' command to procure a sword (Luke 22:36) and the statement "not peace but a sword" (Matt

---

7. Regarding the paucity of Jewish officialdom in Galilee at the time of Jesus see fn 66 on page 42.

8. Vermes, *Jesus the Jew*, 50.

9. Freyne, *Galilee*, 68.

10. Crossley, *Christianity*, 42.

10:34).[11] To this might be added the possible identification of Judas Iscariot as a member of the *Sicarii*[12] and the response of the Jerusalem authorities to Jesus which indicates that they regarded him as such a serious threat to national security that they sent "spies" to keep him under surveillance.[13]

Despite these arguments, most scholars, including Donaldson himself, now reject this theory. Surely the strongest argument against it is the general tenor of Jesus' teaching: repeatedly he advocated love and prayers for one's enemies and forgiveness for one's traducers and persecutors. His recorded teaching contains no anti-Rome sentiment—on the contrary, he taught that Jews should pay Roman taxes. Furthermore, the Romans who were certainly competent military tacticians apparently saw no threat in him; the gospels depict Pilate as wishing to release him and reluctant to crucify him. It is significant that the Romans at first took no action against the apostles, dismissing them as a harmless religious sect.

In regard to Simon the Zealot, although the epithet *zēlōtēs* is suggestive of the Zealot revolutionaries who participated in the uprising of 66 CE, the word may denote any zealous person, an enthusiast or ardent supporter, without any connotations of violence. The LXX applies it to God in Ex 20:5 and Deut 4:24. Christophe Mézange has demonstrated that it is most likely that Simon the Zealot acquired this epithet because he was a particularly ardent disciple; he could not have been connected with the Zealot revolutionaries for the simple reason that at the time of Jesus the Zealot party had not been founded.[14] It is true that by the time that Luke wrote about Simon the Zealot, the term had become associated with the revolutionaries, but surely Simon had acquired the epithet before those Zealots did and Luke need not have intended any connection.

In conclusion, then, the recognition by most recent scholarship that Jesus was not a violent revolutionary appears to be amply justified. But, as we shall see, although Galilee suffered no severe uprisings during the reign of Antipas, the high taxation and exploitative attitudes of the landowners led to widespread underlying discontent amongst the peasantry.

---

11. Donaldson, "Zealot."

12. For further see fn 22 on page 119.

13. This is suggested, for example, by the use of the verb *paratēreō* in Luke 6:7 (and Mark 3:2); 14:1 and 20:20, all referring to officialdom keeping Jesus under observation. For further see *Under Surveillance* on page 123.

14. Mézange, "Simon le Zélote," 489.

GALILEE AS A CENTRE OF HELLENISM

As we saw in chapter 2, by the time of Jesus Palestine, including Galilee, had been thoroughly Hellenized.[15] Galilee was more susceptible to foreign influence than Judea was. Unlike Judea, Galilee was traversed by important international trade routes; these brought Galileans into frequent contact with foreign travelers, inevitably leading to the interchange of ideas. Moreover, since 4 BCE Galilee had been ruled on behalf of the Romans by Herod Antipas, whose Graeco-Roman upbringing was Hellenistic and whose ambition was to make Galilee a premier province of the Roman empire.

At first Antipas established his capital in Sepphoris. The largest[16] city in Galilee, it was strategically located at the intersection of the west-east road from Ptolemaïs on the coast to Tiberias on the Sea of Galilee with a north-south mountain road from Jerusalem. Following its devastation by Varus when he quelled the uprising by Judas son of Ezekias, Antipas restored and fortified it; it remained the provincial capital until 15 CE when he reassigned that function to Tiberias. Sepphoris's location, however, commanded sufficient passing trade to ensure its continuing importance.[17] Antipas intended it to become a major cosmopolitan city, attracting settlers from across the Roman Empire. Archaeologists excavating its site have discovered synagogues[18] and an amphitheatre capable of seating 4500.[19] Despite Antipas's cosmopolitan intentions, all of the houses discovered had been occupied by observant Jews.[20]

15. See under *Hellenistic Influences* on page 16.

16. Estimates of Sepphoris's population at the time of Jesus vary: Jonathan Reed (*Archaeology*, 80) suggests 8000–12,000, while Nathan Schumer of Columbia University claims that a more accurate (but still rough) figure is 2500–5000 ("Population," 19).

17. Crossan, *Historical Jesus*, 18.

18. According to Lee Levine (*Ancient Synagogues*, 4), there were no fewer than 18 synagogues in Sepphoris. Zeev Weiss (*Sepphoris Synagogue*, 3) claims that an excavated example is believed to date from the early 5th century CE. Both sources as cited by Ilka Gray ("Archaeology," 3).

19. Apparently this figure is given in a leaflet issued by the Israel Nature and Parks Department to visitors to the site (Gray, "Archaeology," 10f). There has been some debate about the age of the structure with estimates ranging from pre-70 to early second century (Charlesworth and Aviam, "Reconstructing," 107). The general consensus is that the theatre was built during the reign of Antipas, but extended later. So it is possible that Jesus was familiar with it—indeed it is possible that, as a locally based *tektōn*, he was involved in its construction.

20. This is J. F. Strange's conclusion from the fact that all the houses examined in one investigation were equipped with underfloor ritual baths (*miqva'ot*) and the stone vessels

Nazareth, the agricultural hamlet in which Jesus grew up, was within walking distance of Sepphoris. It is possible that Jesus or his father or both worked on Sepphoris.[21] Even if Jesus did not, he could hardly have avoided some contact with Sepphoris's Greek culture. Some scholars have argued that this greatly influenced him, but even if this is true, that does not make him a Cynic philosopher, as some have claimed.[22]

Scholarship has moved on, few today arguing that Jesus was a Greek philosopher. That, however, is not to deny the importance of Hellenism in Christian origins. As stated in chapter 2, Christianity was Hellenized from its very origin, the New Testament originating within a deeply Hellenized Judaism.[23] Since Jesus was influenced by Hellenistic ideas within a society that was itself already Hellenized, it is not these that made him distinctive.

GALILEE'S SOCIO-ECONOMIC CONDITIONS

Galilee's fertile soils and the productive fisheries of the "Sea" had long made the province potentially wealthy and therefore attractive to settlers. Indeed, Andrew Overman claims that the large number of settlements in lower Galilee, the area which includes Nazareth and Sepphoris, makes it one of the most densely populated regions in the Roman Empire.[24]

As mentioned earlier,[25] this high population density was partly the consequence of a succession of resettlement schemes. At the time of Jesus the most recent of these was Herod Antipas's project to populate his developing Hellenistic cities of Sepphoris and Tiberias. Seán Freyne regards the introduction of these immigrants as a greater drain on the region's resources than the building projects. Surely the point that he is making is that these incomers, whom he identifies with the Herodians mentioned in the gospels,[26] needed to be fed from the land—that is, by the labor of the local

---

used by the city's inhabitants had all been cut from the chalkstone near Abila; this apparently is a reliable indication that the inhabitants were observant Jews (Strange, "Recent Discoveries," 127).

21. For further see *Galilee's Socio-economic Conditions* (below).

22. For Crossan's suggestion of this see fn 66 on page 18.

23. See fn 72 on page 19.

24. Overman, "Urban Christians," 165, 168, as cited in Crossan, *Historical Jesus*, 19.

25. See under *Galilee as a Hotbed of Revolutionary Activity* on page 22.

26. Freyne, *Jesus*, 134. The "Herodians" whom Freyne identifies as the incomers whom Antipas invited are in some ways analogous to the "Hasmoneans." These folk would have been indebted to Antipas and to some extent dependent upon him, obliging

peasantry—and they were paid using money that probably had been raised by taxing that same peasantry, but they themselves did not contribute directly to the productivity of the land. They were therefore a nett drain on the local resources.

Jonathan Reed gives a detailed explanation of the impact of these new developments on the subsistence farmers who had until recently constituted most of Galilee's indigenous Jewish population. To feed the growing population required more intensive agricultural practice. Formerly Galilee's economy had consisted mainly of peasant families struggling for self-sufficiency and paying their surplus in kind to Hasmonean officials. Increasingly, however, they were now forced to become tenant farmers who paid taxes and rents in kind and increasingly in cash. Polycropping gave way to the monocropping needed to produce the higher yields required to satisfy tax demands. Some peasant farmers aggregated together their fragmented holdings to create economies of scale for grain, but more often peasant holdings were forced together into larger estates (*latifundia*) by rulers or wealthy elites. Some peasants sold their land to pay off their taxes and then stayed on it as tenants paying rent. Others left the land altogether to ply an artisan trade.[27]

Richard Horsley notes the two and sometimes effectively three layers of rulers and demands on their produce faced by farmers in Roman Judea and Galilee. After yielding up tribute (to Rome), taxes (to the local ruler), and tithes (to the temple) families could no longer feed themselves and they fell into ever deeper debt. He points out that these are the kind of conditions that often give rise to popular movements.[28] Craig Blomberg makes a similar point about taxation, pointing out that the average Jew in the early first century, after paying Jewish tithes, temple tax and other occasional offerings, and tribute to Rome, paid between 30% and 50% of his income in taxes.[29]

---

them to support him. The identification is certainly plausible: as John P. Meier concludes from his analysis of the three gospel references to "Herodians" (Mark 3:16; 12:13 and Matt 22:16, based upon Mark 12:13) (Meier, "Historical," 745). The problem is that with so few occurrences, it is impossible to be absolutely certain whom the word denotes. This study will assume that Freyne's identification of them is correct and will use the word to denote the settlers whom Antipas encouraged into Galilee.

27. Reed, *Archaeology*, 86f.

28. Horsley, *Prophet*, 82.

29. Blomberg, *Poverty*, 89.

Freyne describes the downward spiral that was experienced by many of Galilee's rural inhabitants. Pressure from the authorities increased poverty so that landowners became tenant farmers, tenant farmers became day laborers, and day laborers became beggars. It is surely significant that, as he observes, these characters all appear in Jesus' parables.[30]

In conclusion, then, this view, widely accepted among current scholarship, paints a bleak picture of the plight of Galilean peasantry at the time of Jesus. Despite the abundant natural resources that originally attracted settlers to the region, these folk faced daily the threat of debt and eviction, the uncertainty of day labor, and, perhaps, ultimately of beggary. The land that—according to Judaism—had been assigned to their tribes and clans in perpetuity was being seized by wealthy elites. The traditional lifestyle that they and their forefathers had pursued for many generations was disappearing before their eyes. If Josephus's claim that Antipas executed John the Baptist for fear that he might incite the populace into rebellion (*Antiquities*, 18:5:2) is correct, this surely confirms the presence of discontent simmering beneath the surface.

This view, however, is not universally accepted. Jensen, for example, argues that although Galilee's inhabitants—like most of the ancient world— suffered harsh living conditions, there is little or no evidence to support the *rapid* deterioration during Antipas's reign that he regards as essential to explain the origin of the Jesus movement.[31] Gradual the decline may have been, but we shall shortly consider motifs within the teaching of Jesus that appear to reflect those harsh socio-economic conditions. Surely these are an accurate indication of the forces impacting him and motivating his ministry.

SOCIAL DIVISIONS BETWEEN JEWISH GROUPS IN GALILEE

The principal division between Jewish groups in Galilee was that between the Hellenistic Jews inhabiting mainly the cities of Sepphoris and Tiberias and the indigenous Jews generally inhabiting the older-established towns and villages. This division is well documented. Paul Rhodes Eddy, for example, refers to it, questioning the claim of some that Jesus from Nazareth, a traditional village, might have been influenced by Sepphoris's Hellenized

30. Freyne, *Jesus*, 134.
31. Jensen, "Purity," 7.

ethos. He regards the silence of the early Jesus tradition regarding Seppho-ris and other Hellenistic cities as evidence that Jesus opposed the ethos and opulence of those urban centers.[32]

Despite this postulated rift, Jews outside Judea were more accustomed to mixing with outsiders than the Judeans were, which may have made them more willing to embrace elements of alien culture. Douglas Edwards argues that Jewish hostility[33] to the Hellenistic cities in their midst was not severe; indeed, he claims that there was a cultural continuum from city to country.[34] The failure of the evangelists to mention Sepphoris or Tibe-rias[35] is not necessarily significant; although Jesus probably knew Greek as a consequence of visits to Sepphoris, many of the Twelve were fishermen from the Capernaum district who may have spoken only Aramaic. So Jesus might have confined his mission to the more traditional towns and villages of Galilee for purely linguistic reasons, giving the evangelists no occasion to mention the Hellenistic cities. Eddy's argument, as he himself admits, is based on silence and arguments from silence are notoriously precarious.

This study conjectures that there was another division within the in-digenous Jewish population of Galilee. The principal victims of Antipas's land-grabbing schemes and those of his father before him were members of the agricultural community, who lost their land or their livelihood or both. Other indigenous Jews who did not own significant land, such as craftsmen and fishermen, were less vulnerable. Indeed, these stood to ben-efit from Galilee's "development" as it opened new markets for their trade. But how eager would they have been to exploit a market created by the very people who were driving their agricultural neighbors off their own land? They faced a moral dilemma not unfamiliar today: "Would you work for the people who put your brother out of work?" Moreover, the ritual purity movement[36] exacerbated cultural differences so that probably some

32. Eddy, "Jesus as Diogenes," 465.

33. The hostility to which Edwards refers was the consequence of hatred of Rome; Sepphoris had a reputation for loyalty to Rome, probably as a consequence of the consid-erable investment that Rome's puppet-king Antipas had made in restoring the city after its destruction by Varus.

34. Edwards, "Urban/Rural Relations," 181f, as cited in Crossan, *Historical Jesus*, 19.

35. Sepphoris is not mentioned in the NT. There is a passing reference to Tiberias in John 6:23; "Sea of Tiberias" is used as an alternative name for the Sea of Galilee in John 6:1 and 21:1.

36. This is ably demonstrated in Jensen, "Purity," 10–25. While Jensen cites the ritual purity movement as a major factor in the foundation of the Jesus movement, he

indigenous Jews refused on principle to have dealings with their Hellenistic neighbors, regarding this as "fraternizing with the enemy." Others, in contrast, might have argued that they needed to earn a living and trade with Hellenistic Jews infringed neither Torah nor Roman law. As we shall see, the conjectured division between Galilean Jews willing to trade with the "Herodians" and those who were not may have played a significant role in the origin of Jesus' ministry.

Jonathan Reed suggests that the socio-economic circumstances of Galilee led Jesus to undertake a ministry resembling those of the Hebrew prophets. True wealth is elusive: like the prophets, Jesus advocated that security was to be found not in the acquisition of objects or human-made structures, but in the divine and the new community's shared vision. Even reliance on the extended family—ultimately upon one's membership of the chosen race—was no longer adequate. The radical response demanded by the new vision led to a critique of most contemporary religious expressions within Judaism, including even the Temple in Jerusalem.[37] But this study hypothesizes that Jesus' preparation for that ministry was completed by mentoring from the John the Baptist.

NAZARETH

Jesus' home for most of his life, Nazareth was an agricultural hamlet set on a hilltop 5 km south east of Sepphoris. Estimates of its population at the time of Jesus vary widely, but the absence of any mention of it in the OT, the Talmud or Josephus suggests that it was not a significant settlement.[38] For this reason the population figure of a maximum of 480 estimated by J. F. Strange[39] is plausible. Nathanael's disparaging question, "Can anything good come out of Nazareth?" (John 1:46), sounds like a trope in common

---

does not say how or why. Moreover, this ignores the evidence in the gospel tradition that Jesus was suspicious of outward displays of purity and concerned primarily with an individual's relationship with God.

37. Reed, *Archaeology*, 220.

38. Although Nazareth is described as a *polis* in Matt 2:23 and Luke 2:39, 51, this may be because the evangelists considered it inappropriate that Jesus should be brought up in a tiny settlement that some seem to have despised as a backwater.

39. Strange, "Nazareth," 4:1050.

use; it may reflect only Nazareth's obscurity, although an evil reputation is also possible.[40]

Jesus' Childhood and Education

The educational opportunities available in such a small community would have been limited.[41] But if, as Luke 4:16f states, Jesus read from the scroll of Isaiah in the synagogue at Nazareth, at some point he had learned to read Hebrew. Moreover, according to John 8:6, he was also able to write, a skill whose comparative rarity at the time accounts for the importance of the *grammateis*.[42] So Jesus appears to have received some education. Although it was not until after 200 CE that elementary schools became formally linked with synagogues,[43] informal arrangements had probably long been in place. So it is possible that some schooling was provided by the synagogue in Nazareth. Such synagogue-based education would probably have focused on reading, especially of Torah, and is unlikely to have included writing. Had Jesus attended a school in Sepphoris? This seems unlikely; in Nazareth to send one's child to school in Sepphoris would surely have been viewed as consorting with Antipas's regime. But although this would explain the suggestions in the NT that Jesus had some familiarity with Greek language and culture, other explanations are possible and there is no definite evidence that he attended school there—or, indeed, anywhere.

Even without a formal school education, through attending synagogue each Sabbath, Jesus would have become familiar with rabbinical Judaism generally and the content of the Hebrew scriptures—although not

40. Surely the implication of Nathanael's question is that Nazareth was associated with ill fortune. The most likely explanation for this is that its proximity to Sepphoris made the farmland around Nazareth a prime target for Herod Antipas's land-grabbing schemes. When he sold or leased those lands, many agricultural laborers living in Nazareth became unemployed. As some of these moved away in search of work, Nazareth possibly became a "ghost town" with a reputation for bringing evil on its inhabitants.

41. Little is known definitely about education in first-century Israel. As James Crenshaw observes, the absence of any mention of schools by the biblical authors may be either because the existence of schools was so well known that no one stated the obvious, or because there were no schools in ancient Israel (*Education*, 90).

42. According to the Liddell & Scott lexicon *grammateus* ("scribe") denotes a secretary or clerk. The significance of this profession was skill in writing as well as reading. Many folk, including even some having influential roles, lacked both skills and writing was rarer than reading.

43. Morris, *School*, 52, as cited in Culpepper, "Education."

necessarily with the reading of the Hebrew text. If his parents traveled to Jerusalem each year for the Passover (Luke 2:41), presumably they were observant Jews. Accompanying them on such visits would have acquainted Jesus with the wider world of Judaism, including Temple worship; moreover at the Passover he would have encountered pilgrims from many parts of the Roman empire and, perhaps, even from beyond its bounds. This experience would have counterbalanced, to some extent, the parochial worldview often engendered by upbringing in a small village. If the incident of Jesus at twelve years old staying behind in the Temple (Luke 2:41–52) is historical,[44] he already demonstrated a religious insight that impressed the Temple's resident scholars, although at that stage he need not have been aware of a special relationship with God or of his destiny.

Jesus' Adult Career

Although many scholars accept that the socio-economic circumstances prevailing in Galilee were important in shaping Jesus' ministry, opinions vary as to the manner in which those factors impacted him.[45] Clearly it was the agricultural sector that was most directly threatened by Antipas's schemes, peasant farmers being at risk of losing their land or their livelihood or both.

The NT's only explicit mention of Jesus' occupation prior to his ministry is in Mark 6:3, which claims that when, in the course of his ministry, he visited his home village of Nazareth and taught in the synagogue there, the congregation recognized him as the community's former *tektōn* (carpenter/builder).[46] Such a small community would not have generated sufficient work to support its own carpenter/builder. Keener suggests that

---

44. Although the story reads like an idealized scene from Jesus' childhood and it could be perceived as foreshadowing later events (his disappearance and reappearance three days later seem especially suggestive), much of scholarship contends that it is true. Nolland, for example, sees evidence for this in Luke's failure to seize any of several possibilities for enhancing the story (*Luke*, 1:128).

45. Morten Jensen cites such scholars as Jonathan Reed, Richard Horsley and Sean Freyne (Jensen, "Purity," 6). Another is James Crossley (*Christianity*, 35).

46. Although the Greek *tektōn* is generally rendered "carpenter" in English versions, BAGD claims that it can also mean "builder." Some of the illustrations Jesus used in his teaching suggest experience of building as well as carpentry; for examples see fn 51 below.

Joseph and Mary might have chosen to settle there (Matt 2:23)[47] because of its proximity to Sepphoris,[48] where Antipas's reconstruction projects could have provided regular work for Joseph. This, however, is questionable, since most Jews would have regarded working for Antipas as equivalent to working for the Romans.

Jean-Pierre Isbouts has suggested[49] that originally Jesus and/or his father were agricultural workers and this is certainly possible; perhaps they were among those mentioned by Reed (above) whom Antipas's schemes had forced off the land and into an artisan trade. Isbouts also insists that Antipas's development schemes[50] would have involved the forced conscription of large numbers of able-bodied men to work on the construction sites in Sepphoris and Tiberias. These schemes, which began in earnest around 6 CE when Jesus would have been about 12, would have had a devastating effect upon local agriculture. Having lost their fittest laborers, many farms would have been unable to meet their quotas and pay their rents. In order to maintain essential food supplies it is likely that many struggling small holdings—especially those close to Sepphoris and Tiberias, where Herodian officialdom could easily supervise them—were amalgamated into *latifundia*, perhaps overseen by wealthy incomers and worked by slaves.

As a Nazareth resident, Jesus lived through these changes; it is possible that he himself was conscripted to work in Sepphoris.[51] If so, he might have

---

47. Keener, *Matthew*, 115.

48. According to Luke 2:4, Joseph and Mary had lived in Nazareth before Jesus was born. But Joseph (or possibly his father) might have chosen to live there because its proximity to Sepphoris ensured a constant supply of work. This assumes that Joseph was working as a *tektōn*, but it is possible that he was an agricultural laborer (see below).

49. Isbouts, *Footsteps*, 117f.

50. Isbouts, *Footsteps*, 121f.

51. If Jesus was conscripted to work on the reconstruction of Sepphoris, this would partly explain his "missing years"—the years from age 12 to 30 concerning which the canonical gospels are silent. The evangelists would have been reluctant to admit that Jesus had effectively worked for the Romans for years, since this would make him appear to be a traitor to Israel. It would also explain how he had acquired the experience as a *tektōn* which is reflected in so many of his parables: (i) in Matt 7:3–5 and Luke 6:41f the parable of the speck in the eye depicts a common occurrence in a carpenter's workshop; (ii) the parable of the two builders (Matt 7:24–27 and Luke 6:47–49) suggests familiarity with building construction; (iii) the parable of the yoke (Matt 11:30) shows experience of making yokes, a frequent task for a carpenter in an agricultural community—he appreciated that to avoid injuring a valuable ox each yoke must be carefully tailored to fit its particular pair of beasts; (iv) in Matt 16:18 Jesus speaks of "building the church" upon a rock as a firm foundation; (v) the following verse refers to the handing over of

experienced opposition from hard-line neighbors who regarded working at Sepphoris, even under duress, as fraternizing with Antipas and his pro-Roman regime and therefore as treachery. He also probably witnessed neighbors in Nazareth being evicted from their land through no fault of their own. He saw the suffering it caused and, if he had any innate sense of justice, he recognized that what was happening was unjust. As he passed through puberty—a time when many boys begin questioning the wisdom of the adult world—he may even have wondered whether there might be something that he could do to alleviate this injustice. Surely these experiences would have made an impression upon Jesus.

HOW JESUS' TEACHING REFLECTS CONDITIONS IN GALILEE

During his later ministry Jesus deliberately based his stories and illustrations upon the everyday experiences of his audience; this ensured that they were both relevant and memorable. So Freyne's observation that the victims of Antipas's schemes appear in Jesus' parables is not surprising.[52] Indeed, by "mirror-reading" the parables and other teachings of Jesus, that is searching them for reflections of the prevailing socio-economic conditions rather than a religious meaning, we can glimpse the everyday experiences of Jesus and of the indigenous Galilean Jewish community generally.

Aggregation of Farms

The aggregation of small farms into larger estates appears to be reflected in the Dishonest Manager (Luke 16:1–14). The huge quantities of farm produce owed by the manager's debtors indicates that these were "gentleman farmers" rather than peasant subsistence farmers. Perhaps they had taken out loans from the manager's wealthy employer in order to buy up smaller farms with which to extend their existing estates and had agreed to make the repayments in the form of produce from the farms.

---

the keys, always a significant occasion for a builder; (vi) in Matt 21:42, Mark 12:10f, and Luke 20:17 Jesus cites the "cornerstone" passage from Ps 118, which itself must have been written by someone having experience of ancient building sites; this would certainly have resonated with a seasoned builder.

52. See fn 30 on page 29.

This buying up of small farms had serious repercussions for Galilee's peasantry. The original occupants were liable to be evicted, leaving the working members of the family jobless. Consequently many unemployed agricultural workers sought casual employment as day laborers. Such day laborers feature repeatedly in the Workers in the Vineyard (Matt 20:1–16) as the unemployed men waiting in the marketplace in the hope that someone would hire them. Theirs was a precarious existence with no guarantee of regular income and no centralized welfare system to act as a "safety net." The repeated appearances of the day laborers in the story imply that such men were a common sight, demonstrating the large numbers of folk displaced from their former workplaces. Moreover, as Stephen Wright observes, "the fact that some were willing to stay all day in the marketplace waiting for someone to hire them is an index of their need for employment, however short-term."[53]

In the original smallholdings the owner usually lived on his farm. When farms were aggregated into great estates, the new owner might live on his estate, but did not always do so. The frequency with which absentee landowners are mentioned in Jesus' stories[54] indicates that this was a common occurrence. Sometimes the landowner lived overseas, but even one who normally resided locally might spend appreciable time abroad for business or pleasure; the *pax romana* facilitated travel. Jesus saw in the figure of the absentee landlord an illustration of how God entrusts his human servants with considerable resources and allows them remarkable freedom in their stewardship of them, but nevertheless expects results; his liability to intervene when least expected is represented by the unpredictable time at which the landowner will return.

Hunger, Debt, and Crime

"Hunger" brackets a broad sweep of conditions from a healthy appetite to starvation. In Jesus' teaching its meaning is generally mid-range— more severe than a healthy appetite, but falling short of starvation; it is the hunger associated with poverty, when people often have insufficient to eat. Only two of Jesus' parables refer to hunger explicitly: the prodigal

---

53. Wright, *Storyteller*, 145.

54. For example, the Tenants (Matt 21:33–46; Mark 12:1–12; Luke 20:9–19), the Steward (Matt 24:45–51; Luke 12:42–46) and both versions of the Talents (Matt 25:14–30; Luke 19:12–27).

son claimed that he was dying of hunger in the distant land (Luke 15:17) and the beggar Lazarus would gladly have consumed the crumbs that fell from the rich man's table (Luke 16:21); the plight of both characters would have resonated with audiences familiar with hunger. Although the Needy Friend (Luke 11:5–8) does not mention hunger explicitly, it implies that it was by no means unusual for a Jew to "have nothing to set before" a friend who visits unexpectedly, that is, to have no presentable food in the home at all. The gospels hint that Jesus and his disciples were no strangers to hunger: "At that time Jesus went through the grainfields on the sabbath; his disciples were hungry, and they began to pluck heads of grain and to eat" (Matt 12:1); "On the following day, when they came from Bethany, he was hungry" (Mark 11:12).

For folk familiar with hunger of this sort Jesus' feeding miracles[55] would have been especially poignant, effectively enacted parables. For example, that those miraculous meals included fish as well as bread may be significant. With destitution widespread in Galilee, it is likely that for many Jews fish had become a luxury rather than the staple that it had been in the past. A meal consisting only of bread would have satisfied hunger, but one including fish as well was more nutritious and satisfying; the implication surely is that Jesus offers more than the bare minimum needed to sustain life.

Perhaps Jesus' most memorable hunger saying is the Beatitude: "Blessed are you who are hungry (*hoi peinōntes*) now, for you will be filled" (Luke 6:21) and "Blessed are those who hunger and thirst for righteousness (*hoi peinōntes kai dipsōntes tēn dikaiosunēn*), for they will be filled" (Matt 5:6). If the simpler Lucan version represents the original form of the saying, its hearers might nevertheless have understood it as having the spiritual meaning that the Matthean embellishment makes explicit, but it would certainly have resonated with hearers who frequently experienced the pangs of physical hunger. That Jesus appreciated the range of symbolism that physical food affords is evident in his institution of the Lord's Supper.

With debt a widespread problem in Galilee, it is surprising that in Jesus' teaching it is mentioned explicitly only in the Debtor Servant (Matt 18:23–35), the Two Debtors (Luke 7:41f), and in the Lord's Prayer.

---

55. The first feeding (five loaves and two fish) appears in Matt 14:13–21; Mark 6:30–44; Luke 9:10–17; and John 6:1–14. The second (seven loaves and an unspecified number of fish) appears in Matt 15:32–38 and Mark 8:1–10.

Nevertheless, its consistent use in these passages to represent moral shortfall or sin presupposes audiences familiar with debt and its devastating consequences.

The toxic combination of debt, hunger, and a lack of opportunities for legitimate gainful employment makes criminality a potent temptation. The frequent allusions to theft, burglary, and robbery in the teaching of Jesus indicate that his audiences were familiar with these and therefore that such crime must have been common and therefore a serious problem.[56]

Slaves

In Jesus' parables slaves are mentioned frequently: they appear as agricultural workers in the Weeds among the Wheat (Matt 13:24–30), as stewards in both versions of the Steward (Matt 24:45–51; Luke 12:42–46), in The Debtor Servant (Matt 18:23–35), and in both versions of the Talents (Matt 25:14–30; Luke 19:12–27). In Matthew's gospel alone *doulos*, "slave," occurs 29 times, all but two occurrences in the teaching of Jesus. That there are so many mentions suggests that slavery was rife in Palestine, including Galilee, despite Torah's prohibition of Jews from keeping other Jews as slaves (Lev 25:46b). Jennifer Glancy observes that Jesus was able to use the figure of the slave in his teachings because he lived in an environment where slaveholding was common.[57]

There is a tendency among Bible translators and exegetes to soften the harshness of life in first-century Israel. This is evidenced in the frequency with which some English versions render *doulos* as "servant." The evangelists certainly knew the difference between a *doulos* and a *diakonos*, "servant." More disturbingly, Glancy draws attention to instances in the parables in which miscreant slaves are subjected to extreme punishment: torturers are mentioned in Matt 18:34 (*tois basanistais*) and a slave is threatened with dismemberment in Matt 24:51 and Luke 12:46 (*dichotomēsei*).[58] The literal meaning of *dichotomeō* is 'cut in two,' but it has been suggested that here it denotes "punish severely," although no other instance is known of it being used in that sense. Perhaps, then, the evangelists intended the literal meaning, "cut in two." Set alongside Matthew's reference to torturers, the evidence is mounting that in first-century Israel slaves were indeed

---

56. For example, Matt 6:19f; 24:43; Luke 12:33, 39; 18:11; John 10:1–10; 12:6.

57. Glancy, *Slavery*, 122.

58. Glancy, *Slavery*, 118–122.

subjected to these extreme punishments. Since Jesus assumed that his audiences were familiar not only with slavery in general, but also with the dire punishments that slaves sometimes incurred, this must have been the *status quo*. Of course, there is always a danger in the literal reading of details in parables; it could be that these references to extreme punishments are hyperbole intended to emphasize the seriousness in God's sight of the sin represented by the slave's offences in the stories. But this conflicts with Jesus' usual policy of making his stories lifelike so that his hearers would identify with them.

It is possible that the slaves in Jesus' parables represented Jewish bonded laborers. Although not technically regarded as slavery (Lev 25:39f), bonded labor was a legal form of slavery. To sell oneself to a fellow Jew as a bonded laborer was an established means of survival in dire financial circumstances; Torah provided some protection for bonded laborers.[59] Perhaps some of Jesus' hearers were such bonded laborers or had been previously or feared that destitution might compel them to sell themselves or perhaps they had relatives or friends in such circumstances. This form of servitude was arguably preferable to day labor or beggary in that normally it ensured a roof over one's head and regular meals. But since Torah's regulations regarding bonded labor expressly prohibit the extreme punishments mentioned earlier, perhaps those parables were intended to depict Gentile slaveholders and/or Gentile slaves; if Jewish slaveholders and slaves were intended, they were blatantly violating Torah.

Beggars

In contrast with bonded laborers, beggars received no protection. Only one beggar appears in the parables of Jesus, namely Lazarus in the Rich Man and Lazarus (Luke 16:19–31). The word *ptōchos*, however, occurs on the lips of Jesus four times in Matthew and nine times in Luke. In classical usage this denotes "beggar," but it has been suggested that by NT times its meaning had moderated[60] justifying those English versions, such as the RSV and NRSV, which render it as "poor" or "poor man." Or is this another

---

59. They could not be subjected to excessive punishment (Ex 21:20)! They must be released if severely injured (Ex 21:26) and allowed to rest on the sabbath (Ex 23:12). They could be held for a maximum of six years (Ex 21:2; Deut 15:12) and on release must be given sufficient provisions to enable them to resume independent living (Deut 15:13f).

60. As evidenced by the transition from *penichran* to *ptōchē* in Luke 21:2f.

example of recent exegesis "softening" the harsh realities of NT times (see above)? Why did Jesus pronounce divine favor upon the *ptōchoi* (Matt 5:3; Luke 6:20)? Surely the commendable element is the needy person's recognition of his or her inability to provide for himself or herself and willingness to seek help; a beggar is by definition someone who solicits help from others. So what Jesus was commending was not the material circumstances of the poor, but their recognition of their total inability to get themselves right with God and consequent willingness to throw themselves upon his mercy. It is true that this saying would have offered little comfort to hearers who had been dispossessed, but Jesus used it to illustrate his understanding of humanity's relationship with God; this, presumably, is why traditionally these sayings have been spiritualized.[61] It is surely significant that in the parable the beggar Lazarus finds solace as Abraham's companion, while the rich man who had ignored many opportunities to help him—representing perhaps the Jewish authorities or the Herodians—is consigned to eternal torment. Those in the greatest danger of beggary were the "the crippled, the blind, and the lame" as their limited capacity for work made them undesirable as slaves and therefore unsellable. Significantly it is these who are invited into the Great Feast (Luke 14:15–24), a parable that would have been especially poignant to a Galilean audience at the time of Jesus.

Consequences of Economic Hardship

Reed mentioned a tendency for unemployed agricultural workers to migrate to cities in search of employment in some artisan trade.[62] Another option for dispossessed Galilean Jews was to leave Galilee altogether, although there is only circumstantial evidence of such a migration.[63] Judea—and especially Jerusalem—might seem the most obvious destination

---

61. If the simpler Lucan version, *Makarioi hoi ptōchoi* (Luke 6:20), represents the original form of this saying, the Matthean embellishment, *Makarioi hoi ptōchoi tō pneumati* (Matt 5:3), may represent an attempt to shift the meaning from a pecuniary condition to a spiritual one.

62. See fn 27 on page 28.

63. Perhaps the younger son's departure to the "distant country" in the Prodigal Son (Luke 15:11–32) is an example; he wished to escape the stringencies in Galilee that were blighting his family and neighbors. In Luke 13:31 some Pharisees advise Jesus to leave Antipas's territory in order to save his life as though such flights were a frequent occurrence.

for Jews seeking a better quality of life,[64] but Galilean immigrants there were unlikely to find a warm welcome for several reasons. The first was that Galileans risked being presumed to be insurgents, as we have seen.[65] Secondly, Galileans who came seeking work were perhaps initially dependent upon charity at a time when Judeans were also under pressure. Thirdly, the incoming Galileans' tales of the injustices they had suffered under Antipas and, possibly, lack of support from Jerusalem (see below) probably caused embarrassment. Fourthly, to Judeans it might have seemed as though Galilee's degree of Hellenization and rapid settlement threatened to overwhelm such traditional Jewish character as it had once possessed; this might have led them to suppose that the Galileans had emulated Jacob in selling their birthright: "they've brought it upon themselves." These factors may explain the Fourth Gospel's depiction of some Judean leaders as contemptuous of Galileans: for example, in John 7:52 Nicodemus's peers on the Sanhedrin insinuate that he must be "from Galilee" because his suggestion that the Galilean Jesus be given a fair hearing was deemed stupid. The clear implication is that those Judeans regarded Galileans as uneducated peasants who did not merit a fair trial.

So Galilean Jews had good reason to believe that they were the victims of unjust treatment from the authorities, both Roman and Jewish. While Antipas was effectively stealing their land, the Jewish hierarchy in Jerusalem turned a blind eye. Ultimately, of course, there was little that it could have done to alleviate the situation; Jerusalem was no longer politically responsible for Galilee, although it had a pastoral obligation to all Jews. Moreover, since Antipas was Caesar's representative, to criticize him or his policies was tantamount to criticizing Caesar himself. But the situation surely led to widespread mistrust of the Jerusalem authorities among Galilean Jews, even though the Jerusalem temple remained the focus of Judaism.

Undoubtedly Galilee's problems were exacerbated by its geographical isolation from Judea. To travel between them necessitated either passing through despised Samaria, which many scrupulous Jews were reluctant to do, or taking a lengthy detour via Perea which involved two awkward crossings of the Jordan. The difficult journey may have been one reason that

---

64. That in Matt 26:73 inhabitants of Jerusalem recognized the Galilean accent instantly (*c.f.* Acts 2:7), showing familiarity with it, might have been a consequence of encounters with Galileans visiting Jerusalem, for example, for the Passover.

65. See *Galilee as a Hotbed of Revolutionary Activity* on page 22.

Jewish officials rarely visited the province,[66] although Sanders points out that there were priests based there.[67] It was probably because Jesus appreciated the scarcity of officialdom in Galilee, having been brought up there, that he retreated there when he fell foul of the Pharisees in Judea (John 4:1–3).[68] Indeed the general acceptance by the scholars of this scarcity of officials has led some to question the veracity of the fourteen episodes in the synoptic gospels on which Jesus encountered teachers of the law (scribes) or Pharisees or both while in Galilee.[69]

66. Anthony Saldarini, for example, points out that the Rabbinic literature places the pre-destruction sages (Pharisees) in Jerusalem and says little about Galilee. This is why he questions the historical reliability of the Galilean tradition derived from Mark which reports scribes and Pharisees in Galilee (*Pharisees*, 291). Geza Vermes states that there was no serious Pharisee presence in Galilee until after the destruction of Jerusalem and the Jewish state in 70 CE (Vermes, *Authentic Gospel*, 63). John Nolland, commenting on Luke's account of Jesus dining with tax collectors and sinners states that the presence of the Pharisees who criticized Jesus' action is unexplained (*Luke*, 245), although it is impossible to determine whether the failure to explain their presence is on the part of the evangelist or subsequent scholarship. E. P. Sanders, commenting on the same incident, says that it is unimaginable that the Pharisees would police Galilee to see whether or not an otherwise upright man ate with sinners (*Jesus and Judaism*, 178). Craig Keener, commenting on Matthew's account of the episode in which Pharisees criticized Jesus for allowing his disciples to pluck heads of grain as they walked through a wheatfield on the Sabbath, says that one would not usually expect to find Pharisees in a Galilean wheatfield on the Sabbath (*Matthew*, 351). This may seem a statement of the obvious, but was it the Sabbath or the setting in Galilee that made the presence of Pharisees so unexpected? In contrast, Alan Storkey claims that the Scribes and Pharisees were probably the next most powerful party in Galilee (*Jesus and Politics*, 44), but the arguments with which he supports this claim seem more appropriate to Judea than to Galilee.

67. These served as judges and teachers of the law (Sanders, *Judaism: Practice and Belief*, 170.) There is Biblical support for this in the healing, presumably in Galilee, of a leper (Mark 1:40–44 and parallels). Jesus told the healed leper, "Show yourself to the priest, and offer for your cleansing what Moses commanded." Since it would surely have been unreasonable to expect a newly healed leper to undertake the long journey to Jerusalem to follow this instruction in the temple, presumably Jesus intended him to visit a local priest.

68. *anechōrēsen* in Matt 4:12 may indicate a flight from a perceived threat. The circumstances of this retreat are considered in chapter 6 under *The Early Judean Ministry* on page 113.

69. The fourteen episodes are listed in fn 37 on page 125.

CAPERNAUM

At some point prior to the start of his public ministry Jesus relocated from Nazareth to Capernaum (Matt 4:13). This was a fishing community on the north-west shore of Lake Galilee. We can only conjecture as to Jesus' reasons for leaving Nazareth, but the following scenario seems plausible. As mentioned earlier, Nazareth was too small a community to support its own carpenter/builder. Jesus may have incurred opposition from his neighbors in Nazareth by working on the reconstruction of nearby Sepphoris, which in their eyes made him a traitor to Israel and her God. This may have led him to begin practicing as an itinerant tradesman, traveling throughout Galilee and undertaking such building and carpentry jobs as he could find. Lake Galilee's thriving fishing industry would have afforded him abundant work opportunities: not only would the fishermen's boats need periodic repair and replacement, but also those men would have owned carts and sheds needing maintenance, not to mention houses. Moreover, locally based *tektones* were likely to have been conscripted to work on the development of Antipas's new capital, Tiberias, which was nearby. Jesus probably chose Capernaum as his new home because he had made friends with some of the fishermen who lived there, having become acquainted with them through his work as an itinerant tradesman.

Four of those fishermen are particularly prominent in the gospels: Simon and his brother Andrew, and James and his brother John (Mark 1:16–20). They had much in common with Jesus. Like him, they probably did not own appreciable land and so were not directly threatened by Antipas's land-grabbing schemes. Furthermore, since many indigenous Galilean Jews were experiencing severe poverty, it is likely that locally the demand for fish as a staple had declined, forcing the fishermen to sell their catches in the comparatively affluent Hellenistic cities of Tiberias and Sepphoris. If they did this, they too were probably regarded by their neighbors as guilty of collaborating with Antipas's pro-Roman regime.

As Jesus and these fishermen worked together, it would have been natural for them to discuss their joys and frustrations. The discovery that they had all experienced hostility from their neighbors for similar reasons created a natural bond between them. Moreover, it enabled them to see that a rift was developing which threatened the social cohesion of Galilee. Since both carpenter/builders and fishermen were essentially practical and self-sufficient people, accustomed to tackling problems as soon as they arose rather than ignoring them or referring them to others, they probably all considered the possibility of demonstrating their solidarity with their community by some kind of political action against the injustices that so many Galilean Jews were suffering. One advantage that they had over their neighbors in the agricultural sector was that they were comparatively wealthy and well fed, able to afford an occasional break from work; in contrast, for most agricultural workers life was a constant struggle simply to survive. If the seeds of Jesus' public ministry had been sown in Nazareth, it was on the shores of Lake Galilee that they took root and began to grow.

From Jesus' discussions with the fishermen an idea emerged. They would organize a special event seeking justice for the suffering Jews of Galilee, particularly those in the agricultural sector. There is circumstantial evidence that it was to take the form of a march of unemployed Galileans to Jerusalem[70] to warn the authorities there that Antipas's policies were causing such discontent that violent insurrection was likely. But neither Jesus nor the fishermen had the skills needed to organize an event of this kind. How could they acquire the very different skill set that they would need? The appearance of John the Baptist provided an answer.

CONCLUSIONS

This chapter has sought to identify factors in Galilee that might have contributed to Jesus' decision to undertake the ministry described in the gospels. Former suggestions that Jesus was an insurgent against Rome or a Cynic philosopher have now been largely discredited. But that Galilee's harsh socio-economic conditions affected Jesus is borne out by the illustrations in his teaching: these suggest that he was familiar with the hardships that Galilean Jews faced, such as unemployment and poverty. His

---

70. That circumstantial evidence is as follows: (i) Jesus was aware that large numbers of agricultural workers were unemployed, as represented by the men waiting in the marketplace in the Workers in the Vineyard (Matt 20:1–16); (ii) when Jesus asked the fishermen to become "fishers of men" (Mark 1:17 RSV), this implies the indiscriminate gathering of large numbers of men rather than the careful recruitment of individuals as disciples; (iii) since Galilee had a reputation for producing insurgents—see *Consequences of Economic Hardship* on page 40—it is easy to understand how garbled reports of the proposed march might have led the Sanhedrin to believe mistakenly that it was a rebel army that Jesus was planning to march into Jerusalem—for further see *Reasons for the Sanhedrin's Hostility* on page 117—and this was sufficient threat to justify the expensive option of placing Jesus under surveillance (see *Under Surveillance* on page 123); (iv) the ultimate aim of the march was to end Antipas's reign; according to Luke 13:31, Antipas regarded Jesus as posing a threat so serious that he plotted to kill him.

discussions with his friends, the fishermen of Capernaum, led to the idea of a campaign to relieve the suffering of Galilean Jews. But they would need to acquire fresh skills if they were to undertake such an project.

4

JOHN THE BAPTIST

THE PREVIOUS CHAPTER CONCLUDED THAT the harsh socio-economic conditions prevailing in Galilee gave Jesus a cause to pursue—justice for Galilee's oppressed indigenous Jews. Nevertheless he remained essentially a carpenter/builder. He may have been passionately concerned about his fellow Galileans, but he lacked the specialist skills of a campaigner and, even if he were to acquire them, it was most unusual for a Jew in his day and age to make so radical a career change; that would require a powerful trigger event. Did the appearance of John the Baptist constitute such an event?

Continuing our search for factors which led Jesus to undertake the ministry described in the gospels, this chapter examines the person and ministry of John the Baptist. All four canonical gospels describe an association between John and Jesus before Jesus' public ministry began. It is not surprising then that many scholars[1] have concluded that the Baptist became Jesus' mentor and therefore, by definition, a person who significantly shaped his subsequent career. The considerable inconsistency in the canonical evangelists' treatment of John may be a consequence of their embarrassment concerning Jesus' subservience to him; this conflicted with their agenda to present Jesus as Lord.

---

1. These are surveyed under *The Relationship between John and Jesus* on page 83.

PRIMARY SOURCES

Apart from the NT and Josephus, few ancient sources mention the Baptist. Robert Webb has surveyed these, concluding that the Slavonic Josephus and the Mandaean literature offer no data of value in a historical study.[2] Among the extra-canonical gospels he confined his attention to those of Thomas, of the Ebionites, and of the Nazareans and the Protevangelium of James, because these are widely believed to have been written no later than the middle of the second century making them less likely to be derived from the canonical gospels. Nevertheless, he concluded that, "The extra-canonical Gospels do not contain the quantity of data concerning John the Baptist found in the canonical gospels. Their concern appears to focus more exclusively upon the relationship between John and Jesus, whereas the canonical Gospels provide some description of John himself and his ministry."[3] A search of the rabbinical literature found no mention of the Baptist,[4] despite the claims of the canonical gospels and Josephus that he made a considerable impact on the Jews. This leaves the NT and Josephus the only useful ancient sources.

A complication regarding the NT's use as a source is that inevitably the evangelists viewed the Baptist retrospectively in the light of the coming of Jesus, which they believed to be the subject—and indeed the fulfillment—of John's eschatological preaching. As Webb sagely observes, there is a danger, therefore, that the evangelists might have tailored their presentation of John's proclamation so that it complies with their understanding of its fulfilment.[5] As will be seen, however, there is evidence that some at least of the evangelists' representation of John's preaching is accurate. A further complication is that the evangelists' primary agenda was to promote Jesus. For them John's importance consisted principally in the role that he exercised in Jesus' career. Moreover, Joel Marcus refers to "serious competition" between John's followers and the Jesus movement which may have affected the evangelists' references to John.[6] These factors contribute to the uneven coverage of John in the NT.

---

2. Webb, *John the Baptizer*, 45.

3. Webb, *John the Baptizer*, 84.

4. This is corroborated by Webb's comprehensive study of John which similarly does not mention the Rabbinical literature as a source.

5. Webb, *John the Baptizer*, 261.

6. Marcus, *John*, 9.

A similar complication concerns Josephus's account of the Baptist.[7] Although its authenticity is more widely accepted than that of his briefer description of Jesus, this is nevertheless the subject of scholarly debate. As Webb observes, most scholars have accepted it although a few reject it as a Christian interpolation.[8] He outlines three objections that have been raised regarding Josephus's account: these concern John's comparative unimportance, the unique vocabulary of Josephus's account, and differences between Josephus's and Christian understandings of baptism; he refutes all three objections convincingly.[9] More recently Marcus has devoted Appendix 2 of his book on the Baptist[10] to a recent claim by Rivka Nir that Josephus's account of John is a Christian interpolation; her argument centers upon Josephus's description of John's baptism, which contains ideas similar to those of Qumran. Marcus refutes her argument on the grounds that the Qumran community's teaching regarding baptism influenced John as well as Josephus, so that Josephus's assertion need not have had a Christian source. But, as we shall see, John's association with Qumran is itself debatable. This study accepts the verdict of most scholarship that Josephus's account of the Baptist is authentic.

So the NT and Josephus are the only primary sources of value in a historical study such as this. Both, however, must be scrutinized critically because of the likelihood that their writers have been influenced by sectarian polemics. In the light of this, reconstruction of "the historical John" is fraught with difficulties. Much of what is widely believed about him is to some extent conjectural.

SECONDARY SOURCES

Recent scholarly literature on John the Baptist is surveyed in *Appendix 3: Literature on John the Baptist* on page 168.

---

7. *Antiquities*, 18:5:2. An English version appears on page 62.

8. Webb, *John the Baptizer*, 39.

9. Webb, *John the Baptizer*, 39–41.

10. Marcus, *John*, 125–7.

JOHN'S BACKGROUND

In Josephus and the canonical gospels except Luke the Baptist appears on the stage of history without any introduction. No account is given of his ancestry, personal circumstances or the background to his ministry. Perhaps the authors reckoned that their intended readers would be so familiar with the Baptist as to need no such information. Alternatively they might have been afraid that to say too much about John might make him seem superior to Jesus.

Luke alone, writing for a Gentile readership which probably had little or no knowledge of John, provides some background material. First he describes an announcement by the angel Gabriel to a priest named Zechariah that his wife Elizabeth, despite her great age, will conceive and bear a son whom they are to name John and who will become a faithful servant of God (Luke 1:5–25); the similarities with Sarah's conception of Isaac at an advanced age (Gen 18:10–12) would not have been noticed by most Gentiles. Next Gabriel visits Mary and informs her that, despite her virginity, she too will bear a son who "will be called the Son of the Most High, and the Lord God will give to him the throne of his ancestor David" (Luke 1:26–38). Here readers learn that Elizabeth and Mary are related, making John and Jesus cousins. Luke next describes a visit by Mary to Elizabeth (Luke 1:39–56) and then John's birth (Luke 1:57–79). Sadly he condenses John's life between his birth and his public ministry into the single sentence: "The child grew and became strong in spirit, and he was in the wilderness (*en tais erēmois*) until the day he appeared publicly to Israel" (Luke 1:80). It would be interesting to discover what led Luke to state that John's childhood was spent "in the wilderness." As will be considered shortly, some scholars have conjectured that John spent at least part of that time in the Qumran community, which would have been literally "in the wilderness"; if so, perhaps Luke is alluding to that. Alternatively he may have used the term figuratively, meaning "in obscurity" in contrast with his explosive appearance on the stage of history at the start of his ministry; Nolland favors this interpretation.[11]

Joan Taylor is skeptical concerning the value of this Lucan material as a historical source. She writes that the infancy narrative of Luke (1:5–80) is generally held to be a literary construct teaching Christians that John was inferior to Jesus and it is questionable whether it contains any historical

---

11. Nolland, *Luke*, 1:91.

material.[12] Her observations seem astute; Luke's attempts to make John into what she describes as an "incipient Christian"[13] seem to conflict with the Elijah-like prophet portrayed elsewhere in the synoptics.

Joel Marcus is also cautious, postulating a non-Christian origin for this biographical material. He also considers that the prophecy that John will be Spirit-filled from his mother's womb (1:15) contradicts the common Christian view, which Luke himself endorses elsewhere, that the Spirit is an exclusive gift of Jesus (Luke 3:16; Acts 19:1–6).[14] But Marcus's objection regarding the Spirit is surely questionable: since the OT prophets were Spirit-filled,[15] surely the statement in 1:15 is intended to place John in the same tradition as they, as many of his contemporaries (Luke 20:6) and recent scholarship recognize.[16]

Taylor and Marcus have good reason for their caution. Thankfully the most important aspects of John that arise from this material—his kinship with Jesus and his priesthood—are peripheral to the Christian faith.

Kinship with Jesus

The authenticity of the posited blood relationship between Jesus and John is one issue raised by this unique Lucan tradition. Since Jewish society attached special importance to blood ties and John plays a prominent role in the gospel narratives, why does only Luke mention it? Of course, it might have been so well known in the early Christian communities that the other evangelists assumed that their readers would be familiar with it. Many commentators, however, consider that the relationship was a Lucan contrivance introduced for theological reasons; perhaps he was attempting to explain the problematic aspects of the relationship between the two men, such as the solidarity between them seen in their willingness to co-operate in what might otherwise appear to be rival missions. Raymond E. Brown, for example, argues that by presenting the Baptist as a relative of Jesus on his mother's side (1:36) Luke is bringing him within the Christian sphere.[17]

12. Taylor, *John*, 9.

13. Taylor may have (perhaps unconsciously) borrowed the term "incipient Christian" from Raymond E. Brown; see the passage referenced in fn 17 (below).

14. Marcus, *John*, 12f.

15. For example, Isa 61:1; Ezek 2:2; 3:24; 11:1; Micah 3:8.

16. For example, the citation from Meyer referenced in fn 38 on page 56.

17. Brown, *Birth*, 285.

It must be remembered that the blood relationship itself is attested in only the three words *hē suggenis sou*, "your relative," in Luke 1:36 and *suggenis*, as Nolland points out, is quite vague.[18] If those words had been omitted, so that no evangelist mentioned any such kinship, the earliest Christians would have assumed that Jesus and John were unrelated.

Priesthood

Another question raised by Luke's account concerns John's priesthood. In Judaism priesthood was hereditary. So if, as Luke states, John's father Zechariah was a priest, of necessity John was also one. Many priests, like Zechariah, administered the cultus in the Temple in Jerusalem. Others, as Sanders points out, exercised a variety of official functions serving, for example, as judges and teachers of the law throughout Judea and Galilee.[19] No source, however, mentions John performing any of the conventional functions of a priest; his only recorded ministry consists in his preaching and baptizing in the wilderness. The evidence for John's priesthood, as for his kinship with Jesus, rests upon Luke's accuracy as a historian. If John was a priest, that he baptized Jesus could be interpreted as an endorsement of Jesus by both law and prophets; otherwise no major Christian doctrine depends upon the authenticity of John's priesthood.

The Qumran Connection

If John was a priest, it is natural to seek a reason for his apparent failure to exercise any of the conventional duties of the priesthood. At one time John's postulated association with the Qumran community[20] seemed to answer this and several other questions about the Baptist.

There may be circumstantial evidence for John's association with Qumran in that all four canonical evangelists claim that the Baptist fulfilled the prophecy, "In the wilderness prepare the way of the Lord" (Isa 40:3).[21] Clearly a tradition in the early Christian communities associated the Baptist with this prophecy, which the Qumran community also appears

18. Nolland, *Luke*, 1:56.

19. Sanders, *Judaism: Practice and Belief*, 170.

20. See *The Qumran Controversy* on page 168.

21. Matt 3:3; Mark 1:3; Luke 3:4; John 1:23. According to John 1:23, the Baptist applied the prophecy to himself.

to have adopted as a kind of mission statement.[22] In what way did the Baptist fulfill this prophecy? Claus Westermann claims that this prophecy compared Babylon's sacred highways, along which cultic processions paraded her gods, with the road through the wilderness which the Israelites are to prepare in the desert and on which they will return from exile.[23] Alec Motyer, however, offers an alternative interpretation; he points out that the Lord's people are not called to prepare that road, because it is ready for them. Instead the passage combines the traditional picture of the Lord coming to his people's aid with the practice of constructing processional ways for visiting dignitaries or for cultic processions.[24] Motyer's interpretation seems preferable because, as will be seen, the Baptist's ministry was concerned primarily with the imminent coming of one who was either God himself or his human agent.

The traditional Christian understanding of the Baptist's fulfillment of this prophecy is that John's ministry in the wilderness "prepared the way of the Lord" by leading the people of Israel into repentance so that they would be ready to receive the mightier personage whose imminent coming he heralded, namely Jesus.[25] At least one scholar, however, connects the prophecy's original setting in the exile with a new exodus to be accomplished in Jesus.[26] As will be considered later in this chapter, this prophecy seems to have held a special significance for the Baptist who believed his to be the voice that it mentions.

Although the work of such scholars as Taylor and Hutchinson has all but disproved the Qumran connection, this leaves a vacuum. If Qumran was not responsible for John's distinctive lifestyle, who or what was? Hutchinson suggests that John should be seen in the role of an Old Testament prophet, namely the eschatological prophet who will herald the Messiah and prepare people for the coming kingdom.[27] This may be correct, but it still leaves questions unanswered. Perhaps the answers are to be found in Craig Keener's observation that the Baptist might have rebelled

22. The Qumran Manual of Discipline states: "They will separate themselves from the midst of the habitation of perverse men to go to the wilderness to clear there the way of the Lord, as it is written: 'In the wilderness clear the way of the Lord; Level in the desert a highway for our God.'"

23. Westermann, *Isaiah 40–66*, 38.

24. Motyer, *Isaiah*, 300.

25. So John Nolland (*Luke*, 1:143). Donald Hagner hints at this view (*Matthew*, 1:48).

26. Keener, *Matthew*, 116.

27. Hutchinson, "John the Baptist," 187.

against his priestly roots (Luke 1:5) and against the corrupt aristocratic Jerusalem priesthood; such a pro-Roman establishment was the very kind of target against which a traditional Israelite eschatological prophet would thunder.[28] Another possibility is

> that more males were being born into priestly families than the cultus needed, so that some selection process was employed and John was one of those whom it rejected. Aware of a divine calling and frustrated by the Temple establishment, John sought an alternative ministry. The vivid eschatological motifs in the snippet of his preaching preserved in Matt 3:7–12 suggest the influence of one of the apocalyptically oriented sects. If John had joined one of those, that and his experience of the Temple hierarchy might explain his radical, anti-establishment stance.[29]

More recently Joel Marcus has revived the theory that John started out as a member of the Qumran community. In his 2018 book *John the Baptist in History and Theology* he lists no fewer than twelve items of circumstantial evidence for this connection,[30] claiming that so many and such varied similarities surely combine to make a strong case for commonality. In fairness, Marcus also acknowledges five significant differences between John and Qumran, pointing out that without these John might have remained with the Sect.[31] As to John's reasons for leaving (or perhaps being expelled from) Qumran, Marcus offers three "reasoned guesses": (i) a developing sense of his own salvation-historical importance, that he was the eschatological Elijah; (ii) a desire to leave the confines of Qumran and proclaim repentance to all Israel; (iii) a more tolerant attitude to the Gentile world.[32]

Inevitably many of Marcus's arguments concern baptism, so characteristic of John the Baptist and widely practiced in the Qumran sect. But this does not necessarily indicate a close connection between John and Qumran. Baptism was the focus of thought and discussion in many Jewish groups at that time; Martin Goodman points out that if Jews were really eager to win converts, the easiest way to increase their number might have been to remove the more onerous requirements laid upon proselytes, notably circumcision; he refers to Epictetus who wrote in the early second

---

28. Keener, *John*, 1:432.

29. Amos, *Hypocrites*, 170.

30. Marcus, *John*, 28–32.

31. Marcus, *John*, 33f.

32. Marcus, *John*, 35f.

century as if the ultimate sign of dedication to Judaism by a convert was baptism.[33] Later Goodman offers the counter argument that circumcision is no more painful or dangerous than other initiation rites and he attributes modern scholarly interest in it to Paul's insistence that it was not required for admission to the Christian community. He is surely justified in his conclusion that it seems naïve to suggest that dropping this one requirement would result in a flood of proselytes.[34]

We may never know for certain whether John was ever at Qumran. Just as the discovery of the DSS led a number of scholars to argue convincingly that John had been associated with that community, only to have their arguments eloquently refuted by others, so Marcus has now initiated a second round of the argument. The Qumran theory is attractive because it not only accords with other ancient sources, but also fills in gaps left by those sources, answering the questions that remained concerning John's origins and providing a plausible explanation for aspects of his later ministry. Attractiveness, however, does not guarantee the correctness of a theory. Marcus has re-laid some foundations upon which others may yet dare to build; perhaps these foundations will prove more secure than those laid soon after the discovery of the DSS.

In conclusion, then, little is certain about John's background. Most scholars are skeptical regarding Luke's statements that his father was a priest and his mother a relative of Jesus, regarding these as a literary construct to explain aspects of John's relationship with Jesus. The attractive hypothesis that John had been associated with the Qumran sect, which answers many questions, has recently been revived by Marcus. It remains to be seen how scholarship will respond to this new round in that debate.

JOHN'S MINISTRY

The synoptic gospels introduce John's ministry as follows:

> In those days John the Baptist appeared in the wilderness of Judea, proclaiming, "Repent, for the kingdom of heaven has come near." . . . Then the people of Jerusalem and all Judea were going out to him, and all the region along the Jordan, and they were baptized by him in the river Jordan, confessing their sins. (Matt 3:1f, 5f)

33. Goodman, *Mission*, 67f.
34. Goodman, *Mission*, 81.

John the baptizer appeared in the wilderness, proclaiming a baptism of repentance for the forgiveness of sins (*kērussōn baptisma metanoias eis afesin hamartiōn*). And people from the whole Judean countryside and all the people of Jerusalem were going out to him, and were baptized by him in the river Jordan, confessing their sins. (Mark 1:4f).

In the fifteenth year of the reign of Emperor Tiberius, when Pontius Pilate was governor of Judea, and Herod was ruler of Galilee, and his brother Philip ruler of the region of Ituraea and Trachonitis, and Lysanias ruler of Abilene, during the high priesthood of Annas and Caiaphas, the word of God came to John son of Zechariah in the wilderness. He went into all the region around the Jordan, proclaiming a baptism of repentance for the forgiveness of sins (*kērussōn baptisma metanoias eis afesin hamartiōn*) . . . (Luke 3:1–3)

The Fourth Gospel introduces the Baptist as follows:

There was a man sent from God, whose name was John. He came as a witness to testify to the light, so that all might believe through him. (John 1:6f)

Its clearest description of the Baptist's ministry is the following extract from his interview with the delegation of officials (see below):

John answered them, "I baptize with water. Among you stands one whom you do not know, the one who is coming after me; I am not worthy to untie the thong of his sandal." (John 1:26f)

The only surviving examples of John's preaching are brief extracts recorded in the synoptic gospels, which we shall consider later.

Whether or not John had been born a priest, his ministry stood firmly in Judaism's alternative prophetic tradition. Mark's description of John's bizarre clothing—"camel's hair, with a leather belt around his waist" (Mark 1:6 and Matt 3:4) may be authentic, reflecting a Petrine reminiscence, but its similarity to that of Elijah (as described in 2 Ki 1:8) may indicate that Mark was influenced by theological interests. In the light of a widespread belief amongst the Jews[35] that Elijah would return to herald the coming of Yahweh himself (Matt 17:10), Mark may have wished to make the public identify John with Elijah and thereby lend credence to his message.

---

35. This was based on the prophecy, "Lo, I will send you the prophet Elijah before the great and terrible day of the Lord comes" (Mal 4:5).

Although John is reported elsewhere as denying that he was Elijah (John 1:21), the synoptic gospels claim that Jesus identified him thus.[36] But if not Elijah, John was claiming to be a prophet and was widely recognized as such.[37]

Meyer identifies John's prophetic claim as significant in itself: "Here was no theologian, no enthusiast, but a prophet. And this alone was taken as a persuasive sign of the truth of his message, a sign of the imminence of the end; for by now Israel had lived so long without prophecy that common expectation postponed its appearance to the day of definitive salvation. The very phenomenon of the return of prophecy made John an eschatological symbol freighted with powerful, if ambiguous, meaning."[38]

Meyer is right in highlighting the impact of John's prophetic ministry, intensified by the social and political *milieu* of mid-first-century Palestine. As Yahweh's chosen people, the Jews resented their subjection to pagan Rome and its interference in their affairs; they were hungry for freedom. Remembrance of previous occasions in their history when Yahweh had intervened to rescue them—the exodus, the return from exile, the Maccabean revolt—now led them to expect a further divine intervention. So when John appeared, proclaiming the imminent arrival of one mightier than himself, the Jews—or some of them at least—imagined that this coming one must be Yahweh's deliverer sent to liberate them from the Romans. Of course, this was exactly what they *wanted* to believe—it is why John attracted a huge audience and exerted such a powerful influence: "for all regarded John as truly a prophet" (Mark 11:32); "they [the Jews] seemed as if they would do anything that he [John] advised" (Josephus, *Antiquities*, 18:118).

Mark

Mark records only the following snippet of John's preaching: "The one who is more powerful than I is coming after me (*erchetai ho ischuroteros mou opisō mou*); I am not worthy to stoop down and untie the thong of his sandals. I have baptized you with water; but he will baptize you with the Holy Spirit" (Mark 1:7f). Other versions of this saying which survive in the

---

36. Matt 11:14; 17:12; Mark 9:13.

37. Matt 11:9 and Luke 7:26; Matt 14:5; 21:26 and Mark 11:32 and Luke 20:6.

38. Meyer, *Aims*, 115.

Fourth Gospel and in the Q tradition preserved in Matthew and Luke will be considered later.

Baptism connects this snippet with Mark's earlier description of John's ministry so that it is possible to make a tentative reconstruction of his understanding of John's *modus operandi*. In Mark 1:7f there is (i) the announcement of a coming one mightier than the Baptist himself. If his hearers identified John with Elijah, they would have expected the mightier one to be Yahweh himself and his imminent coming would have implied judgment (see later). To prepare for this in Mark 1:5 there is (ii) a call to repentance and (iii) an invitation to those responding to demonstrate the sincerity of their repentance through water baptism. Finally (iv) there is the promise that the coming one will perform a more profound baptism, an immersion in not water, but the Holy Spirit. Many of John's hearers would have recognized the Holy Spirit as the inspirer of the prophets of old.[39] In particular they might have remembered the apocalyptic prophet Joel's prediction that in the last days God would pour out his spirit on all humanity (Joel 2:28–32).[40] John's hearers, then, would have understood his message as intimating that the new age foretold by Joel was imminent. In this age God's Holy Spirit would be bestowed on all the faithful rather than, as in the past, only those whose office warranted it, such as prophets and kings. The expected personage mightier than John himself who would inaugurate this age of the Spirit would be Yahweh himself or, perhaps, a specially endowed human representative. Either way, a new divine intervention in human history was at hand. Repentance authenticated by water baptism was the essential prerequisite for sinful humanity's impending personal encounter with God or his representative; either entailed an element of judgment.

The Q Tradition

A longer fragment of John's preaching is preserved in Matt 3:7 12 and Luke 3:7–9, 16f; these incorporate a parallel (Matt 3:11; Luke 3:16) to the snippet

---

39. Compare, for example, Isa 61:1; Ezek 2:2; 3:24; Dan 4:8f; Mic 3:8.

40. The Book of Acts tells of the coming of the Holy Spirit on the community of disciples of Jesus gathering at Pentecost and how the consequent glossalalia drew crowds whom Peter addressed using this prophecy, leading to about three thousand conversions (Acts 2). So the early Christian movement certainly understood itself as a community created through the action of the Holy Spirit in fulfillment of this prophecy and the preaching of John the Baptist concerning the coming mightier one who would baptize with the Holy Spirit.

preserved in Mark 1:7f considered above. The similarity of the two passages has led many scholars to conclude that both are derived from the same hypothetical source document, Q.

Matt 3:7–12	Luke 3:7–9, 16f
But when he saw many Pharisees and Sadducees coming for baptism, he said to them,	
	John said to the crowds that came out to be baptized by him,
"You brood of vipers! Who warned you to flee from the wrath to come?	"You brood of vipers! Who warned you to flee from the wrath to come?
8 Bear fruit worthy of repentance.	8 Bear fruits worthy of repentance.
9 Do not presume to say to yourselves, 'We have Abraham as our ancestor'; for I tell you, God is able from these stones to raise up children to Abraham.	Do not begin to say to yourselves, 'We have Abraham as our ancestor'; for I tell you, God is able from these stones to raise up children to Abraham.
10 Even now the axe is lying at the root of the trees; every tree therefore that does not bear good fruit is cut down and thrown into the fire.	9 Even now the axe is lying at the root of the trees; every tree therefore that does not bear good fruit is cut down and thrown into the fire."
	16 John answered all of them by saying,
11 I baptize you with water for repentance,	"I baptize you with water;
but one who is more powerful than I is coming after me;	but one who is more powerful than I is coming;
I am not worthy to carry his sandals.	I am not worthy to untie the thong of his sandals.
He will baptize you with the Holy Spirit and fire.	He will baptize you with the Holy Spirit and fire.
12 His winnowing fork is in his hand,	17 His winnowing fork is in his hand,
and he will clear his threshing floor and will gather his wheat into the granary;	to clear his threshing floor and to gather the wheat into his granary;
but the chaff he will burn with unquenchable fire."	but the chaff he will burn with unquenchable fire."

Although the verbal agreement in the spoken words is 97%, the highest of any Q passage, the narrative sections are quite different. This suggests that Q contained only the spoken words, without any indication of the circumstances in which they were uttered; this left Matthew and Luke to deduce these from their content and possibly other sources. Consequently in Matthew the passage is addressed to a presumably investigative deputation of Pharisees and Sadducees, but in Luke to the crowds who came seeking baptism. Recent scholarship generally favors the Matthean version, Hagner, France and Nolland giving various reasons for their decision.[41] Certainly the polemical nature of John's address—especially its opening question—makes it easy to imagine him addressing self-righteous Jewish officialdom (Matt 3:9 and Luke 3:8), but such content would hardly be appropriate for the sin-burdened tax collectors and prostitutes who, apparently, constituted a fair proportion of John's baptismal candidates.[42]

The following consideration assumes that the Matthean identity for the audience is correct even though John appears to be under the misapprehension that the officials had come seeking baptism. The NRSV's "for baptism" is probably a more appropriate rendering of *epi to baptisma* in Matt 3:7 than the NIV's "to where he was baptizing," although both are possible. It was an easy mistake to make if "all the people of Jerusalem were going out to him" (Mark 1:5), which must have put John and his disciples under considerable pressure. Inevitably reports of his proclamation of the imminent coming in judgment of the mightier one had reached officialdom in Jerusalem. Perhaps John thought that the officials had believed his message and had come to avail themselves of what he proclaimed as the only escape route, namely repentance authenticated through water baptism. The reference to fleeing from wrath in this context suggests that he was comparing them with snakes (a brood of vipers) cannily fleeing before a spreading bush fire; perhaps he had seen this happen in the wilderness.

John's rejection of these officials as candidates for baptism demonstrates that he subjected all applicants to some kind of appraisal. Thus the rite of baptism was administered only to those whose sincerity was demonstrated by "fruit worthy of repentance." Presumably this means that their inward repentance manifested itself outwardly in a changed lifestyle; John believed that in the absence of repentance the rite itself conferred no benefit. His "fruit" analogy is possibly derived from Psalm 1, of which there are other possible echoes in later verses.[43] This psalm's binary contrast of the faithful and the wicked, recalling the Wisdom literature, provides an eminently suitable theme for prophetic preaching. Its depiction of the

---

41. Hagner, *Matthew*, 1:49; France, *Matthew*, 110; Nolland, *Matthew*, 142.

42. See *John's Target People* on page 72.

43. Similar imagery appears also in Jer 17:7f.

faithful as "trees planted by streams of water, which yield their fruit in its season, and their leaves do not wither" (Ps 1:3) would have resonated with predominantly agrarian folk inhabiting a sometimes arid climate, as would the contrasting fate of the wicked which John describes later: "the chaff he will burn with unquenchable fire."

Next John focuses upon an error that he identified in the attitude of the Jewish leaders. They assumed that their membership of the chosen race ("We have Abraham as our ancestor") exempted them from God's judgment. John claims that this is the antithesis of the truth: election entails responsibilities and therefore confers greater liability to judgment. The prophet Amos had identified the same error: "Hear this word that the Lord has spoken against you, O people of Israel, against the whole family that I brought up out of the land of Egypt: You only have I known of all the families of the earth; therefore I will punish you for all your iniquities" (Amos 3:1f). John's repudiation of Jewish privilege stands firmly in the prophetic tradition.[44]

Perhaps the sight of rocks along the banks of the Jordan prompted John's next development of this argument: "God is able from these stones to raise up children to Abraham." The drama of this saying was enhanced by a poetic play on words in Aramaic, which presumably was the language that John was using: "from these stones (*ebeni*) . . . children (*beni*)."[45] John is underscoring his previous statement of the danger of trusting in divine election alone. Ethnicity counted for nothing. God could turn even lifeless stones, obviously devoid of human ancestry, into "children to Abraham," who, by implication, would be at least as worthy of the title as the Jewish religious leaders in the delegation. So the title is worthless. Indeed, as will be shown, the Baptist dismissed race, nationality and social status as

---

44. If John considered that Jewish ethnicity conferred no advantage, presumably he also considered that Gentiles suffered no disadvantage, making all peoples equal.

45. In the early Christian community stones were sometimes used to represent believers, for example, in 1 Peter 2:4f. Jesus himself uses the analogy in Luke 19:40: when Pharisees tell him to stop his disciples singing about him as the king coming in the name of the Lord, he replies, "I tell you, if these were silent, the stones would shout out." Perhaps the analogy began with the Baptist, but it is also possible that the compiler of Q read what was a frequently used analogy in the Christian community into the preaching of the Baptist.

irrelevant. In contrast, what mattered was a recommitment to God demonstrated through the baptismal analogy to the re-entering of the Promised Land.[46]

Returning to the fruit-and-tree analogy, John emphasizes the imminence of the judgment: "Even now the axe is lying at the root of the trees; every tree therefore that does not bear good fruit is cut down and thrown into the fire." There may be no connection in thought with the fruit of repentance that John had mentioned earlier (Matt 3:8; Luke 3:8), but as Marcus points out[47] traditionally Israel had been represented as a tree (Jer 11:16) or even a vineyard (Isa 5:1–7), whose destruction represents judgment upon her. Even if John's hearers failed to recognize the echoes of scripture, as a primarily agricultural people, they would have understood the metaphor: the owner of an orchard who identifies diseased trees—the absence of fruit being a symptom—will destroy them quickly to prevent the disease from spreading. By implication the Pharisees and Sadducees in the delegation are like diseased trees: they may appear healthy, but are failing to yield the fruit that is the sole reason for their existence. So they must expect God's judgment.

At this point Luke inserts some material peculiar to his gospel (Luke 3:10–15) in which various persons question the Baptist concerning practical ways in which to demonstrate the "fruit" of repentance.[48] Unfortunately in Luke this interrupts the connection in thought between verses 9 and 16.

Having warned of imminent judgment Q next describes the judge himself. This version of the Baptist's saying about the mightier one coming after him is similar to the Marcan form considered earlier, but both Matthew and Luke append the detail *and fire* to the statement that the mightier one will baptize with the Holy Spirit. Opinion is divided concerning the significance of this fire, but the context suggests that it symbolizes divine retribution, as often in the NT,[49] making it yet another prognostication of judgment. Its close association with the Holy Spirit is a further reminder that God's gifts are attended by responsibilities; more will be expected of those on whom the Spirit is bestowed.

The Q speech closes with a further dramatic illustration of the imminent judgment, the Baptist exchanging the imagery of the orchard for that

---

46. See under *Forgiveness of Sins* on page 66.

47. Marcus, *John*, 39.

48. These verses are considered later on page 72, especially fn 80.

49. For example, Matt 7:19; 13:40; 25:41; 1 Cor 3:13; Jude 7; Rev 19:20.

of the threshing floor: "His winnowing fork is in his hand, and he will clear his threshing floor and will gather his wheat into the granary; but the chaff he will burn with unquenchable fire" (Matt 3:12). The material gathered at grain harvest consisted of the valuable grain mixed with worthless chaff. Separation was by winnowing which involved tossing this mixture into the air on a day when there was a gentle breeze. The heavy grain fell back to earth, while the lighter chaff was carried away by the breeze; occasionally it was collected and used as fuel for burning. The implication is that an analogous separation process will be applied to humanity, retaining the useful and discarding the worthless, recalling the binary emphasis of Ps 1.

Josephus

Josephus mentions the Baptist only in the following passage:

> Now some of the Jews thought that the destruction of Herod's army came from God, and that very justly, as a punishment of what he did against John, that was called the Baptist: for Herod slew him, who was a good man, and commanded the Jews to exercise virtue, both as to righteousness towards one another, and piety towards God, and so to come to baptism; for that the washing [with water] would be acceptable to him, if they made use of it, not in order to the putting away [or the remission] of some sins [only], but for the purification of the body; supposing still that the soul was thoroughly purified beforehand by righteousness. Now when [many] others came in crowds about him, for they were very greatly moved [or pleased] by hearing his words, Herod, who feared lest the great influence John had over the people might put it into his power and inclination to raise a rebellion, (for they seemed ready to do any thing he should advise,) thought it best, by putting him to death, to prevent any mischief he might cause, and not bring himself into difficulties, by sparing a man who might make him repent of it when it would be too late. Accordingly he was sent a prisoner, out of Herod's suspicious temper, to Macherus, the castle I before mentioned, and was there put to death. Now the Jews had an opinion that the destruction of this army was sent as a punishment upon Herod, and a mark of God's displeasure to him. (*Antiquities*, 18:5:2)

The differences between this account and the evangelists' accord with Josephus's primary interest in political events. As many have pointed out, there is no inherent contradiction between Josephus and the gospels; Josephus gives as the reason for Antipas's arrest and execution of John his fear that John might incite the people to rebellion, whereas the gospels claim that it was on account of John's denunciation of Antipas's illegal marriage (Mark 6:17f). Perhaps in his public preaching John referred to the Herod dynasty's amoral conduct as one possible reason for the imminent divine judgment. If Antipas heard about this, he might have feared—in view of John's authority over the people—that this preaching would stir the people to rebellion.

What is striking in Josephus's description of John is his interpretation of the purpose of John's baptism. This, he claims, is "not in order to the putting away [or the remission] of some sins [only], but for the purification of the body; supposing still that the soul was thoroughly purified beforehand by righteousness." This might seem to contradict the synoptists' claim that it was *eis afesin hamartiōn* (Mark 1:5; Luke 3:3). But while an uncritical reading of those passages might give the impression that John's water baptism cleansed the soul of sin by some mystical process analogous to its removing physical dirt from the body, the "Q" tradition hints at a deeper understanding, more akin to Josephus's understanding. There John insists that his candidates "Bear fruit(s) worthy of repentance" (Matt 3:8; Luke 3:8). The clear implication is that this baptism is efficacious only if the candidate demonstrates a desire for a new life, for righteousness. Herein, perhaps, is the germ of the Pauline understanding of baptism: "Therefore we have been buried with him by baptism into death, so that, just as Christ was raised from the dead by the glory of the Father, so *we too might walk in newness of life*" (Rom 6:4). Clearly the Baptist could not have identified baptism with Jesus' death and resurrection, but it is possible that Josephus, writing towards the end of the first century, had encountered early Christian communities and perhaps had witnessed Christian baptismal services using liturgy similar to the Pauline passage. This might have led him to write sacramental elements into his description of John's baptism.

THE DISTINCTIVE FEATURES OF JOHN'S MINISTRY

In six respects John's ministry is strikingly different to those of most other prominent Jewish figures of his day: (i) his asceticism; (ii) his offer of forgiveness of sins; (iii) his repudiation of institutional Judaism; (iv) the diversity of his target people; (v) his use of water baptism; and (vi) his proc-lamation of the coming mightier one.

Asceticism

John's lifestyle and especially his clothing were so radically different from those of most Jews that Mark (perhaps recalling Peter's eyewitness account) took the trouble to describe them: "Now John was clothed with camel's hair, with a leather belt around his waist, and he ate locusts and wild honey" (Mark 1:6 and Matt 3:4). Thus both his food and the material for his cloth-ing occurred naturally in the wilderness, in contrast with their conventional equivalents which would have been processed by human hand.

Although second-temple Judaism had no command to such austerity, various groups practiced forms of asceticism. At the moderate end of the spectrum were the Essenes of whom at least some lived communally; the evidence suggests that they wore substantial clothing, although this was held in common,[50] and that their diet was conventional. Similar to them in some respects were the Therapeutae, described by Philo, who renounced property and regarded temperance as a prime virtue.[51] That the Baptist was not unique in his more extreme asceticism, however, is evident from Jose-phus's description of his mentor Banus.[52]

So why did John dress and live as he did? Although one possibility is that he had embraced Cynic ideas and practices,[53] that is unlikely. It is true that itinerant Cynic sages were poorly dressed, but their lifestyle was essentially urban, begging for their food rather than foraging for it in the wilderness. Moreover, to command repentance in view of a coming

50. According to the description of the Essenes in Philo's *Hypothetica*, as cited by Joan Taylor, "Scrolls and Hellenistic Jewish Literature," 145f.

51. "When, therefore, men abandon their property without being influenced by any predominant attraction . . . they depart, not to another city . . . but they take up their abode outside of walls, or gardens, or solitary lands, seeking for a desert place, not be-cause of any ill-natured misanthropy . . . but because of the associations with people of wholly dissimilar dispositions to which they would otherwise be compelled, and which they know to be unprofitable and mischievous." (Philo, *De Vita Contemplativa*, 17–20)

52. "when I was informed that one, whose name was Banus, lived in the desert, and used no other clothing than grew upon trees, and had no other food than what grew of its own accord, and bathed himself in cold water frequently, both by night and by day, in order to preserve his chastity, I imitated him in those things, and continued with him three years." (Josephus, *Life* 2)

53. See on pages 17f.

judgment would be most unlike a Cynic and none of the principal authors on John[54] has associated him with Cynicism. Joan Taylor offers as an explanation for John's use of camel hair for garments that camel or goat hair was used for sackcloth, which would have been a highly appropriate material for John to wear, because it was the appropriate attire for someone who was repentant.[55] On this basis, then, John's ascetic attire was an attempt to identify himself with the candidates to whom he administered his "baptism of repentance for the forgiveness of sins." Alternatively he might have wished to dissociate himself from institutional Judaism and, especially, the lavish lifestyle of many Jewish leaders of his day, whom he believed to be corrupt. Yet again he may also have been seeking to demonstrate his total commitment to his calling: his mission took top priority in his life, his own physical needs being, in comparison, unimportant. In effect, he was seeking to exemplify in a visible manner that a right relationship with Yahweh, restored by repentance and baptism, is ultimately the top priority in life; all else is secondary. Joel Marcus, however, insists that the brief references to the Baptist's attire in Mark 1:6 and Matt 3:4 do enshrine a historical memory, which might reflect his Elijan self-image.[56] He draws attention to the similarity between the descriptions of John's attire in the gospel narratives and Elijah's in 4 Kings 1:8 LXX. One significant difference, however, is that 4 Kings 1:8 LXX describes Elijah as a hairy *man* (*anēr dasus*), while Mark 1:6 has John wearing a *garment* of camel hair. According to Marcus, in order to model himself on Elijah, John deliberately made his appearance like that of his biblical prototype, but as he himself was not hairy, he wore a hairy garment, one of camel's hair.[57] Marcus's suggestion is ingenious and, indeed, plausible. The only flaw in it is that the ancient sources show John as so committed to his mission that it is surely debatable whether he would have taken the trouble to fabricate a camel-hair garment simply to imitate Elijah's hairiness.

Whether or not the Jewish people identified John with Elijah, according to the NT they certainly recognized him as a prophet.[58] Meyer regards

54. Cynicism is not mentioned in the books on John by Webb, Dapaah, Taylor or Marcus.

55. Taylor, *John the Baptist*, 35–37.

56. Marcus, *John*, 49f.

57. Marcus, *John*, 53f.

58. According to, for example, Matt 11:9 and Luke 7:26; Matt 14:5; 21:26 and Mark 11:32 and Luke 20:6.

the return of prophecy to Israel after a long absence as significant.[59] The very appearance, then, of one so widely identified as a prophet heightened the expectancy of the people that a new divine intervention was imminent.[60]

Forgiveness of Sins

The three synoptists associate John's baptism with the forgiveness of sins. Strictly, Matthew mentions only confession, but arguably that implies the seeking of forgiveness, while according to Mark and Luke forgiveness of sins was the express purpose of this baptism (*eis afesin hamartiōn*). The Fourth Gospel does not mention forgiveness and Josephus appears to deny any such connection, although the passage is somewhat ambiguous. Perhaps surprisingly forgiveness is not mentioned explicitly in the preserved excerpts of John's preaching, although it may be implied in repentance.

But precisely who was being forgiven and for what kind of sin? It might appear that the scholars are divided, some believing that John's baptism remitted the sins of individuals and others the sins of the nation. N. T. Wright, for example, seems to argue that for first-century Jews "forgiveness of sins" could never be simply a private blessing, although the DSS reveal that sometimes it was. The state of the nation under Roman rule took priority as Israel yearned for God's blessing. So when Mark and Luke claim that John's baptism was "for the forgiveness of sins," they understood it as ushering in the redemption which Israel sought.[61]

Meyer makes the same point, taking judgment as his starting point:

> It is historically out of the question that John conceived judgment along the individualistic lines characteristic of later Western thought. Rather, he conceived judgment in collective, or better, "ecclesial," terms, *i.e.*, in terms of "God's people, Israel." . . . Judgment is turned against *Israel* and *Israel* is the object of salvation. John's summons to baptism in the wilderness was accordingly directed not simply to all Israelites but to all Israel, *i.e.*, to the nation as an ecclesial entity or to Israel as people of God. The response to his summons therefore could not be merely so many responses of

---

59. See the passage cited earlier, fn 38 on page 56.

60. See *Messianic Expectations* on page 13.

61. Wright, *Victory*, 271.

individuals within Israel; it had to be the response of Israel as such. "Prophet" is locked, as always, in engagement with "people."[62]

The paradox in the extract from Wright is highly significant. Although the Decalogue attributes an "ecclesial" property to guilt (Ex 20:5f)—so that in theory Jews did not apportion the blame for sin to a particular individual or group, but rather attached it to the whole community which ultimately was the nation—by Second Temple times, as Wright observes, for many Jews guilt and forgiveness had become an individual matter. It appears, then, that "national" and "personal" sin coexisted in a kind of tension so that there was no longer a hard-and-fast distinction between them; all sin was to some extent both "national" and "personal."

Crossan expresses a similar view, but with a more pronounced eschatological emphasis. He sees significance in John's exclusive use of the Jordan for baptism.[63] Although the Jews did not regard the Jordan as sacred *per se*, it held symbolic importance for them: it marked the final frontier in the exodus, which as God's definitive intervention to save his chosen people from oppression in Egypt had become the root metaphor of Judaism. Crossan describes John's baptism in terms of people crossing over into the desert and being baptized in the Jordan as they return to the Promised Land.[64] Colin Brown offers a similar theory, although he relates it to the return from exile rather than the exodus: first John crossed over, and baptism consisted in heeding John's call to leave the land and follow him in penitence into the Jordan and return as consecrated members of a renewed Israel.[65] Brown, then, like Crossan, regards those receiving John's baptism as reenacting the conquest of the Promised Land, giving the nation a symbolic rebirth. There may be some value in this interpretation: ritual reenactments of God's saving events were an important part of Judaism, as the Passover meal demonstrates.

There may, however, be an alternative and purely practical explanation for John's exclusive use of the Jordan for baptism. He understood his mission in terms of "a voice crying in the wilderness," fulfilling Isaiah's

---

62. Meyer, *Aims*, 117f.

63. Although John used various sites along the Jordan's course, there is no record of him baptizing away from the Jordan with the possible exception of "Aenon near Salim" (John 3:23) whose location is uncertain; it is as though he regarded Jordan water itself as an essential ingredient in his baptism.

64. Crossan, *Historical*, 231.

65. Brown, "John the Baptist," 45f.

prophecy: he baptized those who responded to his voice, that is, his call for repentance. In the Judean wilderness water deep enough for baptism by immersion[66] is generally scarce. But the Jordan flowed through that wilderness, making it the most suitable location for a wilderness-based baptizing ministry. This explains the paradox that John, who understood his mission as targeting all Israel, avoided urban areas, even though they offered a wider public, in favor of the Jordan in the wilderness.

Meyer sees an alternative symbolism in John's confinement of his ministry to the wilderness: "It can be no accident that the wilderness chosen by John was within easy distance of Jerusalem. Bent on confronting the whole of Israel with his proclamation, he was no doubt acutely conscious that the way Jerusalem went the nation would go. But John would not himself go to Jerusalem, for example to preach in the temple. No; he called Jerusalem out to him, to the wilderness, away from the whole network of current structures and commitments. He called the nation to a new beginning."[67] As we shall consider shortly, John repudiated institutional Judaism, including the temple and its cultus, which he regarded as corrupt. The wilderness distanced people from familiar human institutions and surrounded them with Nature, created by God alone. The repentance and the renewed relationship with God to which he called people marked the start of a new era. Meyer's view of John's baptism accords with this interpretation: "It was designed to symbolize and seal the conversion of Israel in the face of the approaching judgment."[68]

Even though Wright, Crossan, Brown, and Meyer all emphasize the "national" or "ecclesial" forgiveness of sins effected by John's baptism, surely most[69] of those who flocked to hear John preach, who responded

---

66. The assumption that John baptized by whole body immersion is based on the use of the Greek verb *baptizō*. Derived from *baptō*, which means "dip," *baptizō* carries the sense "cause to be dipped," that is, immerse. Immersion requires a considerable depth of water, in contrast with affusion (sprinkling) for which a few centimeters would suffice. That John practiced total immersion is corroborated by the observation that "John also was baptizing at Aenon near Salim because water was abundant there (*hoti hudata polla ēn ekei*)" (John 3:23). In other words, only certain sites were deep enough to suit John's ministry and Aenon was one of these.

67. Meyer, *Aims*, 116.

68. Meyer, *Aims*, 116.

69. There may have been some who considered that they were performing a patriotic duty: they believed that if all—or if *enough*—Jews demonstrated repentance in this dramatic way, God would once again look favorably upon his chosen people and deliver Israel from the Romans. There may even have been some who were swept along on a

to his message and received his "baptism of repentance," were seeking remission primarily for their personal sins. Sanders highlights the personal emphasis in the language used of John's baptism: candidates were baptized "confessing their sins" (Matt 3:6 and Mark 1:5) and the Baptist is said to have urged his hearers to bring forth "fruit worthy of repentance" (Matt 3:8 and Luke 3:8).[70] Undeniably this is the language of individual sin, not national. Moreover, the evangelists' claims that John's baptismal candidates included such "sinners" as tax collectors and prostitutes[71] is more consistent with the seeking of forgiveness for personal rather than national sin; it is hard to imagine tax collectors and prostitutes trekking into the wilderness to seek forgiveness for national sin, while for their personal moral lapses it is more credible. Surely only the most saintly—those who identified themselves with the sins of the nation—would seek baptism in order to atone specifically for the sins of the nation.[72]

Irrespective of the kind of forgiveness offered by John's ministry, for John to mediate forgiveness at all reveals a significant point about his ministry that is widely overlooked. Through the Temple cultus Judaism already operated an official process for the remission of sins (Lev 4:1–5:13; 6:24–30). Indeed, the Hebrew scriptures testify to a remission of sins apart from the cultus: Ps 32:1–5, for example, states explicitly that confession of sins directly to God is sufficient to secure divine forgiveness; no doubt the Temple hierarchy, however, would have insisted that a pious Jew would wish to respond to such directly obtained forgiveness by offering the appropriate levitical sacrifice. To some extent, then, John had set himself up as an alternative to the Temple. Webb comments that "John's repentance-baptism, as a rite which mediated forgiveness indicated that the usual means of forgiveness, the Temple cultus, had been made invalid, probably by the actions and policies of the Temple establishment. Thus, John's baptism functioned as a protest against the perceived abuses by the Temple establishment."[73] Undoubtedly Webb is correct in stating that the Baptist considered the Temple cultus invalid; his repudiation of the Jewish establishment will be discussed

flood-tide of religious mass hysteria.

70. Sanders, *Jesus and Judaism*, 109.

71. See under *John's Target People* on page 72.

72. Consider, for example, Moses who asked Yahweh to forgive the sin of the Israelites in creating idols, but if this was not possible to "blot me out of the book you have written" (Ex 32:32). He was offering himself for the sins of the nation.

73. Webb, *John the Baptizer*, 215f.

shortly. His statement that John regarded his baptism as a protest against such abuses, however, flies in the face of the evidence. John's ministry focused primarily, as stated above and will be considered again later, on the imminent coming of the mightier one with his Holy Spirit baptism. It was not so much a protest *against* an evil as the announcement of imminent judgment *upon* evil; it was too late to protest against it.

There probably was, however, an element of protest in John's ministry considered as a whole. For example, as mentioned above, the gospels state that many "sinners" and tax collectors responded to his ministry. Morton Smith believes that John's ministry met a widely felt need: when Jews could offer sacrifices only in Jerusalem—and its services were expensive, John introduced a new, inexpensive rite, effective for the remission of all sins.[74] Strictly speaking, Jerusalem was not the only place in the country where Jews could legally offer sacrifices. The so-called "lustral sacrifices" concerned mainly with cleansing and the remission of sin could be offered anywhere[75] and there were priests throughout the country who could administer them.[76] The suggestion, however, that Qumran and some other Jewish sects were beginning to regard baptism itself as capable of remitting sins has been largely discredited.[77] John appears to have modeled himself to some extent upon the charismatic prophets of the OT who were indeed not particularly concerned with ritual piety (see below). As for anti-Temple sentiment, it is abundantly clear that Jesus and the early Christian movement believed the Temple an outmoded institution; although undocumented, there may have been earlier groups holding such views.

---

74 Morton Smith, *Clement*, 208. Smith's reference to "all sins" may reflect the fact that the levitical sin offerings were effective only for unwitting sins; they could not remit sins committed intentionally. John's baptism, in contrast, appears to have remitted all kinds of sin. So John may have intended his ministry as a protest concerning what he perceived as inadequacies in the services offered by the Temple. Another such inadequacy was the Jewish establishment's treatment of the "sinners" whom it had marginalized.

75. These were the sacrifices that the Qumran community offered (Brownlee, "John," 37).

76. Sanders, *Judaism: Practice and Belief*, 170. There is a possible example in Mark 1:44, when Jesus instructs a newly cleansed leper to "show yourself to the priest." Matthew expands this to "show yourself to the priest, and offer the gift that Moses commanded" (Matt 8:4). The Marcan context suggests that this happened in Galilee. It seems unlikely that Jesus would have expected a newly cleansed leper, probably impoverished, to make the long journey to Jerusalem in order to offer the appropriate levitical sacrifice. So it was probably a local priest to whom the man was sent.

77. Taylor, *John*, 29f.

Repudiation of Institutional Judaism

As mentioned above, by offering forgiveness of sins apart from the levitical sacrifices administered by the Temple priesthood John's ministry was an implicit denial of the validity of the cultus. In fact John repudiated the whole of institutional Judaism. In so doing he was following the praxis of the prophetic wing of Judaism which had always maintained that the state of a person's inner life took precedence over the outward observance of religious ceremonial, including even that prescribed in Torah. For example, the hyperbole in the following saying of the prophet Micah carries more than a hint of cynicism regarding the Temple cultus:

> With what shall I come before the Lord, and bow myself before God on high? Shall I come before him with burnt offerings, with calves a year old?
>
> Will the Lord be pleased with thousands of rams, with ten thousands of rivers of oil? Shall I give my firstborn for my transgression, the fruit of my body for the sin of my soul?
>
> He has told you, O mortal, what is good; and what does the Lord require of you but to do justice, and to love kindness, and to walk humbly with your God? (Mic 6:6–8)

The prophet Amos is even more audacious when, as Yahweh's mouthpiece, he expresses a similar truth:

> I hate, I despise your festivals,
> and I take no delight in your solemn assemblies.
> Even though you offer me your burnt offerings and grain offerings, I will not accept them;
> and the offerings of well-being of your fatted animals I will not look upon.
> Take away from me the noise of your songs;
> I will not listen to the melody of your harps.
> But let justice roll down like waters,
> and righteousness like an ever-flowing stream. (Amos 5:21–24)

John's repudiation of the cultus included rejection of the authority of the priests and the teachers of the law. Presumably, then, he considered himself called directly by God and accountable to him alone. There is evidence to support this in, for example, his attitude to the Pharisees and Sadducees (if Matthew's identification of them in Matt 3:7 is correct), whom he mistakenly believed had come seeking baptism. In marked contrast with the deference to them paid by the masses (Matt 23:6f), in Matt 3:8f John effectively tells this delegation, which included Sadducees representing the nation's religious *elite*, that their need for repentance and restoration to a right relationship with God is the same as that of the rest of sinful humanity; neither their office nor their ancestry conferred any spiritual advantage. Perhaps the offence that they took at this statement explains the Jewish establishment's refusal to endorse his ministry.[78]

It is tempting to ask whether John's faith retained *any* of the distinctive features of Judaism. The gospels depict him as believing in God, sin, judgment, repentance, and forgiveness and he appears to have had some familiarity with the Hebrew scriptures.[79] Water baptism, as will be seen, was an accepted rite in Judaism, albeit a specialized one. If Mark's observation is true, the Jewish populace "all regarded John as truly a prophet" (Mark 11:32), so that he was widely recognized as not only a Jew, but a genuine messenger of Yahweh. But it is important to remember that most of what we know about John is derived from the gospels which have a specific agenda; they tend to show him as "an incipient Christian." Although the historical John might have differed in some respects from the picture presented in the gospels, we may be certain that he was a Jew and that he baptized.

John's Target People

John's denial of any inherent benefit in Jewish ancestry (Matt 3:9 and Luke 3:8) indicates that he regarded all people as equal, each individual accountable directly to God as he himself was. All stood equally in need of the divine forgiveness mediated through his baptism of repentance. That John's mission is generally regarded as being to all Israel may be a legacy of the absence of any definite record of him encountering Gentiles.[80] Marcus

---

78. This is implicit in the occasion when another deputation of Temple officials declined to answer Jesus' challenge: "Did the baptism of John come from heaven, or was it of human origin?" (Matt 21:25).

79. In John 1:23 the Baptist cites Isa 40:3. His preaching as preserved in Q may allude to Ps 1 (see above).

80. It is possible that the "soldiers" with whom John engaged according to Luke 3:14 were Roman troops and therefore Gentiles; although it is unlikely that Roman soldiers would have been given the extended leave needed to prepare for John's baptism, Luke does not state that these were baptismal candidates; they might have been spectators who found themselves challenged by John's preaching. These "soldiers" could, however, have been Jewish: there are several possibilities for their identity. If the encounter took

considers the "others" of Josephus's *Antiquities* 18:118 to be Gentiles,[81] but it is impossible to be certain. That John appears to have welcomed some types whom pious Jews had marginalized, such as the underclass of tax collectors and "sinners,"[82] makes it likely that he also welcomed Gentiles, whom some Jewish teachers regarded as on a par with tax collectors (Matt 5:46f; 18:17):

> For John came to you in the way of righteousness and you did not believe him, but the tax collectors and the prostitutes believed him; and even after you saw it, you did not change your minds and believe him. (Matt 21:32)

> Even tax collectors came to be baptized, and they asked him, "Teacher, what should we do?" He said to them, "Collect no more than the amount prescribed for you." Soldiers also asked him, "And we, what should we do?" He said to them, "Do not extort money from anyone by threats or false accusation, and be satisfied with your wages." (Luke 3:12–14)

> And all the people who heard this, including the tax collectors, acknowledged the justice of God, because they had been baptized with John's baptism. (Luke 7:29)

The first of these passages implies that the tax collectors and the prostitutes who "believed" John demonstrated their trust by submitting to his baptism. The reference to prostitutes indicates that John baptized women. This contrasts with some Jewish water rites, such as those specific to priests, which were administered to men only. Since recent scholarship

---

place in Galilee or Perea, they could have been regular soldiers in the service of Herod Antipas whom the Romans allowed to maintain a small army for defensive and policing duties. That Antipas arrested him indicates that John did sometimes venture into his territory. Another possibility is suggested by the word translated "soldiers" in Luke 3:14, *strateuomenoi*, part of the present participle of *strateuomai*. Its literal meaning, "people serving as soldiers," might indicate individuals pursuing a soldier-like occupation although not members of a regular army. They might have been temple police, who probably formed part of the band that arrested Jesus. Most commentators, however, consider that these "paramilitaries" were employed by tax collectors as bodyguards and debt collectors; in Luke 3:12–14 their association with tax collectors and the reference to extortion is consistent with this possibility.

81. Marcus, *John*, 135f.

82. For further see *The "Sinners"* on page 8.

has established that Qumran admitted women as well as men,[83] John's willingness to baptize women may be evidence of a connection with Qumran.

It is interesting to speculate concerning the future that the Baptist envisaged for the repentant "sinners" whom he baptized. As there is no evidence that he invited them to become permanent members of his community or any other, presumably he sent them back to their regular homes and occupations. In view of his repudiation of the Jewish establishment, it is unlikely that he expected—or even wanted—them to be reinstated in the observant Jewish society of his day. Indeed, as mentioned in chapter 2, the evidence suggests that the establishment refused to revoke their excommunication; in its sight they remained "sinners," excluded from regular Jewish society. So what future did John have in mind for them? Overarching every aspect of John's ministry was the imminently expected figure of the mightier one whose baptism in the Holy Spirit would complete the transformation begun through their repentance and submission to his water baptism. Surely, so far as the Baptist was concerned, the future of his baptismal candidates was in the hands of the mightier one, who would inaugurate a new age and a new society. Neither the NT nor any other ancient source provides any more specific information concerning John's understanding of the eschata.

Water Baptism

The titles "Baptist" and "Baptizer" indicate that this was the aspect of his ministry for which John was chiefly remembered. In fact mainstream Judaism practiced many forms of ritual ablution, some prescribed in the OT and some in the literature of the Second Temple period. Ritual immersion was central to the ritual purity movement which encouraged all Jews to perform the cleansing rituals that Torah specified for the priesthood.[84] The Qumran community made extensive use of such practices. Some Jewish ablutions involved only hand washing or foot washing. A few involved total immersion of the body. Some were required only of the priests. Some were concerned with ritual purity rather than hygiene. A few were associated with repentance, forgiveness of sins, and conversion. Qumran not only immersed candidates on their initiation to the community, but also practiced

---

83. Cecilia Wassén, "Daily Life," 548.

84. For further see *Purity* on page 6.

regular on-going immersions, all purificatory in function. Webb has undertaken a detailed survey of these.[85]

In the light of this John's use of baptism was not in itself a radical departure from routine Jewish practice. Its association with the forgiveness of sins was considered earlier. It appears that John adapted an established rite—albeit a specialized one—to suit his own mission. What was unique about John's baptism was its association with the dominant theme of his preaching, namely the coming mightier one who would baptize with the Holy Spirit. Webb summarizes the connection as follows: "John's baptism expressed a person's turning to God, but the expected figure will complete the conversion by baptizing the person with a holy spirit. John's baptism cleansed the person but, through the expected figure's ministry, the cleansing will be full and final."[86] So John's water baptism could be regarded as a down payment, the balance to follow later at the hands of the mightier one.

The Coming Mightier One

As will be shown shortly, the coming figure, "one who is more powerful than I," is central to John's ministry. As Meyer succinctly expresses it, "The clear points are two: (1) John's own mission was wholly relative to that of the coming judge (2) whose messianic epiphany was imminent."[87] But who was this figure? That he was so much "more powerful" than John, that he would baptize with the Holy Spirit and that his coming would be attended by judgment (implicit in John's calls for repentance) limit the possibilities. For example, the expected figures of Elijah and "the Prophet" (John 1:21) may be eliminated, since neither was associated with baptism in the Holy Spirit nor with the administration of judgment. This leaves two possibilities.

The first is Yahweh himself. The baptism in the Holy Spirit and the judgment might seem to confirm this indisputably. Moreover, belief that Yahweh would visit his people in person is attested in the Hebrew scriptures. Perhaps the clearest example is the prophecy which all four canonical evangelists associate with the Baptist:

> A voice cries out: "In the wilderness prepare the way of the LORD,
>   make straight in the desert a highway for our God." (Isa 40:3)

85. Webb, *John the Baptizer*, 95–132 for mainstream Judaism and 133–162 for the Qumran community.

86. Webb, *John the Baptizer*, 215.

87. Meyer, *Aims*, 117.

The way to be prepared in the wilderness is the highway along which Yahweh will come in person to judge and rescue his people. Other instances include the following:

> For the LORD comes out from his place
>> to punish the inhabitants of the earth for their iniquity;
> the earth will disclose the blood shed on it,
>> and will no longer cover its slain. (Isa 26:21)

> See, the LORD God comes with might, and his arm rules for him;
>> his reward is with him, and his recompense before him.
> He will feed his flock like a shepherd; he will gather the lambs in his
>> arms, and carry them in his bosom, and gently lead the
>> mother sheep. (Isa 40:10f)

The second possibility is the Messiah. As discussed in chapter 2, Jewish ideas concerning the person and role of the Messiah were flexible, to say the least. Some thought that John himself might be the Messiah (Luke 3:15; John 1:19f), although for the Messiah (or anyone) to proclaim his or her own imminent advent is clearly absurd. Moreover, the only recorded occasion on which John used the word "Messiah" is in John 1:20 when he denied being the Messiah himself.

A case can be made for John's mightier one being the Messiah. John's preaching insisted that the mightier one would baptize with the Holy Spirit. Some Jewish contemporary groups associated the Messiah with the bestowal of the Holy Spirit: Brownlee, for example, considers that "so will he sprinkle[88] many nations" (Isa 52:15 NIV) reflects an endowment that equips God's servant to anoint others. He claims that the Messiah is similarly described in the Damascus Document and that the Qumran Community Rule mentions "a man upon whom God will sprinkle . . . the Spirit of Truth as purifying water," a similar analogy to that in Mark 1:8: "I have baptized you with water; but he will baptize you with the Holy Spirit."[89]

If the evidence seems divided between John's coming mightier one being God himself and one of his human servants, these are not necessarily mutually exclusive—a resolution is possible. John's language that seems to deify the coming one may be figurative; Brownlee points out in connection with Isa 9:6's description of the Messiah as "Mighty God" that such godlike

---

88. KJV and NIV read "sprinkle," while RSV and NRSV read "startle." The Hebrew root is *nazah*, which denotes "spirt" or "sprinkle."

89. Brownlee, "John the Baptist," 43f.

names do not necessarily claim that their bearer is God, but indicate that attributes of God may be evidenced in the bearer's life.[90] The meaning, then, may be that the Messiah is to be mightier than ordinary mortals in that his person reveals aspects of God. The Jews appreciated that God had often acted through devoted human agents such as Moses, David, and the prophets. It is therefore plausible that John was expecting a human with extraordinary God-given powers—indeed, one able to bestow the Holy Spirit upon others because the Spirit had been bestowed liberally upon himself.

JOHN'S PURPOSE

Deducing the purpose of the Baptist's ministry from the limited portrait of him painted by the NT and Josephus involves a precarious tight-rope walk. On one hand we need to extract as much information as possible from such source material as is available and on the other to resist the temptation to read into that more than it is saying. The Fourth Gospel includes an account of a visit to John by an investigative delegation of Jewish officials who asked him questions not unlike those that a present-day researcher might wish to do. While few would insist that this is the *verbatim* transcript of a historical interview, Matthew's account of Pharisees and Sadducees approaching John (Matt 3:7–12) perhaps corroborates that such encounters with officialdom took place; if so, this confirms the authorities' interest in him. Since scholarship is now increasingly recognizing the Fourth Gospel's value as a historical source,[91] this account may provide a useful starting point:

> This is the testimony given by John when the Jews sent priests and Levites from Jerusalem to ask him, "Who are you?"
> [20] He confessed and did not deny it, but confessed, "I am not the Messiah."
> [21] And they asked him, "What then? Are you Elijah?" He said, "I am not." "Are you the prophet?" He answered, "No."
> [22] Then they said to him, "Who are you? Let us have an answer for those who sent us. What do you say about yourself?"
> [23] He said, "I am the voice of one crying out in the wilderness, 'Make straight the way of the Lord,'" as the prophet Isaiah said."

90. Brownlee, "John the Baptist," 41.
91. See, for example, fn 2 on page 114.

²⁴ Now they had been sent from the Pharisees. ²⁵ They asked him, "Why then are you baptizing if you are neither the Messiah, nor Elijah, nor the prophet?"

²⁶ John answered them, "I baptize with water. Among you stands one whom you do not know, ²⁷ the one who is coming after me; I am not worthy to untie the thong of his sandal." (John 1:19–27)

The questions asked are, for the most part, those to be expected of such an investigative team and are relevant to our present quest. Unfortunately the Baptist's reported answers are not straightforward and require elucidation.

In answer to "Who are you?" the evangelist maintains that the Baptist cited the prophecy of Isa 40:3, identifying himself with "the voice of one crying out in the wilderness." It would be easy to accuse the Baptist, the evangelist or the translators of most English versions of misinterpretation concerning "the voice of one crying out in the wilderness." Although the NT depicts the Baptist as crying out in the wilderness, in the original prophecy the voice itself is not in the wilderness; "in the wilderness" forms part of the message that the voice is bidden to proclaim; this was where the way was to be prepared. As the original Greek texts lacked punctuation it could be argued that the English versions of the Fourth Gospel faithfully reproduce the ambiguity of the Greek. But did the Baptist really give this as his answer? The verse reads as though it were a contrived attempt by the evangelist to introduce Isa 40:3 into his gospel; moreover, it is the only occasion on which speech attributed to the Baptist contains a definite quotation of scripture. Nevertheless, it could be genuine. As explained earlier, Isa 40:3 was effectively the Qumran community's mission statement. If the Baptist had been a member of that community, but left it in order to undertake what he considered to be the correct interpretation of its mission statement, he might well have identified himself with "the voice" and, moreover, he cried out in the wilderness. And if he were never at Qumran, he might nevertheless have heard of that community's use of the text, but felt that the ministry to which he was called fulfilled it more adequately. Or he might have been unaware of Qumran's use of the text, but his own familiarity with this scripture challenged him to become that voice. It is surely significant that all four canonical evangelists associate this verse with the Baptist. On this basis his answer to the two questions in verse 22 is reasonable.

The question of verse 25, why John was baptizing, raises numerous issues. It implies that if John had identified himself with the Messiah[92] or Elijah[93] or "the prophet,"[94] his baptizing ministry would have been understandable.[95] But as he denied being any of these, his ministry required an explanation. The answer he gives in the Fourth Gospel is unsatisfactory. It is as though the evangelist originally intended at this point to insert material similar to Luke 3:16, "I baptize you with water; but one who is more powerful than I is coming; I am not worthy to untie the thong of his sandals. He will baptize you with the Holy Spirit and fire." This would have answered the question insofar as it made the Baptist the herald of the coming mightier one, preparing the people for his arrival and making John's water baptism a precursor or foretaste of his more potent baptism. But the evangelist appears to lose the thread of the argument, not mentioning the climactic Spirit-baptism until verse 33 in a different context. Effectively this leaves the Baptist's reply to "Why are you baptizing?" as "I baptize with water," which does not answer the question.

It is arguable that there is theological significance in the unique wording that the fourth evangelist introduces after the water baptism statement—indeed it may have been the need to insert this that caused him to lose his thread: "Among you stands one whom you do not know, the one who is coming after me." This reads as though it were a genuine saying of the Baptist recalled by someone who was present when it was spoken. If so, it indicates that the Baptist was aware that the mightier one whose coming he proclaimed had now arrived and was already circulating unrecognized amongst his entourage. Although some of the claims that the Baptist makes about this figure seem more appropriate to God, as stated above, they could also apply to a godly human being.

---

92. According to Luke 3:15 some thought that the Baptist *was* the Messiah: "As the people were filled with expectation, and all were questioning in their hearts concerning John, whether he might be the Messiah . . . "

93. Paradoxically John denies being the historical Elijah, although as mentioned earlier he may have dressed in garments like Elijah's in order to identify with him or, at least, to show that he was a prophet.

94. It appears that some Jews were expecting a figure known as "the prophet," who was distinct from the Messiah and Elijah. "The prophet" is mentioned five times in John's gospel (1:21, 23, 25; 6:14; 7:40). This expectation may be based on the eschatological prophet mentioned in Deut 18:15–19.

95. Why this should be so is unknown. There is no evidence that first-century Jewish thought associated baptism with the Messiah, Elijah or "the prophet."

The nearest that the Fourth evangelist makes to an explicit statement of the Baptist's purpose comes later, in verse 31. This claims that on the day after the visitation by the delegation of officials, John saw Jesus walking towards him and declared: "I came baptizing with water for this reason, that he [Jesus] might be revealed to Israel." On this basis, then, the purpose of John's baptizing ministry was to reveal Jesus to Israel. It is not immediately obvious how John's ministry would accomplish this. The evangelist does, however, explain how the Baptist came to recognize Jesus as the expected mightier one:

> And John testified, "I saw the Spirit descending from heaven like a dove, and it remained (*kai emeinen*) on him. I myself did not know him, but the one who sent me to baptize with water said to me, 'He on whom you see the Spirit descend and remain is the one who baptizes with the Holy Spirit.' And I myself have seen and have testified that this is the Son of God." (John 1:32–34)

This recollection is the closest that the Fourth Gospel gives to an account of Jesus' baptism. The detail that the Spirit descended from heaven "like a dove" (*hōs peristeran*) is also attested in the three synoptic accounts of the baptism. Although the further detail that the Spirit was to remain on him appears to be an important aspect of the sign, the closest to a parallel to this in the synoptics is Matthew's "alighting on him (*erchomenon ep' auton*, literally 'coming upon him')." The Baptist's testimony that Jesus is the Son of God may reflect the synoptic tradition's reports of the divine voice at the baptism acclaiming Jesus as Son and Beloved. It seems remarkable that John's gospel contains no explicit account of the baptism itself which, as mentioned in chapter 1, proved to be a major turning point for both Jesus and the Baptist: this was the occasion on which it was revealed to John that Jesus was the expected mightier one and to Jesus that God was calling him to a significant ministry.

Although the gospels provide clues to the Baptist's purpose, nowhere is it stated explicitly. It is therefore necessary to deduce it from an analysis of those elements of his ministry whose authenticity is beyond question. John's saying which links his baptism with the coming mightier one surely falls into this category. The versions in the four canonical gospels represent multiple attestation (Mark, Q, and John) and the remarkable absence from them of any specifically Christian *motifs* bespeaks the antiquity and authenticity of this tradition.[96] So this saying may contain the key to the

96. Inevitably all four evangelists, as stated at the start of this chapter, viewed the

Baptist's agenda. The four versions are set out below in parallel columns for ease of comparison:

Matt 3:11	Mark 1:8a, 7, 8b	Luke 3:16	John 1:26f, 33
I baptize you with water for repentance,	I have baptized you with water;	I baptize you with water;	I baptize with water.
			Among you stands one whom you do not know,
but one who is more powerful than I is coming after me;	7 The one who is more powerful than I is coming after me;	but one who is more powerful than I is coming;	27 the one who is coming after me;
I am not worthy to carry	I am not worthy to stoop down and untie	I am not worthy to untie	I am not worthy to untie
	the thong of	the thong of	the thong of
his sandals.	his sandals.	his sandals.	his sandal.
He will	8b but he will	He will	33 He
			is the one who
baptize you with the Holy Spirit and fire.	baptize you with the Holy Spirit.	baptize you with the Holy Spirit and fire.	baptizes with the Holy Spirit.

What is common to these versions is as follows: (i) the imminent coming of one so much mightier than and superior to the Baptist himself; (ii) the necessity for repentance (implicit except in Matthew); (iii) the necessity to demonstrate that repentance by water baptism; and (iv) that the mightier one will baptize with the Holy Spirit.

Baptist retrospectively in the light of the coming of Jesus. So it would have accorded with their agendas for them to amend this saying to identify the coming mightier one more closely with Jesus. For example, they might have changed "the one who is more powerful than I is coming after me" to "the Christ who is more powerful than I is coming after me." Significantly the synoptists have resisted this temptation, all three referring to the mightier one as though unaware of his identity. Surely this can only be because these words were regarded as sacrosanct since they were an authentic saying of a prophet. Arguably only the author of John's gospel has yielded to the temptation and that in a low-key manner by identifying the coming one with the unknown personage already present amongst the Baptist's retinue.

While the centrality of water baptism in John's ministry is reflected in the titles "Baptizer" and "Baptist," this was nevertheless a means to an end, not an end in itself. John baptized people because they were repenting and they were repenting because they had believed his message concerning the imminent coming in judgment of the mightier one. It is therefore the coming of the mightier one that was the primary driver of John's ministry. For this reason the purpose of John's ministry can only have been to prepare Israel for the coming of the mightier one. Insofar as the mightier one proved to be Jesus, the Fourth Gospel correctly identifies the Baptist's agenda as "I came baptizing with water for this reason, that he might be revealed to Israel" (John 1:31).

This identification of the purpose of John's ministry raises further questions. A time came when Jesus joined John's company of disciples and John began training him for a mission similar to his own. Did this training begin before or after Jesus' baptism and John's recognition of him as the mightier one? That the synoptists emphasize that Jesus' temptation in the wilderness followed soon after his baptism surely indicates that the baptism took place at the end of Jesus' time with John. If so, the training took place before the baptism and at the start of the training process both men would have been unaware that Jesus *was* the mightier one.[97] So did John begin training Jesus also to proclaim a coming mightier one? This would accord with Sanders's suggestion that Jesus proclaimed the imminent coming of the Son of Man, a heavenly figure distinct from himself.[98]

CONCLUSION

John the Baptist has a unique place in the gospel records. Standing in the tradition of the great OT prophets, he rejected the authority of institutional Judaism and its hierarchy, considering himself called directly by God and answerable to him alone. He proclaimed the imminent coming in judgment of One mightier than himself who would baptize with the Holy Spirit. To prepare for his coming Jews should repent and demonstrate the sincerity of their repentance by submitting to his "baptism of repentance for the remission of sins." Jesus himself submitted to John's baptism and, according to the Fourth Gospel, John recognized him as the Mightier One whose coming he had proclaimed and began preparing him for a mission similar to his own.

97. This statement assumes that Jesus was unaware of his calling until his baptism.

98. Sanders, *Historical Figure*, 180, 247.

5

How John Affected Jesus

In this chapter we first consider the relationship between John and Jesus and then seek to determine the extent to which Jesus was affected by John. To do this we identify the distinctive features of Jesus' ministry and compare these with the distinctive features of John's ministry identified in the previous chapter.

THE RELATIONSHIP BETWEEN JOHN AND JESUS

When Jesus first approached John, his quest—which we have identified as justice for the oppressed indigenous Jews of Galilee—was one that in today's western thought would be considered purely political. John's ministry, in contrast, would be regarded as primarily religious: he administered a "baptism of repentance for the forgiveness of sins." It may appear then that there was little common ground between John and Jesus, even though the Jews drew no hard distinction between politics and religion. So what prompted Jesus to approach John? There are several possible explanations. Firstly, he might have desired to show solidarity with his fellow Jews who were coming to John for baptism. But this seems unlikely; Mark's report that it was "people from the whole Judean countryside and all the people of Jerusalem" who flocked to John in droves (Mark 1:4f) suggests that John's audiences were mainly Judeans, not Galileans. Indeed Mark states explicitly that Jesus traveled from Nazareth in Galilee, as though highlighting that for a Galilean like Jesus to approach John was unusual (Mark 1:9).[1] Secondly, Jesus might have been motivated by the thought that if *enough* Jews repented, God would intervene and deliver the nation from the Romans and—in Galilee—from Antipas whom Rome sponsored. Thirdly—and perhaps most likely—it might have been the hope that from John, who was making such an impact on the people of Judea, he might learn techniques that would help him in his own mission.

Whatever led Jesus to approach John, the Fourth Gospel alone suggests that Jesus spent an extended period with the Baptist.[2] Many scholars believe that John became Jesus' mentor, training him for a mission or ministry similar to his own. Jerome Murphy-O'Connor claims that Jesus became John's assistant, as Elisha assisted Elijah.[3] Daniel Dapaah in what is probably the most detailed study of the relationship between John and Jesus agrees with Murphy-O'Connor.[4] Marcus gives a detailed comparison of John and Jesus with Elijah and Elisha.[5] Sanders recognizes that Jesus had been a disciple of John[6] and Joan Taylor with characteristic caution suggests that Jesus had studied under John.[7] Insofar as Jesus seems to have been ill equipped for his ministry prior to his time with the Baptist and well prepared for it afterwards, the evidence for John's mentoring role is compelling and this study assumes its authenticity.

At some point during his time with the Baptist Jesus was baptized by him; the three synoptics state this explicitly[8] and the Fourth Gospel implies it (John 1:32–34). The attendant theophanic phenomena described in the gospels indicate that the evangelists regarded this as a highly significant occasion for Jesus, perhaps constituting his conversion or call to ministry.

---

1. According to John 1:35–42, Andrew and Simon Peter were among the Baptist's entourage at the same time as Jesus. Probably they had traveled with Jesus to spend time with the Baptist—see later.

2. An uncritical reading of the synoptics may give the impression that Jesus journeyed to John at the Jordan, was baptized immediately, and went off at once into the wilderness to be tempted, all in the space of a few hours; this is most unlikely. In contrast, "The next day . . . " in John 1:29 and 35 suggests a stay of several days and perhaps considerably longer.

3. Murphy-O'Connor, "John the Baptist," 362.

4. Dapaah, *Relationship*, 144.

5. Marcus, *John*, 87–89.

6. Sanders, *Historical Figure*, 94.

7. Taylor, *John the Baptist*, 278.

8. Matt 3:13–17; Mark 1:9–11; Luke 3:21f.

The prominent bestowal of the Holy Spirit upon him is suggestive of the commissioning of a prophet, c.f. "The spirit of the Lord God is upon me, because the Lord has anointed me; he has sent me to bring good news to the oppressed, to bind up the brokenhearted, to proclaim liberty to the captives, and release to the prisoners" (Isa 61:1).[9] It is also significant that in John 1:35–42 the Baptist appears to have directed some of his own entourage to become followers of Jesus. But since these men were from Galilee and included Andrew and Simon, it is likely that they were Jesus' friends who were accompanying him on his visit to John.[10] If the Baptist was aware of this, perhaps he was effectively telling them, "This man, your friend Jesus, has a special commission from God. Go with him and do as he says; he will need all the help you can give him." On this basis John not only trained Jesus but also participated in the formation of the band of disciples that would support him throughout his earthly ministry.[11]

Despite the previously mentioned difference in emphasis between Jesus' quest and John's mission, there is common ground. Both the dispossessed Galileans and the "sinners"—such as the tax collectors and prostitutes so prominent amongst John's baptismal candidates (Matt 21:32)—were victims of injustice perpetrated by a corrupt establishment. The message of imminent divine judgment that would punish the unjust and bring relief to their victims was a regular part of the prophetic calling: "to proclaim the year of the Lord's favor, and the day of vengeance of our God; to comfort all who mourn; to provide for those who mourn in Zion—to give them a garland instead of ashes, the oil of gladness instead of mourning, the mantle of praise instead of a faint spirit" (Isa 61:2f). Indeed, the most characteristic aspect of Jesus' later ministry—his compassion for the "sinners"[12]—is surely a legacy of his time with the Baptist, during which he must often have witnessed their sincere repentance prior to baptism. In this way John revealed to Jesus that the same spiritual malaise was afflicting all humanity,

9. According to Luke 4:16–21, during his ministry when he visited the synagogue at Nazareth Jesus claimed to be the fulfillment of this prophecy.

10. See *Capernaum* on page 43.

11. It is interesting that no ancient sources mention Jesus' disciples receiving John's baptism. Since Simon and Andrew were also present with Jesus on his visit to John, it might seem strange that Jesus was baptized, but not they. Or are we to assume that they were? Perhaps the evangelists are reluctant to state that the disciples were baptized as this makes Jesus less unique. Apparently no scholars have researched this matter, but that may simply reflect the lack of source material.

12. For further on this see *Concern for the "Sinners"* on page 98.

including the Jewish establishment: both the dispossessed Galileans and the marginalized sinners were its symptoms as well as its victims.[13] It was John who demonstrated to Jesus that the "sinners" were more open to God than the nation's religious leaders were and this is reflected later in Jesus' reply to a deputation of Jewish leaders: "Truly I tell you, the tax collectors and the prostitutes are going into the kingdom of God ahead of you. For John came to you in the way of righteousness and you did not believe him, but the tax collectors and the prostitutes believed him . . . " (Matt 21:31f).

That Jesus in his later ministry frequently alluded to John the Baptist[14] surely bespeaks the importance that he attached to him. Perhaps most significant is the implicit parallel that Jesus drew between himself and John:

> As he was walking in the temple, the chief priests, the scribes, and the elders came to him and said, "By what authority are you doing these things? Who gave you this authority to do them?" Jesus said to them, "I will ask you one question; answer me, and I will tell you by what authority I do these things. Did the baptism of John come from heaven, or was it of human origin? Answer me." They argued with one another, "If we say, 'from heaven,' he will say, 'Why then did you not believe him?' But shall we say, 'Of human origin'?" — they were afraid of the crowd, for all regarded John as truly a prophet. So they answered Jesus, "We do not know." And Jesus said to them, "Neither will I tell you by what authority I am doing these things." (Mark 11:27–33)

In this passage Jesus gives a veiled answer to the Jewish leaders' question by implying that his authority, like that of John the Baptist, comes directly from God. The Jewish leaders had failed to recognize John's authority despite the revival amongst the "sinners" which he initiated and, by implication, they would do the same with Jesus. Such was their incompetence.

The Relationship between John and Jesus: Conclusions

John acted as Jesus' mentor, revealing to him that the injustices suffered by the indigenous Jews of Galilee and those suffered by the "sinners" were

---

13. The sinners were victims of injustice because the Jewish establishment had excluded them from mainstream Jewish society and was unwilling to reinstate them even though they demonstrated sincere repentance.

14. For example, Matt 11:7–15 and Luke 7:24–28; Matt 17:10–13; 21:25–27 and Mark 11:30–33 and Luke 24:2–8; Matt 21:32.

all aspects of the same spiritual malaise at the heart of society. John also trained Jesus for a mission similar to his own.

HOW JOHN AFFECTED JESUS

If, as we have established, John acted as Jesus' mentor, by definition he shaped Jesus' ministry. We now seek to determine the extent to which John influenced Jesus by first identifying the distinctive elements in Jesus' earthly ministry and then comparing them with those of John's ministry identified in the previous chapter.

The Distinctive Elements In Jesus' Earthly Ministry

The methodology adopted for identifying the distinctive features of Jesus' ministry was to scan the canonical gospels for those occasions when the people around him expressed amazement concerning his sayings or actions, indicating that they considered these to be extraordinary. Clearly the primary source is the NT canon and, especially, the gospels. Since we are here concerned with aspects of Jesus that were unusual and therefore particularly likely to be remembered, the gospel passages concerned are probably accurate reminiscences of Jesus.[15]

Authority

The earliest occasion in the synoptic narratives on which the evangelists record Jesus as provoking astonishment is the following:

> They went to Capernaum; and when the sabbath came, he entered the synagogue and taught. They were astounded at his teaching, for he taught them as one having authority, and not as the scribes. (Mark 1:21f)

Matthew has recontextualised the Marcan passage, adapting it as the conclusion to the Sermon on the Mount:

> Now when Jesus had finished saying these things, the crowds were astounded at his teaching, for he taught them as one having authority, and not as their scribes. (Matt 7:28f)

15. For further on this see *Criteria of Authenticity* on page 164.

Luke 4:32 also records the Capernaum congregation's astonishment at his authority, but does not mention the scribes, probably because it is unlikely that his intended Gentile readership would have understood their significance.

For our purposes the difference between the Marcan and Matthean versions is immaterial; what is significant is that both mention astonishment at the *authority* inherent in the newcomer Jesus' teaching style; this apparently contrasted sharply with that of the traditional scribes or teachers of the law to whom the people were accustomed. Although the evangelists compiled their gospels some decades after the events that they describe, that the congregation's astonishment at his authority still featured in the source material that they used suggests that it was remembered and was deemed an important aspect of Jesus' ministry.

It may be significant that Mark and Matthew clearly imply that the scribes who normally taught Jesus' hearers *lacked* such authority. France, commenting on Matt 7:28f, explains that while scribal teachers appealed to earlier interpreters of the law to lend weight to their arguments, Jesus set himself up as an authority with his confident "*I* tell you," exemplified in Matt 5:17–48.[16] Jesus, then, taught as though acting with God's direct authority, indeed as God's spokesman, a role firmly in Judaism's prophetic tradition. Despite this, it is remarkable that Jesus is nowhere recorded as using the archetypal prophetic expression "Thus says the Lord." In the NRSV this phrase occurs 418 times in the OT, usually spoken by prophets, but only once in the NT and that in a citation of an OT passage. Although Jesus is not recorded as having used this expression, the gospels frequently record the people as acclaiming him a prophet, presumably because they recognized divine authority in him.[17]

Personal Relationship with God

Jesus self portrayal as God's spokesman probably arises from the intimate personal relationship with God that he claimed to enjoy. This is evidenced in his addressing God as "Father,"[18] one of the most characteristic features

---

16. France, *Matthew*, 299.

17. Matt 13:57; 16:14; 21:11, 46; Mark 6:4, 15; 8:28; Luke 9:8, 19; 24:19; John 4:19; 6:14; 7:40, 52; 9:17.

18. In the NRSV text 43 times in Matthew, 4 in Mark, 19 in Luke, and 105 in John.

of his ministry.[19] While the Jews had long regarded Yahweh as the father of Israel,[20] the OT never speaks of God as the father of any individual. Before Jesus there is no evidence that any Jew had presumed to address God as "my Father." To Jews—who reverentially refused even to pronounce the divine name Yahweh—such an appellation was tantamount to blasphemy. And yet in calling God "Father" Jesus put into perspective doctrines to which most Jews of his day would have readily assented. If God is their Creator, he gave them life as their earthly fathers had done. If God is omniscient, he knows them thoroughly, even more intimately than an earthly father knows his children (*c.f.* Ps 139). If God is merciful, surely they may enter his presence to crave his pardon, as children enjoy a right of access to their earthly fathers. God should be approached naturally and sincerely. Jesus' practice simply extended this fatherhood motif to its logical conclusion: if God was in any sense a father, he could be addressed in a familiar manner, as children address their earthly father as "Daddy." Indeed, on at least one occasion Jesus does address God in this way, the Aramaic *Abba* in Mark 14:36.

Moreover, far from claiming exclusive rights to his filial intimacy with God, Jesus opened it up to embrace his followers. Of the 43 occasions in Matthew on which Jesus speaks of God as "Father," in all but seven "Father" is qualified by a possessive adjective: "your" (18 times), "my" (15 times), "our," "their" and "his" (once each). His instruction to his disciples to address God as "Our father" (Matt 6:9) rather than "my father" implies that the disciple's filial relationship with God depends upon Jesus as its mediator and this is confirmed in such sayings as "No one comes to the Father except through me" (John 14:6) and "no one knows the Father except the Son and anyone to whom the Son chooses to reveal him" (Matt 11:27). So all who follow Jesus are admitted into this personal relationship with God.

While the familial intimacy of the Christian's relationship with God became one of the most characteristic features of the Christian faith,[21] Jesus himself was aware that a counterbalancing truth was needed. God is also holy and therefore unapproachable by fallen humanity. Although he

19. It may be significant that at his baptism the divine voice declared Jesus as his Son (Matt 3:17; Mark 1:11; Luke 3:22; *c.f.* John 1:32–34). The fatherhood of God then became the keynote of Jesus' public ministry as well as his personal devotional life.

20. This is explicit or implicit in a diversity of OT passages, such as Ps 68:5; 103:13; Prov 3:12; Jer 3:4, 19; 31:9; Hos 11:1; Mal 1:6; 2:10.

21. For example, Paul adapted it in his depiction of Jesus' followers being adopted into God's family in Rom 8:22f, 29.

may be addressed as Father, he is not a human being and the reverence of the Jews has a proper place; he is other-worldly and must be held in awe. It may be significant that of Jesus' 43 references to God as "Father" in Matthew, 20 qualify the homely imagery of "Father" as either "heavenly" or "in Heaven."

Ultimately the channel of this personal relationship with God is the Holy Spirit. In the OT the Holy Spirit was conferred only upon certain individuals such as prophets and kings, who held special responsibilities, allowing them alone to have a personal relationship with God. In the NT Jesus has the power to confer the Holy Spirit on every Christian disciple,[22] fulfilling the prophecy of Joel 2:26 and the Baptist's preaching.

Repudiation of the Religious Establishment

The prophets of old differed from the ministers employed by the religious establishment, such as the priests, in two significant ways. Firstly, the prophets' authority came directly from God; they were his spokespersons. Secondly, many of them distanced themselves from the religious establishment; sometimes, indeed, the messages they delivered were severely critical of it.[23] As we have seen, Jesus regarded himself as called directly by God and in this regard he followed the tradition of the prophets of old—but did he dissociate himself from the establishment?

In general Jesus appears to repudiate the establishment and, especially, its hierarchy. Surely the most graphic example of this is the cleansing of the temple, which Sanders regards as the most significant action in Jesus' ministry, a symbolic destruction.[24] According to Matthew's gospel, in the ensuing confrontation with officialdom when representatives of the establishment challenge Jesus' authority, his reply includes the Stories of the Two Sons (Matt 21:28–22) and the Wedding Feast (Matt 22:1–10); it is surely significant that both depict unsuitable servants bring replaced by more satisfactory ones.

There are some passages in which Jesus appears to uphold the establishment, but under close scrutiny the situation is more complex. For

22. Luke 11:13; John 20:22; 1 Cor 12:3.

23. Perhaps the clearest examples are the passages in which Jeremiah and Ezekiel denounce the "shepherds," *i.e.* the priests (for example, Jer 23:1–4; Ezek 34:1–10). See also the texts cited under the heading *Repudiation of Institutional Judaism* on page 71.

24. Sanders, *Jesus and Judaism*, 69f.

example, in Mark 1:40–44 and parallels Jesus instructs a newly healed leper, "go, show yourself to the priest, and offer for your cleansing what Moses commanded." Since apparently this incident took place in Galilee, it was surely one of the locally based priests[25] to whom Jesus sent the leper; it seems unlikely that Jesus would send a newly healed leper on the arduous trek to Jerusalem when the requisite ritual could be performed locally. It was the *Jerusalem* hierarchy which Jesus refused to recognize on account of its failure to help the beleaguered Jews of Galilee. Locally based priests were surely as familiar as he with the hardships of Galilean Jews and perhaps as critical as he was of the shortcomings of the Jerusalem hierarchy.

In the Sermon on the Mount Matthew records Jesus as saying, "Do not think that I have come to abolish the law or the prophets; I have come not to abolish but to fulfill. For truly I tell you, until heaven and earth pass away, not one letter, not one stroke of a letter, will pass from the law until all is accomplished" (Matt 5:17f). If this is a genuine saying of Jesus, he upheld Torah rigorously and that presumably would include the cultus which it enjoined. But to accept the divine institution of the cultus as set out in sacred scripture is not the same as accepting the human institutions that currently were supposedly administering that cultus; surely Jesus would have argued that the cultus operating in Jerusalem in his time was invalidated by the corruption of its ministers. In Matt 5:20, "For I tell you, unless your righteousness exceeds that of the scribes and Pharisees, you will never enter the kingdom of heaven," Jesus arguably acknowledges some virtue in the scribes and Pharisees, but clearly regards it as inadequate—he demands higher standards of his own followers. A similar accusation regarding the scribes and the Pharisees appears in his injunction, "The scribes and the Pharisees sit on Moses' seat; therefore, do whatever they teach you and follow it; but do not do as they do, for they do not practice what they teach" (Matt 23:2f). Jesus' is not renouncing Torah or the institutions enshrined within it, but the human personnel who were inadequately executing its ordinances.

Destruction of the Temple

According to the synoptic gospels Jesus explicitly predicted the destruction of Herod's Temple (Mark 13:1f and Matt 24:1f), although he did not explain when, how or why this would happen. At Jesus' trial some witnesses

25. For further see under *Priesthood* on page 51, especially fn 19.

claimed that Jesus had threatened to destroy the Temple himself and build a new one (Mark 14:56–59 and Matt 26:59–61), although this may have been a garbled recollection of a figurative saying comparing his own body with a temple, as in John 2:19ff. According to Sanders, that Jesus became involved in a controversy concerning the Temple is one of the "almost indisputable facts" concerning his ministry.[26]

These sayings and actions constituted a controversy because, as the focal point of Judaism, the Temple held an unique place in Jewish culture. It was the seat of the cultic worship prescribed in the Pentateuch, commanding the loyalty of the Pharisees and the Sadducees, despite their many differences; only the most radical sects, such as the Qumran community, were sceptical concerning the Temple. Herod's Temple was regarded as one of the wonders of the ancient world and attracted both Jewish pilgrims and visitors of other races and religions. Such was Jewish pride in Herod's Temple that Jesus' prediction of its total destruction—"Not one stone will be left here upon another; all will be thrown down"—would have been deeply shocking to most Jewish hearers, indeed bordering on heresy. This ensured his hearers' attention and that the saying was remembered and committed to writing.

What, then, did Jesus mean by this prediction? Although it found literal fulfillment in the traumatic events of 70 CE, it is unlikely that Jesus was referring only to the destruction of a physical building, albeit one of such unique significance. Surely his meaning was deeper, rooted in the Temple's symbolism. As the centerpiece of Judaism, it represented that religion itself, much as some folk today refer to "Rome," denoting the whole of Roman Catholicism. If so, Jesus was predicting not the destruction of the physical Temple, but the ending of institutional Judaism as God's preferred way for humanity to engage with himself. Its replacement would be a structure built from people, not stones, the new community that he had already begun to assemble. His prediction of the Temple's demise (and its replacement) is therefore parallel with the Stories of the Two Sons and the Wedding Feast which depict God's dismissal of his original servants and their replacement by others.

26. Sanders, *Jesus and Judaism*, 11.

Jesus' New Egalitarian Community

An inevitable consequence of Jesus' repudiation of the religious establishment is his insistence that his followers are directly accountable to himself, not to any other human agency. This teaching is "low key," however, in that these are implications of his teaching which become apparent only upon reflection. For example, a recurring *motif* in Jesus' teaching is the imagery of shepherd and sheep as a metaphor for himself and his followers.[27] An extension of the same imagery used in the OT to portray Yahweh's relationship with Israel, sometimes mediated through human leaders,[28] it became a root metaphor of the Christian movement, originating the ecclesiastical usage of such terms as "pastor" and "flock." The bucolic imagery of Jesus as shepherd,[29] however, extends beyond the comforting assurance that he will lead, feed and protect his followers: the sheep in a flock are all equal; sheep have no hierarchy such as those found in Judaism and some church structures; the sole responsibility of each individual is to follow the shepherd. So this metaphor indicates that each disciple has only one master, Jesus himself, and therefore that all disciples are equal under him. This equality of disciples underlies Jesus' diatribe against honorific Jewish titles:

> But you are not to be called rabbi, for you have one teacher, and you are all students. And call no one your father on earth, for you have one Father—the one in heaven. Nor are you to be called instructors, for you have one instructor, the Messiah. The greatest among you will be your servant. (Matt 23:8–11)

This passage envisages a community in which distinctions of rank or class are abolished so that all are equal under God's unique earthly representative. All disciples therefore have equal access to God through Jesus, eliminating the need for other human intermediaries such as priests.

Indeed all disciples inherit the privileges of the upper echelons of the Jewish hierarchy. It is surely significant that Matthew records two instances of the authority to bind and loose—that is, to forgive sins—being given to

---

27. For example, Matt 7:15; 9:36; 10:6, 16; 15:24; 18:12ff; 26:31; Mark 6:34; Luke 15:3–7; John 10:1–18; 21:15–17.

28. For example, Ps 80:1; Isa 40:11; Ezek 34:1–35; Zech 10:2.

29. There is a shock element in the concept of the shepherd itself, since shepherds in first-century Jewish society were included amongst the "sinners" banished from respectable society (see *The "Sinners"* on page 8).

disciples: first to Peter as the prototype Christian (Matt 16:19) and later to the disciples generally (18:15–20).

Although ultimately all disciples are accountable only to Jesus and not to any intermediary, that does not isolate them or diminish the importance of relationships between them. On the contrary, Jesus insisted that discipleship entails a duty of care towards fellow disciples; this is a mutual responsibility.[30] In the Parable of the Sheep and the Goats, a graphic depiction of the final judgment, when the King (Jesus) commends the righteous for their acts of mercy towards him when he was in need, they reply, quite understandably,

> "Lord, when was it that we saw you hungry and gave you food, or thirsty and gave you something to drink? And when was it that we saw you a stranger and welcomed you, or naked and gave you clothing? And when was it that we saw you sick or in prison and visited you?" And the king will answer them, "Truly I tell you, just as you did it to one of the least of these who are members of my family, you did it to me." (Matt 25:37–40)

The passage suggests that Jesus counts any act of mercy towards "one of the least of these who are members of my family"—meaning, presumably, even the most obscure of disciples—as though he himself were its recipient and, by implication, will reward the carer accordingly. Ultimately, then, each disciple has a "pastoral" responsibility for all others; this is a mutual obligation among equals.

But although this pastoral obligation applies only to fellow disciples,[31] Jesus has a broader equality in view. The new community that he envisages has a mission to those outside its fold—to proselytize them. Moreover, this is global in scope: to "make disciples of all nations, baptizing them . . . " (Matt 28:19). The distinction between Jews and Gentiles is thereby abolished: the new community is one that welcomes all races and nationalities. Indeed, it is to be a community in which *all* human divisions—including

---

30. Jesus taught that devotion to God and to one's fellow disciples are inextricably interlinked, each an expression of the other. This principle is well exemplified in 1 John 4:20: "Those who say, 'I love God,' and hate their brothers or sisters, are liars; for those who do not love a brother or sister whom they have seen, cannot love God whom they have not seen."

31. That is not to deny the value of deeds of mercy towards outsiders. Jesus taught that the second most important commandment was to love one's neighbor as oneself (Mark 12:31 and parallels) and he told the parable of the Good Samaritan (Luke 10:30–37) to illustrate that this neighbor may be someone from another race or religion.

those based upon race, sex, age, wealth, and social status—are null and void. Jesus advocated "equality" and "diversity" long before the advent of "political correctness." This was explicitly the teaching of the apostles;[32] that it was previously the teaching of Jesus himself becomes apparent from interpretation of some of his parables. The Mustard Seed (Mark 4:30–32 and parallels) views the kingdom as expanding from small beginnings to a tree so large that birds—which in Jewish thought symbolized Gentiles—can roost in its branches. The Yeast (Matt 13:33; Luke 13:20f) shows a little yeast (the fledgling community of disciples) as nevertheless sufficient to transform a vast batch of dough (the whole of humanity). In the Parable of the Great Feast, when the originally invited guests (the Jews and especially their leaders) refused to attend, the host's servants are sent out into the streets to invite "all the people they could find, both good and bad" (Matt 22:10) or "the poor, the crippled, the blind, and the lame," that is, the marginalized (Luke 14:21). The new community is to welcome even those most despised by the outside world and within it they will be on a par with all their peers.

Reversal of Fortunes

One occasion when Jesus' disciples expressed astonishment at him was following his encounter with the wealthy young man who was reluctant to follow Jesus' instruction to sell his possessions and give the proceeds to the poor. Jesus told the disciples:

> "How hard it will be for those who have wealth to enter the kingdom of God! . . . Children, how hard it is to enter the kingdom of God! It is easier for a camel to go through the eye of a needle than for someone who is rich to enter the kingdom of God." They were greatly astounded and said to one another, "Then who can be saved?" (Mark 10:23 26)

At the time of Jesus popular Jewish piety regarded wealth as evidence of God's blessing and poverty as a consequence of divine disfavor. That Jesus' disciples shared this misconception is evident from their reaction to Jesus' pronouncement. Jesus was proposing the antithesis of common

---

32. For example, Paul wrote, "for in Christ Jesus you are all children of God through faith. As many of you as were baptized into Christ have clothed yourselves with Christ. There is no longer Jew or Greek, there is no longer slave or free, there is no longer male and female; for all of you are one in Christ Jesus" (Gal 3:26–28).

Jewish understanding, so it is not surprising that the disciples "were greatly astounded."

Elsewhere Jesus pronounced God's blessing on the poor, especially beggars. As pointed out in chapter 3,[33] in the sayings "Blessed are you who are poor, for yours is the kingdom of God" (Luke 6:20) and the Matthean variant, "Blessed are the poor in spirit, for theirs is the kingdom of heaven" (Matt 5:3) the Greek word inadequately rendered as "poor" in many English versions is *ptōchos*, which in classical Greek denoted a beggar and probably still implied someone dependent upon the help of others. So both versions of this saying could be paraphrased, "God's favor rests upon those who are not ashamed to admit their own insufficiency and who come to him sincerely begging for his assistance on the grounds of his grace alone. These are the ones who will find themselves in the kingdom of heaven." Jesus expands upon this "divine dependency culture" when he compares disciples with children:

> Truly I tell you, unless you change and become like children, you will never enter the kingdom of heaven. Whoever becomes humble like this child is the greatest in the kingdom of heaven. Whoever welcomes one such child in my name welcomes me. (Matt 18:3–5)

The significance of this saying is that in the ancient world children had no rights or resources of their own and therefore were entirely dependent for all their needs upon their parents or other guardians. Jesus sought to inculcate in his disciples an analogous wholehearted dependence upon God. Wealth was an obstacle to this: why trust in God for the next meal when one has sufficient funds to purchase it? Moreover, wealth itself is deceptive: as the Parable of the Rich Fool (Luke 12:15–21) and the following passage from the Sermon on the Mount teach, material possessions are vulnerable and everyone leaves them behind upon death:

> Do not store up for yourselves treasures on earth, where moth and rust consume and where thieves break in and steal; but store up for yourselves treasures in heaven, where neither moth nor rust consumes and where thieves do not break in and steal. For where your treasure is, there your heart will be also . . . But strive first for the kingdom of God and his righteousness, and all these things will be given to you as well. (Matt 6:19–21, 33)

---

33. See under *Beggars* on page 39.

Some exegetes view the motif of seeking heavenly treasure with suspicion because it appears to introduce an element of greed, the seeking of reward, into discipleship. But, while we cannot with any certainty predict the nature of the promised reward, we may be confident that it will not be of the sort that appeals to earthly human appetites.

Even if Jesus advocated poverty, he was certainly no ascetic. In contrast with John the Baptist, Jesus dressed conventionally[34] and attended formal dinners,[35] even attracting the epithet "a glutton and a drunkard" (Matt 11:19; Luke 7:34). Nevertheless, there is arguably an incipient asceticism is his instructions to his disciples when preparing them for a preaching and healing mission:

> Take no gold, or silver, or copper in your belts, no bag for your journey, or two tunics, or sandals, or a staff; for laborers deserve their food. (Matt 10:9f)

In other words, the disciples are to take no provisions for their journey, but to depend for their sustenance upon the hospitality of the communities that they visit. There is no suggestion that Jesus instructed them to beg; because their mission was to Jews only (Matt 10:5f), he considered that they should have no need to do so; a tradition of hospitality obliged all Jews to care for travelers in need. Although these instructions to the disciples have often been compared with the precepts of Cynicism, Jesus' refusal to beg and his insistence upon conventional dress stand in sharp contrast with the teachings of the Cynics. Nevertheless, throughout much of his ministry he and his disciples pursued an itinerant lifestyle sufficiently arduous to deter some candidates: he told one would-be disciple, "Foxes have holes, and birds of the air have nests; but the Son of Man has nowhere to lay his head" (Matt 8:20). Disciples, by definition, are persons under *discipline*.

---

34. Even to the detail of wearing tassels as a reminder of Torah (*kraspedon* in Matt 9:20; 14:36; 23:5; Mark 6:56; Luke 8:44).

35. Mark 2:15 *etc*; Luke 19:5 (implied); Luke 7:36; 11:37; 14:1.

Concern for the "Sinners"

One aspect of Jesus' ministry that drew a sharp response from the Pharisees[36] and murmured complaints from the wider populace[37] who accepted Pharisaic teaching was his attitude to the "sinners."[38] The popular piety promoted by the Pharisees taught that observant Jews should despise the "sinners." Moreover, the ritual purity movement[39] so influential in first-century Judaism exacerbated observant Jews' concerns about defilement through contact with something or someone considered unclean. For example, although Torah did not explicitly prohibit Jews from entering the homes of "sinners," social contact and, especially, dining with them with them was discouraged as it introduced the risk of consuming food that did not comply with the Judaism's purity laws as then widely understood.

In striking contrast with the conventions of his society, Jesus was concerned about the "tax collectors and sinners." His saying, "I have come to call not the righteous but sinners" (Mark 2:17 and parallels) is almost his mission statement. Another term which Jesus sometimes used apparently as a synonym for the "sinners" was "the lost" (*to apolōlos* or *ta apolōlota*[40]). This vividly reflects the lot of the "sinners," as they were banished irrevocably from the mainstream life of Israel. Jesus linked this to his favorite shepherd-and-flock metaphor when he compared his mission to that of a shepherd seeking a lost sheep,[41] although he also used the imagery of a housewife seeking a lost coin (Luke 15:4) and a father welcoming a returned son feared lost (Luke 15:24, 32).

Amidst Luke's collection of parables about "the lost" Jesus makes what is surely a key statement for understanding his mission: "I tell you, there will be more joy in heaven over one sinner who repents than over ninety-nine righteous persons who need no repentance" (Luke 15:7). There is a

36. For example, the Pharisees criticized him for dining with tax collectors and "sinners" (Matt 9:10f; Mark 2:15f; Luke 5:29f).

37. Such as the disparaging epithet, "friend of tax collectors and sinners" (Matt 11:19; Luke 7:34; 15:2).

38. This study, for reasons given under *The "Sinners"* on page 8 and *Excommunication: a Hypothesis* on page 10, assumes that these "sinners" were Jews who had been excommunicated by the establishment for failure to comply with the Pharisaic twofold law.

39. For further see on *Purity* on page 6.

40. From the verb *apollumi*, widely used in the NT, which transitively can mean "destroy," "abolish," "lose" or "get rid of," or passively, "perish."

41. Matt 10:6; 15:4; Luke 15:6.

similar saying in verse 10: "I tell you, there is joy in the presence of the angels of God over one sinner who repents." Nolland links these sayings with the tradition in Matt 18:13: "And if he [the shepherd] finds it [his lost sheep], truly I tell you, he rejoices over it more than over the ninety-nine that never went astray." Astutely Nolland points out that the passage highlights God's delight in restoration and the value he sets on individuals.[42] Catastrophically at the time of Jesus institutional Judaism appeared content to let "sinners" languish in hopelessness. Jesus, in contrast, was concerned for them, dismissing as little more than superstition the purity movement that was instrumental in creating so many of them. According to Mark 7:15–23, when accused of allowing his disciples to eat without observing the approved hand-cleansing procedure, he replied, "there is nothing outside a person that by going in can defile, but the things that come out are what defile . . . Do you not see that whatever goes into a person from outside cannot defile, since it enters, not the heart but the stomach, and goes out into the sewer? . . . It is what comes out of a person that defiles. For it is from within, from the human heart, that evil intentions come: fornication, theft, murder, adultery, avarice, wickedness, deceit, licentiousness, envy, slander, pride, folly. All these evil things come from within, and they defile a person." In other words, people are defiled by their thoughts and actions, not what they consume.

Internalizing the Commandments

Surely one of the greatest shocks that Jesus gave his hearers is in the sayings that have become known as the *Antitheses*. For example, "You have heard that it was said to those of ancient times, 'You shall not murder'; and 'whoever murders shall be liable to judgment' . . . But I say to you . . . " (Matt 5:21). No Jew would have objected to the initial statement. But as he began the second there would surely have been a sharp intake of breath—for two reasons. The first was the sheer effrontery of Jesus for setting his own authority on a par with that of Moses (*But I say*). The second was that it must have seemed as though he were about to abrogate the sixth commandment: "But I'm telling you that murder is permissible."

Of course, what Jesus proceeded to tell his hearers was that, far from murder being permissible, God accorded equal gravity to the anger that gives rise to murder, even when it leads to no outward action. Instead of

42. Nolland, *Luke*, 2:773.

99

relaxing the commandment, Jesus has replaced it with a more stringent one. He has *internalized* the original commandment, identifying and disparaging the processes in the human psyche that lead to murder. In the second antithesis (Matt 5:27f) Jesus treats the seventh commandment in the same way, replacing the prohibition of adultery with the prohibition of lust. The shock element in these sayings—analogous to that in many of his parables—would have made them memorable, so it is likely that they are authentic.

Clearly Jesus considered that unthinking, literal observance of the Decalogue prohibitions was insufficient. What he sought in his followers was an inward reorientation to the will of God, of which Torah's commandments were an imperfect expression. What Jesus proposes is the very antithesis of the antinomianism of which some have accused him.[43] It is not unduly difficult to refrain from the literal act of murder, but to live a lifetime without anger is surely unattainable. Similarly most Christian men manage to avoid committing the act of adultery, but surely few are innocent of lust. Jesus' commandment is a counsel of perfection. Benno Przybylski refers to this process as "fencing Torah," that is, banning lesser indiscretions so that people never have an opportunity to commit the more serious offences.[44]

What is significant here is that both reinterpretations shift the offensive element from the outward act to the state of mind that gives rise to it. Because the offence has now become an episode in a person's inner life, it could never be tried in an earthly court of law. Jesus was not the first Jewish thinker to look beyond Torah's commandments to the state of mind that led people to infringe them. Although he is sometimes thought to have invented the "double commandment of love"[45] whose faithful observance would ensure conformity with the whole of Torah, the two commandments occur separately in the Pentateuch[46] and Maccoby claims that their apposition was an established part of Pharisee thinking.[47] Ellis Rivkin states that the Pharisees were the first to teach that what God demands of humanity is

43. For example, G. Barth ("Law," 159–64) argues that Matthew wrote to counter groups who disputed that the law and the prophets still hold for the church. Evidence for this, he claims, can be seen in Mt 5:17ff; 7:15ff, and 24:11ff.

44. Przybylski, *Righteousness*, 81f.

45. Matt 22:34–40; Mark 12:28–31; Luke 10:25–28.

46. "You shall love the Lord your God with all your heart, and with all your soul, and with all your might" (Deut 6:5); "you shall love your neighbor as yourself" (Lev 19:18).

47. Maccoby, *Jesus*, 121.

not just outward observance of the commandments, but conformity in the individual's inner life as well: see the passage cited earlier.[48]

Even if the Pharisees were exploring the principles underlying Torah—and the very nature of their oral law indicates that they were indeed doing this—it was Jesus' teaching that caught the people's imagination. While the Pharisees were effectively multiplying laws and so laying an intolerable burden upon ordinary Jews (Matt 23:2–4), Jesus was simplifying them and promising relief to the weary (Matt 11:28–30).

Attitude to Rome

Jesus never mentions Rome *per se* and his only recorded reference to Caesar is in the saying, "Render therefore to Caesar the things that are Caesar's, and to God the things that are God's."[49] It is tempting to retroject into this saying the sharp distinction between sacred and secular spheres that characterizes present western world culture, a legacy of the Protestant Reformation, but that would divorce this saying from its context. At the time of Jesus most Jews—with the notable exception of the Sadducee high priestly classes—hated Rome on account of its crippling taxes, cruel punishments and general interference with Jewish affairs. Understandably many wished to expel the Roman presence from Palestine by military means and some thought that Jesus might be the leader whom God had sent to raise an army for that purpose.[50] According to the gospel records, however, Jesus showed no interest in raising an army and never spoke out against either Rome or those who opposed Rome; he displayed perfect neutrality. According to the Marcan account, it was "some Pharisees and some Herodians" who in order "to trap him in what he said" asked Jesus whether it was lawful to pay Roman taxes. This question was a cunningly contrived trap: if Jesus advocated that Jews should pay Roman taxes, his followers—whom his questioners assumed to be solidly anti-Rome—would surely be so disillusioned with him that they would desert him and he would lose his influence. But if he forbade the payment of Roman taxes, he could be reported to the authorities for inciting rebellion against Rome. The genius in Jesus' reply lies in his insistence that one of his supposedly anti-Rome questioners produce

48. See fn 73 on page 19.

49. Matt 22:17; Mark 12:17; Luke 20:25 RSV.

50. For example, the unnamed disciples in Acts 1:6 who ask Jesus, "Lord, is this the time when you will restore the kingdom to Israel?"

an example of the coin for the capitation tax. This was a Roman denarius, which of course bore Caesar's image. That the questioner was able to do so showed that he himself was guilty to some extent of compromise with Rome inasmuch as he was carrying Roman coinage. Moreover, since the coin bore Caesar's image—and images were offensive to Jews—and an inscription describing him as "son of God"—which Jews found offensive—the integrity of the questioner's own Jewish piety had been called into question.

Forgiveness of Sins

Jesus' first recorded confrontation with Jewish officialdom in Galilee was provoked by his pronouncement of a paralysed man's sins forgiven (Mark 2:5–7 and parallels). Not only did he claim authority to forgive sins (or, perhaps more strictly, to pronounce sins forgiven), but also to confer this authority upon his followers. This latter tradition is preserved in three places in the gospels:

Matt 16:19	Matt 18:18	John 20:22f
I will give you the keys of the kingdom of heaven, and		
	Truly I tell you,	
		When he had said this, he breathed on them and said to them, "Receive the Holy Spirit.
whatever you bind on earth will be bound in heaven, and whatever you loose on earth will be loosed in heaven.	whatever you bind on earth will be bound in heaven, and whatever you loose on earth will be loosed in heaven.	If you forgive the sins of any, they are forgiven them; if you retain the sins of any, they are retained."

The two sayings in Matthew are addressed respectively to Peter as an individual and to the disciples as a whole. Although they do not mention forgiveness explicitly, it is arguable from the context that it is primarily in connection with forgiveness that God delegates authority to his human servants. In Matthew 16 the saying follows Jesus' promise to give Peter "the keys of the kingdom of heaven," a potent symbol of authority. If Peter holds the keys of the kingdom, presumably he can choose those whom he will admit and those to whom he will deny access, admission to the kingdom depending surely upon a right relationship with the king. As the king is holy God, unforgiven sin will hinder a person's relationship with him. In Matt 18 the saying is followed by others concerning the innate presence of Jesus in gatherings of his followers and then by Peter's question about the number of times he should forgive his fellow. That in turn is followed by the Parable of the Unforgiving Servant. Since Matthew tends to aggregate material on related themes, it is likely that he understood "binding" and "loosing" to refer to forgiveness as a function of Jesus' indwelling in his disciples.

The Johannine saying explicitly empowers the disciples to forgive sins or withhold forgiveness; the prior anointing with the Holy Spirit is presumably a prerequisite, equipping the disciples for their role in mediating God's forgiveness. If this saying represents the Johannine version of the commissioning of the church, it implies that forgiveness of sins is the church's most important function.

Matthew's gospel refers more frequently than the other gospels to Jesus' authority to offer divine forgiveness, but Jesus' offer of forgiveness is always conditional upon the recipient in turn forgiving others:

> Blessed are the merciful, for they will be shown mercy. (Matt 5:7)

> Forgive us our debts, as we also have forgiven our debtors. (Matt 6:12)

> For if you forgive men when they sin against you, your heavenly Father will also forgive you. But if you do not forgive men their sins, your Father will not forgive your sins. (Matt 6:14f)

This condition, which stands in striking contrast with the free grace emphasized by Paul (for example, in Rom 8:1), is also reflected in the other gospels, although less prominently. In fact, the clearest example in Matthew is the Parable of the Unforgiving Servant (Matt 18:23–35), which Jesus tells in response to a question from Peter about the propriety of repeatedly forgiving the same offending brother; it explains why disciples must *always* forgive their fellows. The message of the parable is that someone who has been forgiven a debt so great that it could never have been repaid, even by a lifetime of devoted service, is under an enduring obligation to forgive others who offend him or her in comparatively trivial ways.

But what in the real world is the counterpart to the single massive act of forgiveness on the part of the king that lays upon its recipient this permanent obligation to forgive others? Although present-day Christian believers inevitably identify this with the atoning death of Jesus on the cross, if the parable is an authentic saying of Jesus, it must pre-date the cross; so how did Jesus understand it? Perhaps the truth is encapsulated in T. W. Manson's observation that Christians should be merciful because God is merciful.[51]

But where does the initiative lie in the interdependence of human and divine forgiveness? In other words, must I forgive my brother *in order that* God may forgive me or *because* God has already forgiven me? Matthew seems ambiguous; the sayings from Matt 5 and 6 cited above suggest the former, while in the Parable of the Unforgiving Servant it is clearly the latter. But because we are describing humans in whom the risen Jesus is indwelling through the Holy Spirit, the distinction between divine and human initiatives is tenuous. Ultimately, the engine that drives the interlinked cycles of divine and human forgiveness is divine mercy, even when I am forgiving my brother.

So What was Distinctive about Jesus?

This section has attempted to identify those aspects of Jesus' ministry that distinguished him from most other Jewish teachers of his day. In particular these aspects are the ones that drew reactions of astonishment from his hearers or that angered Jewish officialdom. We may summarize them as: (i) his authority directly received from God, (ii) his personal relationship with God as "Father," (iii) his repudiation of the religious establishment, (iv) his eschatological teaching regarding the destruction of the Temple, (v) his new egalitarian community, (vi) his teaching regarding the reversal of fortunes, (vii) his concern for the "sinners," (viii) his internalizing of the commandments, (ix) his ambivalent attitude to Rome, and (x) his authority to pronounce the forgiveness of sins and to confer this authority upon others. Not all of these were peculiar to Jesus, but many were and the aggregation of so many radical ideas in one teacher is certainly unique.

51. Manson, *Sayings*, 214.

COMPARISON OF JOHN'S DISTINCTIVES WITH JESUS'

Having identified the distinctive elements of Jesus' ministry, we shall now compare them with those of John the Baptist's ministry. Chapter 4 identified six distinctive features of John's ministry and this chapter ten of Jesus' ministry. This section will work through the six distinctive features of John's ministry in the order in which they were considered in chapter 4 and examine the extent to which each was also present in Jesus' ministry. The six distinctive features of John's ministry that were identified in chapter 4 were: (i) his asceticism, (ii) his claim to forgive sins, (iii) his repudiation of institutional Judaism, (iv) the diversity of his target people, (v) his use of water baptism and (vi) the centrality of the coming mightier one. We shall then briefly consider other distinctive features of Jesus' ministry before attempting to gauge the extent to which Jesus was affected by John.

Asceticism

Judaism had no commandment to practice asceticism; for this reason the few Jews who practiced it attracted attention. So John's asceticism, reflected in his clothing and diet, was his deliberate lifestyle choice; it made such an impression on Mark that he mentioned it early in his description of John's ministry (Mark 1:6).

Of the six distinctives of John's ministry, as will be seen, this one is unique in that Jesus did not adopt it. In no way was Jesus an ascetic: he dressed conventionally, even to the detail of wearing tassels as a reminder of Torah,[52] although he criticized the over-long tassels that some Pharisees wore, perhaps to make them appear extra pious (Matt 23:5). Moreover, his diet was conventional. He appears to have enjoyed food, accepting dinner invitations from tax collectors (Mark 2:15 and parallels) and Pharisees[53] alike and sometimes even inviting himself into the homes of new converts (Luke 19:5). The criticism that this behavior evoked may have been directed more at the company that he kept rather than what he ate: "For John came neither eating nor drinking, and they say, 'He has a demon'; the Son of Man came eating and drinking, and they say, 'Look, a glutton and a drunkard, a friend of tax collectors and sinners!'" (Matt 11:18f). Evidently, then, Jesus felt no obligation to pursue the ascetic practices of his former mentor.

52. See fn 34 on page 97.
53. Luke 7:36; 11:37; 14:1.

It could be argued that Jesus did exhibit a mild form of asceticism inasmuch as—after the start of his public ministry—he had no permanent home; he told one would-be follower, "Foxes have holes, and birds of the air have nests; but the Son of Man has nowhere to lay his head" (Matt 8:20). Moreover, when sending his disciples on a mission he commanded them to carry no provisions, but to rely on the hospitality of others for their daily needs (Matt 10:6–14). Nevertheless, so far as we are aware, his disciples dressed conventionally and ate whatever fare they were offered.

Forgiveness of Sins

As we have seen, John administered "a baptism of repentance for the forgiveness of sins" (Mark 1:4; Luke 3:7). Probably one reason for John's popularity was that he offered an inexpensive alternative to Judaism's official process for the remission of sins through the temple cultus.

When the paralyzed man was let down through the roof and Jesus told him, "Son, your sins are forgiven (*aphientai sou hai hamartiai*)" (Mark 2:5 and parallels), the Jewish officials present were enraged. They regarded this as blasphemous: "Who can forgive sins but God alone?" Of course, the use of the passive voice may indicate that Jesus was acting as God's spokesman, pronouncing God's forgiveness of the man's sins, rather than forgiving them himself. But to the Jewish officials who had probably been instructed specifically to seek grounds for Jesus' arrest, the subtle distinction was immaterial. Jesus, however, effectively proved his authority to forgive sins by pronouncing the man healed of his paralysis and demonstrating this to be so; if his word was efficacious over physical illness, so it was over the spiritual dimension. Indeed Jesus not only had the authority to forgive sins, but also to confer this authority upon others (Matt 16:19; 18:18, John 20:22f). Herein lies the precedent for Christian ministers granting absolution to followers of Jesus.

Repudiation of Institutional Judaism

That John repudiated institutional Judaism is an inference from his confinement of his ministry to the wilderness, far from temple and synagogue, and his offer of forgiveness of sins in competition with Judaism's official process through the temple cultus. Jesus' relationship with institutional Judaism is more complex. The gospels record that he attended synagogue and even taught in the synagogue until the occasion when he narrowly avoided a lynching by the congregation in Nazareth (Luke 4:16–30). Although he firmly upheld the sanctity of Torah and the prophets (Matt 5:17–19) and appears to have respected the temple as God's supposed dwelling place and centrepiece of Judaism—he taught in it during the final week of his earthly ministry—his cleansing of the temple was a symbolic destruction, suggesting that he regarded it as obsolete and he even foretold its future destruction (Mark 13:1–8). Moreover he considered the priesthood based there corrupt: if such sayings as "No one comes to the Father except through me" (John 14:6) and "no one knows the Father except the Son and anyone to whom the Son chooses to reveal him" (Matt 11:27) are genuine, they indicate that he regarded himself as the sole intermediary between God and humanity, thereby making other priests unnecessary. Although in the earlier period of his ministry Jesus appears to have respected the lay leaders, the Pharisees and teachers of the law, he later became estranged from them as evidenced by the diatribe in which he denounced them as hypocrites and blind guides (Matt 23:11–36).

Target People

The NT depicts both John and Jesus as targeting only Jews. Although Jesus is recorded as having some encounters with Gentiles and being pleasantly surprised by their faith (for example, Matt 8:5–13; 15:21–28), it was the Gentiles themselves who sought him out rather than *vice versa*. What was unusual about John's clientele is that it included "sinners," including tax collectors and prostitutes (Matt 21:32; Luke 3:12–14; 7:29), whom "respectable" Jews shunned. In the later phase of his ministry (after the healing of the paralyzed man) Jesus also targeted "sinners," including tax collectors, and even acquired a reputation as "a friend of tax collectors and sinners" (Matt 11:19; Luke 7:34).

Water Baptism

Water baptism had long had a purificatory role in Judaism, but it was his widespread and public use of it that earned John the epithet "Baptist." That Jesus and his disciples had also practiced baptism is less obvious in the gospels, but there is clear evidence that they had done so. For example, when Jesus asked his disciples, "Who do people say that I am?", the first of several answers was "John the Baptist" (Matt 16:13f; Mark 8:27f; Luke 9:18f.). If people now reckoned that Jesus was John *redivivus*, Jesus' ministry must have resembled John's closely. So if John's ministry was characterized by baptism, presumably Jesus' was too.

It was not only the public at large who were saying that Jesus was the Baptist restored to life; according to two of the synoptists, when Herod Antipas heard about Jesus' ministry, his immediate conclusion was that this was John the Baptist risen from the dead, returning to haunt his killer (Matt 14:1f; Mark 6:14–16). Of course, there were other possible reasons besides his administration of baptism that might have led to the identification of Jesus with John, but surely it was because Jesus baptized, performing the rite that in the public consciousness was so strongly associated with John that people were now saying that Jesus *was* John returned from the dead.

Although the synoptic gospels do not mention Jesus' baptizing ministry explicitly, the Fourth Gospel does:

> After this Jesus and his disciples went into the Judean countryside, and he spent some time there with them and baptized . . . [26] They came to John and said to him, "Rabbi, the one who was with you across the Jordan, to whom you testified, here he is baptizing, and all are going to him." (John 3:22–26)

> Now when Jesus learned that the Pharisees had heard, "Jesus is making and baptizing more disciples than John" [2] — although it was not Jesus himself but his disciples who baptized — [3] he left Judea and started back to Galilee. (John 4:1–3)

Even if John's Gospel had not been written or if the above passages had been omitted from it, it would still be possible to deduce from the synoptic gospels that Jesus had exercised a baptizing ministry. In the Great Commission Jesus instructs the apostles to "make disciples of all nations, baptizing them . . . " (Matt 28:19). This is the only mention of water baptism in the synoptic gospels aside from the ministry of John the Baptist. Consequently a hypothetical reader of Matthew unfamiliar with John's Gospel might be startled to see Jesus enjoining his disciples to perform the rite that otherwise seemed the prerogative of the Baptist alone. And yet Jesus' instruction implies that those apostles are familiar with the administration of the rite; it is as though they had been performing it for years. If so, why have the synoptists failed to mention what must have been an important element in

Jesus' ministry? The most likely explanation, as France comments,[54] is that the early Christian communities were well aware that their own baptism of converts was the continuation of the routine practice of Jesus and his disciples.

Centrality of the Coming Mightier One

The main theme of John's eschatological preaching was the imminent coming in judgment of the "one who is more powerful than I" (Mark 1:7). It was to prepare for his coming that John preached that people should repent and receive baptism.

Far more of Jesus' preaching is preserved than John's; this shows Jesus covering a range of eschatological topics. One such motif in Jesus' teaching is the "Son of Man," which occurs 85 times in the NRSV NT, 30 times in Matthew alone. A Hebraism that normally means "human being," sometimes Jesus uses it to denote himself, especially in contexts that stress his human vulnerability (for example, Matt 8:20; 26:24). Often, however, Jesus uses the term in an eschatological context with unmistakably Messianic overtones:

> The Son of Man will send his angels, and they will collect out of his kingdom all causes of sin and all evildoers . . . (Matt 13:41)

> Truly I tell you, there are some standing here who will not taste death before they see the Son of Man coming in his kingdom. (Matt 16:28)

> Then the sign of the Son of Man will appear in heaven, and then all the tribes of the earth will mourn, and they will see "the Son of Man coming on the clouds of heaven" with power and great glory. And he will send out his angels with a loud trumpet call, and they will gather his elect from the four winds, from one end of heaven to the other. (Matt 24:30f)

The words in quotation marks in the last snippet above appear to be a citation of Dan 7:13f, a passage that held special significance for the Jews at the time of Jesus, perhaps because Daniel was the last of the canonical prophets, having been written—as some scholars believe—during the second century. For further on Daniel see under *Messianic Expectations* on page 13.

54. France, *Matthew*, 1116.

Other Distinctive Elements in Jesus' Ministry

Some of the distinctive aspects of Jesus identified earlier in this chapter appear not to correspond with any of John's distinctives identified in chapter 4. These are: authority directly received from God, a personal relationship with God as "Father," the new egalitarian community that he advocated, the reversal of fortunes, internalizing of the commandments, and his attitude to Rome.

In fact, many of the distinctives identified above are interdependent and relate to distinctives which Jesus shared with the Baptist. Jesus' special relationship with God—manifest in his addressing him as "Father"—is a consequence of the authority that he considered that he had received directly from God. John also believed that he had been commissioned directly by God to undertake his baptizing ministry; many of the OT prophets who were critical of the religious establishment shared this belief. Few would deny that on occasions God bypasses the routine procedures of established religion and calls individuals to specific missions, even though they lack the formal qualifications approved by the establishment.

The egalitarian nature of the faith community that Jesus envisaged is a further extension of his directly received divine authority. Those whom Jesus calls receive access to God through him, eliminating the need for hierarchies. As Paul expresses it, "those whom he foreknew he also predestined to be conformed to the image of his Son, that his Son would be the firstborn among many brothers and sisters" (Rom 8:29 NET).

The reversal of fortunes—Jesus' teaching that material wealth hinders faith, while poverty fosters true dependency upon God's provision—is arguably yet another outcome of directly received divine authority. Although there is no indication that John the Baptist taught this, his ascetic lifestyle is a possible indication that he practiced it.

Jesus' internalization of the commandments (forbidding anger rather than murder and lust rather than adultery) was, in fact, a regular aspect of Pharisee thinking and his disciples were probably familiar with it. What shocked the disciples when Jesus pronounced, "You have heard that it was said to those of ancient times . . . But I say to you . . . " was not only his presumption of authority on a par (at least) with that of Moses, but also the form of words that he used which suggested that he was about to abrogate the prohibitions on murder and adultery; Jesus was a skilful teacher who knew how to command his audience's attention.

An apparent indifference to Rome was most unusual for a Jew at that time. It is impossible to determine whether Jesus inherited this attitude from John, since the preserved examples of John's sayings have no occasion to mention Rome. Nevertheless, it seems likely that John avoided mentioning political concerns because he regarded humanity's primary problem as spiritual. Jesus may have inherited the same attitude.

CONCLUSION

Since five of the six distinctive aspects of John the Baptist identified in chapter 4—that is, all except his asceticism—tally closely with five of Jesus' distinctives identified in this chapter, it is tempting to conclude that Jesus acquired these from John. If John as Jesus' mentor prepared him for a mission similar to his own, surely it is likely that Jesus "learned" these from John. Moreover, it is possible that many of the other distinctives of Jesus' ministry identified in this chapter were derived from John. One of the principal difficulties when comparing Jesus and John is the paucity of material from John's preaching and teaching that has been preserved.

Of course, there may be other explanations for the similarities between Jesus and John. They might both have been members of some sect which held and advocated these beliefs and practices. Alternatively both might have come under the influence of some individual teacher holding these beliefs. But there is no definite evidence to support either theory. In the absence of such evidence, the most likely explanation is, as many scholars claim, that John mentored Jesus, training him for a mission similar to his own. And if he did that, similarities between them are surely to be expected.

6

AN OVERVIEW OF JESUS' MINISTRY

THE PURPOSE OF THIS CHAPTER is to discover whether it is possible to re-construct Jesus' ministry from his leaving the Baptist to his confrontation with officialdom in the Temple, taking into account what we have learned about his mission and the conditions in which he was living. Do these form a coherent picture? While the primary sources are, inevitably, the gospels, some hypothesis will be proposed to fill in the gaps.

THE WILDERNESS

The synoptic gospels record that after Jesus' baptism but before he began his public ministry, "the Spirit immediately drove him out into the wilderness. He was in the wilderness forty days, tempted by Satan; and he was with the wild beasts; and the angels waited on him" (Mark 1:12f). Although this period in the wilderness is described as a time of "temptation," it was probably more a period of reflection, during which Jesus considered what he had learned while with the Baptist and what he had experienced at his baptism, and decided upon the particular course that his ministry should take. Undoubtedly it must have included many episodes of temptation.

Although he never abandoned his original intention to campaign for justice for the beleaguered indigenous Jews of Galilee, John's mentoring had broadened the scope of his mission to encompass all the marginalized in Israel, especially the tax collectors and other "sinners" who were being effectively locked out of mainstream Jewish society, despite genuine repentance (Matt 13:13). This study hypothesizes that while in the wilderness Jesus made what was probably the most revolutionary decision of his career: he would begin his ministry by attempting to change the attitude of institutional Judaism towards the groups that it had marginalized. Like the prophets of old, by preaching and teaching he would call Israel back to a wholehearted commitment to serve Yahweh. If this was successful, he would have achieved his intention in that the leaders of Judaism would willingly readmit sinners who repented. But if it failed, he would switch to an alternative agenda. Abandoning institutional Judaism as a lost cause, a failed religion, he would inaugurate an alternative community that would welcome all on the basis of faith alone; these would include the needy and dispossessed, including the repentant "sinners," who would indeed become his primary target. It is impossible to know how Jesus expected to recognize that the time had come to make this transition. Perhaps he hoped that it would never become necessary, but if it did, then he would "know it when he saw it."

THE EARLY JUDEAN MINISTRY

As stated above, Jesus had decided to start his ministry by attempting to change the attitude of institutional Judaism. The most sensible starting point was its leaders: if they could be persuaded to renew their relationship with Yahweh, surely the change would "trickle down" through the hierarchy to the laity, bringing justice for all. Since the Sanhedrin was the highest Jewish court, this was the obvious prime target. Jesus' ministry therefore needed to begin in Jerusalem, where he could engage with the chief priests and principal scholars.

Although the synoptic gospels concentrate on Jesus' ministry in Galilee, two of them acknowledge that Jesus had previously ministered elsewhere. According to Mark 1:14, "Now after John was arrested, Jesus came to Galilee, proclaiming the good news of God." Matthew 4:12 suggests a reason: "Now when Jesus heard that John had been arrested, he withdrew to Galilee," his *anechōrēsen* suggestive of a flight from a perceived threat.[1] Surely what is implied is that Jesus feared that what had happened to John might happen to him too.

---

1. BAGD suggests that in this context *anachōreō* denotes "withdraw, retire, take refuge."

The Fourth Gospel, in contrast, describes several significant episodes during at least two visits that Jesus made to Judea, presumably prior to the withdrawal to Galilee mentioned in Mark and Matthew. Recently scholarship has begun to acknowledge that this gospel, long regarded by many as theological reflection rather than historical narrative, may have a historical basis, especially in its account of Jesus' early ministry.[2]

The first such Judean episode is the cleansing of the Temple (John 2:13–25) during what might have been a brief visit to Jerusalem for the Passover. Jesus appears to have been alone on this visit; there is no mention of anyone accompanying him. The synoptists, of course, set the cleansing during the last week of Jesus' ministry and at least one commentator considers that the author of the Fourth Gospel has placed it artificially early for theological reasons.[3] But if John's were the only account of this episode, no-one would question his timing: it is undeniably the kind of action that one might expect of an ardent reformer. If the Temple was crowded with Passover pilgrims, Jesus would have scored a magnificent publicity coup, making himself and his desire for reform known to a wide cross section of Jews, including some from the diaspora. It would certainly provoke robust debate amongst the Temple authorities. Significantly for subsequent developments, it led the Sanhedrin to brand Jesus a troublemaker from the beginning of his ministry.

The Fourth Gospel's next episode describes Jesus' meeting with the Pharisee Nicodemus (John 3:1–21). As this carries no time reference, the evangelist may have intended his readers to infer that it took place soon after the cleansing, which is certainly possible. Nicodemus was precisely the kind of leader that an aspiring reformer might hope to influence: John describes him as "a leader of the Jews," by which he probably means a member of the Sanhedrin, and he presents Jesus as addressing him as "a teacher of Israel," suggesting that he had a reputation as a scholar. The surprising detail that it was Nicodemus who visited Jesus and that "by night," rather than Jesus calling on him in an appropriate daytime location, may be a consequence of the cleansing of the Temple. Jesus' recognition by the hierarchy as a troublemaker might have prevented him from obtaining an audience with Nicodemus through the regular channels, but this meeting was

2. For example, J. A. T. Robinson in "Baptism," 190. J. H. Charlesworth's most informative paper, "The Historical Jesus," especially pages 3–13, also argues persuasively that the Fourth Gospel is in some respects a superior historical source to the synoptics and Josephus.

3. Beasley-Murray, *John*, 38f.

Nicodemus's own initiative. As a member of the Sanhedrin, he would surely have heard about the cleansing and he might even have witnessed it. If he was already disaffected with the Jewish establishment,[4] something about Jesus might have resonated with him, leading him to seek a discussion with him. Nevertheless, fear that his enviable reputation would be tarnished if it became known that he had consulted the troublesome upstart Jesus led him to make his visit secretly, under the cover of darkness.

These two units of tradition dovetail together so well that the authenticity of John's timing for the cleansing surely deserves reconsideration. If the cleansing took place towards the end of Jesus' ministry, as the synoptists claim, either Jesus performed two similar cleansings[5] or in this early period he performed some other provocative action—probably in the temple—intended to draw attention to his cause and John, writing long after those events, has inadvertently inserted a description of the later cleansing in its place.

The next episode presumably happened on a later and longer visit to Judea. John writes, "After this Jesus and his disciples went into the Judean countryside, and he spent some time there with them and baptized" (John 3:22). Since Jesus was now accompanied by an entourage of disciples and he was baptizing, perhaps he was building a disciple base there.[6] Clearly he enjoyed considerable success as the evangelist next describes a period in which Jesus and John the Baptist were exercising simultaneous baptizing ministries in Judea, with a hint of rivalry between them (John 3:25–30).[7] Eventually Jesus was baptizing greater numbers than the Baptist, which according to the following somewhat cryptic passage caused the Jewish authorities some concern: "Now when Jesus learned that the Pharisees had

4. The exchange described in John 7:45–52 suggests that Nicodemus was at odds with many of his peers.

5. There is undoubted appeal in this suggestion: the two cleansings form an *inclusio* around Jesus' earthly ministry, symbolizing his rejection of institutional Judaism and its failure to recognize his authority.

6. There is circumstantial evidence that Judas Iscariot answered Jesus' call to discipleship during this early Judean period. The appellation "Iscariot" may mean "man of Kerioth," that being a community in Judea. That Judas became one of the Twelve and, moreover, was entrusted with special responsibility as treasurer (John 13:29) implies the kind of trust earned through long service, supporting an early calling.

7. It is difficult to determine whether "all are going to him" (John 3:26) means that the public were now approaching Jesus for baptism in preference to John or that John's disciples were now deserting him and following Jesus instead. John's response, especially verse 30, is consistent with either scenario.

heard, 'Jesus is making and baptizing more disciples than John' . . . he left Judea and started back to Galilee" (John 4:1–3). This presumably is the same retreat to Galilee that Matthew and Mark mention (see above).

By "the Pharisees" almost certainly John means the Sanhedrin.[8] The reason that the Sanhedrin was so concerned about what might appear to be simply the comparative followings of two preachers and baptizers is that the monitoring of religious and political developments formed part of its maintenance of the uneasy balance between the Roman political supremacy and the freedom of Jews to practice Judaism whose borderline with fervent nationalism was somewhat tenuous.[9] When John the Baptist's ministry began attracting attention, it had sent a deputation to investigate him, according to John 1:19–28. So, when Jesus' Judean ministry began overtaking John's, it is likely that it investigated him too. Although that investigation is not mentioned in the gospels, John 4:1–3 may reflect its findings. These led the Sanhedrin to decide upon a drastic course of action: to arrest him or even, perhaps, to have him killed.[10] So Beasley-Murray is not exaggerating when he comments that Jesus' withdrawal to Galilee was presumably intended to avoid a conflict which could have brought his ministry to a premature end.[11]

---

8. The nature of Jesus' response indicates that these "Pharisees" exercised sufficient authority to cause him severe difficulties. In several other places John uses the term "the Pharisees" where he clearly intends to denote the Sanhedrin (for example, 7:32, 45; 9:13; 11:46f). Perhaps this was because he considered the Pharisees to dominate the Sanhedrin (*c.f.* Josephus, *Antiquities* 18:1:4), just as he sometimes uses "the Jews" to denote the Pharisees. In the Fourth Gospel the precise nuance of both terms must always be deduced from the context.

9. The influential Pharisees and the Sadducees were both products of the Maccabean rebellion (Rivkin, *Revolution*, 220f) and Josephus (*Antiquities* 18:1:2–6) describes a militant offshoot of the Pharisees, whose openly declared aim was to overthrow the Romans by violent means.

10. The reason for such extreme action will be discussed shortly. Passages such as John 5:18 and 7:1 mention official plots to kill Jesus; this would have been illegal unless the intention was to hand Jesus over to the Roman authorities as an insurgent against Rome. A death sentence was mandatory for this—and, of course, this is eventually what happened. The alleged reason for the plot mentioned in John 5:18 is the healing of a paralyzed man on the Sabbath for which the death penalty prescribed in Torah would have been illegal under Rome; the reason for the later plot is not specified. Both, however, may be a legacy of the decision that precipitated his withdrawal to Galilee as described in John 4:1–3.

11. Beasley-Murray, *John*, 59.

Reasons for the Sanhedrin's Hostility

Although the Sanhedrin had regarded Jesus as a firebrand since the cleansing of the Temple (or whatever form his action there took), that alone hardly justifies such severe action; there must have been some other more compelling reason for it. Ultimately any identification of the cause of the Sanhedrin's alarm is hypothesis, but circumstantial evidence suggests that it suspected Jesus of raising an army in order to overthrow the Roman presence or the Jewish authorities or both. That evidence is as follows.

Firstly, Matthew and Mark associate Jesus' return to Galilee with the Baptist's arrest. Josephus states that the Baptist's arrest was occasioned by Antipas's fear that he might use his influence over the people to incite them to rebellion (*Antiquities* 18:5:2).[12] And because of the association between the Baptist and Jesus and their many similarities, Jesus probably expected the Sanhedrin to assume that he too was raising a rebel army and to target him next—as indeed it did.

Secondly, John 4:1 implies that it was the *number* of disciples ("more . . . than John") that Jesus was winning that led the Sanhedrin to decide upon action against him. There is evidence that at this point the evangelist intended to mention the Baptist's arrest,[13] which Matthew and Mark regard as a significant factor, but he inadvertently omitted to do so. If so, perhaps his meaning is that following the Baptist's arrest many of his disciples, deprived of their charismatic leader, began following Jesus instead.[14] When these were added to the disciples that Jesus had gained by his own efforts, his body of followers was larger than John's had been at the time of his arrest. It was the size of Jesus' following that alarmed the Sanhedrin ("the Pharisees") and spurred it to take the drastic action that forced his withdrawal. This interpretation harmonizes the synoptic and Johannine accounts.

Thirdly, according to Acts 1:6, even after Jesus' death and resurrection his disciples were asking him, "Lord, is this the time when you will restore the kingdom to Israel?" That question could be rephrased, "Are you now

12. Josephus's account of the Baptist is considered in chapter 4 under the heading *Josephus* on page 62.

13. The evangelist's statement in John 3:14, "John, of course, had not yet been thrown into prison," leaves readers expecting to hear more about this, although he does not mention it again.

14. There is a precedent: according to John 1:35–37, even during his ministry John had suggested to some of his disciples that they should become followers of Jesus.

going to liberate Israel from the Romans?" The author of Acts, then, appears to believe that even at the end of Jesus' earthly ministry those who knew him best envisaged him as an opponent of Rome, although his teaching as recorded in the gospels never suggests this. If his closest associates believed this, it is likely that the public at large and the authorities did too.

Lastly, to eliminate common misconceptions, it was not a doctrinal difference that provoked the Sanhedrin's action. There was nothing in Jesus' public ministry that conflicted with the teaching of the Pharisees who dominated the Sanhedrin.[15] And if the minority Sadducees in the Sanhedrin had taken offence at some aspect of Jesus' ministry, they would surely have been outvoted by their Pharisee peers. It was not a crime to administer baptism.

So, with Messianic expectations riding high, it is understandable that the Sanhedrin might suspect that Jesus was a militant leader intent upon insurrection and this prompted its decision to take drastic action against him. Presumably someone[16] warned Jesus before the proposed action took place and Jesus judged the threat sufficiently serious to warrant an immediate "tactical withdrawal."

THE GALILEAN PERIOD

That Jesus returned to Galilee suggests that there he expected to escape the unwelcome attention of Jewish officialdom.[17] As he had lived in Galilee for most of his life, he was presumably familiar with its religious *ambience* and considered it a suitable and safe location in which to continue his reforming ministry.[18] He must have assumed that the local community leaders

15. N. T. Wright, *Jesus*, 372.

16. Nicodemus perhaps? Jesus appears to have had at least one supporter in the Sanhedrin. There are several episodes in the Fourth Gospel which, if authentic, can only have originated from someone present in meetings of the Sanhedrin. Examples are John 4:1; 7:32, 45–52; 9:13–34; 11:45–53; 12:9–11; and 18:28–32. Matthew's Gospel also includes tradition that must have originated within the Sanhedrin, such as Matt 26:3–5 and 57–68. If Jesus had adversaries in high places, he also had allies there.

17. The reason for the paucity of Jewish officials in Galilee is discussed in chapter 3; see especially fn 66 on page 42.

18. Although Jesus presumably hoped to convert Jews in Galilee to his way of thinking, clearly this would have little impact on the powerhouse of Judaism that was Jerusalem. Perhaps he hoped that he might make a fresh assault upon Jerusalem later, when the fuss had died down and by which time he would have gained more experience in the art of persuasion and more followers.

would be more amenable to his activities than those in Judea. His expectations seem to have been justified: the synoptics record only two encounters with officials during the early phase of his ministry which followed his withdrawal from Judea. One is the friendly meeting with a solitary teacher of the law described in Matt 8:19f.[19] The other is when he healed the paralyzed man let down through the roof, but that is the "watershed incident" which led Jesus to abandon his reforming agenda, bringing the first phase of his ministry to a close. This will be considered shortly.

Jesus' Choice of Disciples

Of the four fishermen from Capernaum whom Jesus had befriended—Simon, Andrew, James, and John—three became the core of the later Twelve.[20] This study hypothesizes that Jesus' ministry had largely grown out of their friendship, which was borne in part out of their common experience of hostility from their neighbors because they had willingly traded with the Hellenistic community, associated with the pro-Rome Herod Antipas. It is interesting to consider what is known about the former occupations of the other members of the Twelve. The only other member of the Twelve whose former occupation is stated explicitly in the NT is the tax collector Matthew or Levi. As a former servant of the pro-Roman regime, he would certainly have experienced severe hostility. Regarding the others we have only a hint that Thomas and Nathanael were also fishermen[21] and the unlikely suggestion that Judas Iscariot's surname means "man of the Sicarii."[22] So of the Twelve nearly half—all of those whose occupation is

19. It is possible that this episode belongs properly in the later phase of Jesus' ministry; the Lucan parallel places it later (Luke 9:57), although Luke describes the would-be disciple as simply "someone" (*tis*) and not as a teacher of the law.

20. To some extent Andrew seems to recede into the background; it is the combination of Simon Peter, James, and John who are Jesus' most intimate companions (Mark 5:37 and Luke 8:51; Mark 9:2 and Matt 17:1 and Luke 9:28; Mark 13:3; 14:33).

21. Their ready agreement to join Peter's fishing expedition (John 21:1–3) surely indicates that they were fishermen; unskilled crew would have been a hindrance on the unpredictable waters of Lake Galilee.

22. This has been suggested, for example, by Paul Badham ("Just War," 26f). These *Sicarii*, literally "dagger men," are mentioned by Josephus: "there sprang up in Jerusalem a class of robbers called Sicarii, who slew men in the daytime, and in the midst of the city. This they did chiefly when they mingled with the populace at the festivals, and, hiding short daggers in their garments, stabbed with them those that were their enemies. The first to be assassinated by them was Jonathan the high priest, and after him many were

stated in the NT—resembled Jesus in that their loyalty to Israel had been questioned. This made them potentially sympathetic to his desire for some kind of action in support of the suffering indigenous Jewish community in Galilee.

Was the hypothesized hostility that Jesus and the fishermen experienced an instance of a broader rift between agricultural workers and others in Galilee? This might explain the surprising fact that, although Jesus was exercising his ministry in predominantly agricultural Galilee, there is no evidence that any of the Twelve were former agricultural workers. This is further compounded by the fact that many of Jesus' stories (the Sower, the Seed Growing Secretly, the Wheat and the Tares, the Tenants, and the Lost Sheep) draw upon the world of agriculture, while only one (the Drag-net) is based upon fishing. Presumably Jesus pitched his stories to suit his audiences who in Galilee were likely to consist mostly of agricultural workers and their families. The lack of agricultural workers amongst Jesus' disciples may be because they viewed Jesus with such suspicion ("It's OK for him— he doesn't face the problems we do") or because the parlous state of agriculture in Galilee meant that they dare not leave their work; their livelihood depended on their labor.

Justice for the Galilean Jews

For a period of uncertain duration Jesus exercised his ministry in Galilee, ironically far from the hub of Judaism. Presumably the copious teaching which survives from this period, such as the classic reforming material in the Sermon on the Mount, indicates that his principal strategy was preaching and teaching the public at large. His message was that Jews should re-dedicate themselves wholeheartedly to Yahweh's service; such a spiritual transformation would result in social renewal and an end to injustice. In many ways his teaching resembled that of the OT prophets:

> Wash yourselves; make yourselves clean;
>> remove the evil of your doings from before my eyes;
> cease to do evil, learn to do good;
>> seek justice, rescue the oppressed,
> defend the orphan,
>> plead for the widow. (Isa 1:16f)

---

slain daily" (*War*, 2:13:3). It seems unlikely, however, that a fanatical assassin would willingly follow Jesus who opposed violence and showed no anti-Rome tendencies.

But Jesus had not forgotten his original intention of campaigning for justice for the suffering Jews in Galilee's agricultural sector. Although his challenge to some of his early Galilean disciples to become "fishers of men" (Mark 1:16–18) has traditionally been interpreted as indicating that his priority was the gathering of disciples, there is another possibility. The fishing metaphor is more appropriate to the gathering of men on an "industrial" scale rather than the careful recruitment and nurturing of individual disciples.[23] His aim might have been the recruitment of unemployed agricultural workers, as many as possible, to join the protest march to Jerusalem postulated earlier.[24] The Jewish leaders, as we have seen, were determined to arrest him and possibly to execute him; if, however, he arrived in Jerusalem accompanied by hundreds or even thousands of supporters, their presence should not only ensure his personal protection from hostile officialdom, but also lend weight to his demands for justice and, perhaps, for Caesar to be informed of the disastrous consequences of Antipas's reign.

But the hypothesized hunger march did not happen. The most likely reason for this is that Jesus cancelled it himself when he discovered that he had been placed under surveillance by the Sanhedrin, indicating that it still suspected him of being a dangerous insurgent leader. He appreciated that in these circumstances the unemployed workers on the march might be mistaken for the rebel army supposedly under his command; if there was a confrontation with the authorities—as was certainly possible in those tense times—they might be killed or injured. Unwilling to subject innocent, deprived men to such a risk, Jesus decided that his quest for justice for the Galileans would have to await another opportunity.

Ironically it was probably Jesus' efforts to organize the protest march that had brought him once again to the attention of the Jerusalem authorities. Just as his disciple-gathering activities in Judea had so concerned the Sanhedrin that it planned the drastic action that forced his withdrawal to Galilee, so Galilean community leaders probably became alarmed when

23. The use of nets enabled commercial fishermen to catch huge quantities of fish, thus securing a worthwhile profit. By analogy the work to which Jesus was calling his disciples was to gather huge quantities of men. The expression "fishers of men" appears to be a new metaphor, coined perhaps by Jesus himself. Cranfield is surely correct in suggesting that this imagery was used here only because it had been suggested by the two men's actions (*St Mark*, 70). There is, however, no connection with the Old Testament's frequent application of a fishing analogy to the gathering of people (for example, Jer 16:16, Ezek 29:4f, Amos 4:2, Hab 1:14–17) for the execution of divine condemnation on the wicked!

24. For the evidence that this was Jesus' intention see fn 70 on page 44.

they heard garbled accounts of what Jesus was planning. With so many agricultural workers out of regular employment the proposed march could have attracted very large numbers; in Judea it had been the numbers of disciples that Jesus was recruiting (baptizing) that triggered the alarm (John 4:1–3). Even though the ethics of the Sermon on the Mount suggest that the intended activities of the marching men would have been non-violent and lawful,[25] the mere sight of such numbers on the march can be intimidating. Probably, then, some Galilean community leaders sent a message to the Sanhedrin expressing their concerns about Jesus' activities.[26]

The Sanhedrin's scrutiny of religious and political developments has already been noted. It should come as no surprise, then, that when it received the message that Jesus was now raising an "army" of disaffected Galileans and planning to march it to Jerusalem, no matter how lawful his agenda, this was bound to ring alarm bells. So far as it was concerned, Jesus already had a record as the rabble-rouser who had previously caused a disturbance in the temple and more recently had narrowly evaded its intended action against him. Moreover, since Galilee had a reputation for producing insurgents,[27] it is perhaps inevitable that the Sanhedrin should interpret this message as indicating that Jesus was planning to lead a huge army of militant rebels into Jerusalem. Popular Jewish piety was expecting the emergence of a charismatic leader who would rally the Jewish people and liberate Palestine from the hated Romans by military action.[28] So if the Sanhedrin's suspicions concerning Jesus' intentions became public knowledge,

25. The objection that Jesus' healings ought to have convinced the authorities that his intentions were benign and incompatible with those of a terrorist is not valid. There is evidence that healers in first-century Palestine were not held in high esteem. Even if some had genuine skills, many were charlatans as evident in Mark's observation: "Now there was a woman who had been suffering from hemorrhages for twelve years. She had endured much under many physicians, and had spent all that she had; and she was no better, but rather grew worse" (Mark 5:25f). This may explain why the officials who witnessed Jesus' healing of the paralyzed man let down through the roof were seemingly unimpressed by the healing and concerned primarily that Jesus had uttered blasphemy (Mark 2:1–12).

26. According to Luke 5:17 at the healing of the paralysed man "Pharisees and teachers of the law . . . (they had come from every village of Galilee and Judea and from Jerusalem)" accompanied the delegation from Jerusalem sent by the Sanhedrin to observe him. Probably those from Galilee were, or included, those who informed the Sanhedrin of their concerns about Jesus.

27. For further see under *Consequences of Economic Hardship* on page 40.

28. That even Jesus' closest disciples considered that Jesus was this expected leader is evident from the question in Acts 1:6 mentioned earlier.

the Jewish populace might assume that Jesus was that long-awaited libera-tor[29] and, with or without him, rise up against the Romans—and possibly against the corrupt Jewish leadership as well—with potentially catastrophic consequences. Although some Sanhedrin members might have supported such a rising, others such as the chief priests had a vested interest in main-taining the *status quo*, uneasy as it was. In order to decide upon the most appropriate course of action the Sanhedrin needed more precise informa-tion concerning Jesus' agenda and to be kept informed of his activities. For this reason this study hypothesizes that it dispatched a surveillance team to Galilee to keep Jesus under observation.

Under Surveillance

That Jesus was kept under surveillance is well attested in the gospels,[30] but scholarship is reluctant to acknowledge that this is what was happening.[31] Perhaps one reason for this is that in the twenty-first century the word "sur-veillance" conjures images of spy cameras, hidden microphones, tapped telephone lines, and computer hackers—technology that obviously was not available in the first century. Another reason may be the fact that the evan-gelists habitually describe the surveillance team as simply "the Pharisees" or "the scribes" or suchlike, which leads many present-day readers—and even expositors—to assume that these officials were either Galilee residents or frequent visitors, whose presence was therefore unremarkable. Con-sequently they fail to appreciate that what the evangelists are describing is surveillance. Even the three occasions on which Luke depicts Jesus as

29. According to John 6:15, there was a popular attempt to make Jesus king after the feeding of the five thousand.

30. As will be demonstrated, many of the gospels' reports of Jesus' encounters with officialdom, especially in Galilee, in fact depict surveillance. One suggestive term is *paratēreō* in Mark 3:2; Luke 6:7; 14:1 and 20:20. According to BAGD this denotes "to watch closely, observe carefully"; there would be a case for rendering it "keep under surveillance." Also significant is *egkathetos*, "spy," in Luke 20:20; according to BAGD this denotes someone "hired to lie in wait."

31. Surveillance is not mentioned in any commentary on the gospels that the author has consulted and references to it in scholarly literature are rare. A search of the ATLA/ EBSCO databases in January 2019 found only the spirited rebuttal of this suggestion by Richard Horsley mentioned below. The only scholar of whom the present author is aware who has published that Jesus was kept under surveillance is Eric Stoddart of St Andrews University, also cited below.

accepting dinner invitations from Pharisees in Galilee[32] were in fact a part of their surveillance of him.

The surveillance team consisted of Pharisees or scribes[33] or both and, apparently, at one stage Pharisees and Sadducees (Matt 16:1), reflecting the composition of the Sanhedrin who sent it. While today's technology allows the subject of surveillance to be unaware that it is happening, there was nothing covert about the surveillance to which Jesus was subjected. He, his disciples, and probably many in the crowds following him were fully aware of the reason for the presence of these conspicuous strangers from Jerusalem.[34] The team mingled with the crowds following Jesus, sometimes engaging with him in debate; some of those exchanges are recorded in the gospels.

Because the synoptic gospels contain so many accounts of Jesus' interactions with scribes and Pharisees—meaning the surveillance team—in Galilee, an uncritical reading may give the impression that Galilee was awash with scribes and Pharisees; it would have been impossible for Jesus—or anyone else—to do anything there without being observed by them. That, however, is the antithesis of the truth. As mentioned previously, scholars have provided convincing evidence that scribes and Pharisees rarely visited Galilee, so that Jesus' encounters with them there were most unusual. Indeed for this reason some scholars dismiss the synoptic gospels' accounts of those encounters as unreliable.[35] Richard Horsley, for example, dismisses Mark's portrayal of the Pharisees keeping Jesus under surveillance as lacking historical credibility. Interestingly he acknowledges that the synoptics—or Mark at least—describe Jesus as under surveillance by officialdom. Moreover, he appears to accept the possibility that Jesus might occasionally encounter scribes and Pharisees in Galilee. But it is

32. Luke 7:36–50; 11:37f; 14:1–6.

33. It is surely significant that many of the gospels' references to the surveillance team mention that it included *grammateis*, usually rendered "scribes" or "teachers of the law" in English versions. The *grammateis* were able to write, a skill which other members of the team may not have shared. The Sanhedrin wanted a written record, *verbatim* or as near so as practicable, of what Jesus said, especially when it contained material that might be considered heretical or blasphemous and so used as the basis of a charge against him. It was the function of the *grammateis* to provide this.

34. They may have been aware that the officials were observing Jesus, but not that the reason for the observation was that the Sanhedrin suspected Jesus of being an insurgent leader.

35. See fn 66 on page 42 for the reasons that many scholars offer that Pharisees and scribes rarely visited Galilee at the time of Jesus.

the repeated coincidence factor—that those officials "just happened to be" present on so many significant occasions that leads him to dismiss surveillance as beyond credibility.[36]

And yet the synoptic gospels record no fewer than fourteen occasions on which Jesus encountered Pharisees and/or scribes in Galilee,[37] a substantial corpus of episodes, which the evangelists treat as factual, unlikely though that may seem. When such an unlikely phenomenon is recorded repeatedly, it is surely as irrational to dismiss it as an anomaly as to accept it uncritically. Many scientific discoveries were made when researchers established that what had appeared to be a string of freak coincidences was in fact the operation of a previously unsuspected process. Perhaps, then, those scribes and/or Pharisees in Galilee did not "just happen to be" where Jesus was: they were there intentionally. They were there, in fact, *because* Jesus was there; this was part of a process, namely surveillance. If we allow the evangelists credence, the surveillance that they describe explains the paradox of Jesus' many encounters in Galilee with officials who normally were rarely seen there, because it gives them a reason to be there. Moreover, those officials behave much as we might expect of a team charged with that particular task. Surely scholarship needs to reconsider the gospels' accounts of Jesus' encounters with scribes and Pharisees in Galilee.

One scholar who does recognize that Jesus was kept under surveillance is Eric Stoddart of St Andrews University. In 2014 he wrote: "Christ was himself under surveillance—not least in his eating with tax collectors and sinners (Matthew 9:11), and for the lack of fasting practiced by his disciples (Matthew 9:14). The Pharisees watched Jesus cast out demons and commit illegal actions on the Sabbath (Matthew 9:34; 12:2). We are told they were plotting against him—a typical reason for surveillance (Matthew 12:14). Luke 6:7 is perhaps the clearest reference to Christ under surveillance: 'So

---

36. Horsley, *Roman Palestine*, 138f.

37. The fourteen encounters are: (i) the would-be disciple (Matt 8:19f); (ii) the healing of the paralyzed man (Matt 9:2–8; Mark 2:1–12; Luke 5:17–26); (iii) dining with tax collectors and "sinners" (Matt 9:10–13; Mark 2:15–17; Luke 5:29–32); (iv) exorcism using demonic power (Matt 9:32–34); (v) plucking corn on the Sabbath (Matt 12:1–8; Mark 2:23 27; Luke 6:1–5); (vi) the healing of the man with a withered hand (Matt 12:9–14; Mark 3:1–6; Luke 6:6–11); (vii) dining in a Pharisee's home (Luke 7:36–50); (viii) exorcism using Beelzebub (Matt 12:22–32; Mark 3:20–29); (ix) the request for a miraculous sign (Matt 12:38–42); (x) breaking the tradition of the elders (Matt 15:1–9; Mark 7:1–13); (xi) scribes and Pharisees are hostile (Luke 11:37–54); (xii) Pharisees (and Sadducees) ask for a sign (Matt 16:1–4; Mark 8:11–13); (xiii) Pharisees warn Jesus to leave Galilee (Luke 13:31); and (xiv) the healing of a man with dropsy (Luke 14:1–6).

the scribes and Pharisees watched Him closely, whether He would heal on the Sabbath, that they might find an accusation against Him.'"[38] While it is reassuring to find a scholar who recognizes that Jesus was kept under surveillance by officialdom, it is a pity that Stoddart does not explain why the Pharisees were plotting against him.

The hypothesized surveillance team traveled around with Jesus and his disciples in order to maintain its observation. Of necessity the personnel in the team would have been changed regularly; perhaps this is reflected in several gospel passages that mention members having recently arrived from Jerusalem.[39] While the gathering of intelligence—especially in regard to Jesus' plans—was the team's primary objective, the gospel accounts suggest a broader remit: it certainly had the arrest of Jesus in view and, to this end, it was to monitor his teaching carefully for any heretical statement and to watch for any unlawful action that might provide grounds for this. Moreover, it was not content to wait for Jesus to make such a slip of his own accord; it played the role of *agent provocateur*, attempting to force Jesus into compromising himself by means of, for example, trick questions.[40] Even if some of its actions were, strictly speaking, beyond the remit of the sending Sanhedrin, they surely reflect the urgency with which that body impressed upon the team its desire to put an end to Jesus' ministry—and that in turn indicates the severity of the threat that they considered him to pose.

Because Jesus' Galilean ministry was itinerant, the dispatched surveillance team would not have known where in Galilee to find him. It is likely, therefore, that it reported initially to the Galilean community leaders whose message to the Sanhedrin expressing their concerns had led to the team's dispatch. This group was probably acquainted with Jesus' movements and might even have employed local spies to keep it informed of these. By whatever means, they learned that Jesus was currently in his home town of Capernaum. Moreover, by accompanying the surveillance team there they

38. Stoddart, "(In)visibility." *Cosmologics Magazine*, in which Stoddart published this in 2014, is a project of the Science, Religion, and Culture program at the Harvard Divinity School, which is not scanned by ATLA/EBSCO.

39. For example, Matt 15:1; Mark 3:22; 7:1.

40. For example, that concerning tribute to Caesar (Matt 22:15–22 and parallels) and that concerning the appropriate punishment for the woman caught in the act of adultery (John 8:1–11). These questions were supposedly so cunningly contrived that irrespective of how Jesus answered them, he would incriminate himself. Those two incidents happened in Jerusalem, later in Jesus' ministry. Perhaps it was only later that the team resorted to such methods.

could ensure that its members, who might not have seen Jesus before, were targeting the right person.

Jesus' Change of Agenda

Jesus' first encounter with the surveillance team—supplemented on this occasion by the local leaders—is preserved in the synoptic accounts of the healing of the paralyzed man let down through the roof.[41] Luke's begins, "One day, while he was teaching, Pharisees and teachers of the law were sitting near by (they had come from every village of Galilee and Judea and from Jerusalem)."[42] This is the first mention of Pharisees or teachers of the law in Luke's gospel; surely the evangelist expects his readers to be surprised at their sudden appearance and to ask themselves, "What are *they* doing here? We've not encountered *them* before. Why have some of them come all the way from Jerusalem?"

And this is not only a new experience for Jesus—or at least a new Galilean one—it is a turning point, a watershed in the gospel. The gospel accounts of this encounter convey the impression that the surveillance team was determined to find fault in Jesus' ministry:[43] any virtue in the healing is dismissed, outweighed by Jesus' supposedly blasphemous absolution of the man's sins. Jesus, it must be remembered, had assumed that by returning to Galilee he would avoid such confrontations, and yet even here officialdom had sought him out and seemed determined to find grounds for action against him.

At this point Jesus recognized that the time had come to switch to his alternative agenda:[44] accordingly he abandoned his reform of institutional Judaism, dismissing it as a lost cause. Since it had declined the invitation that he had extended to it, that invitation would now be offered instead to others outside its bounds, such as the tax collectors and "sinners," whom it

---

41. Matt 9:2–8; Mark 2:1–12; Luke 5:17–26.

42. Some scholars, such as Nolland (*Luke*, 1:234), consider that Luke's description of the home districts of these officials is not to be taken literally. But if they included the hypothesised surveillance team, that some had come from Judea and Jerusalem is plausible.

43. A similar action is described in Mark 7:1f and parallels when "the Pharisees and some of the scribes who had come from Jerusalem gathered around him, they noticed that some of his disciples were eating with defiled hands, that is, without washing them."

44. See *The Wilderness* on page 112.

had excommunicated.[45] Jesus' time with the Baptist had revealed that large numbers of these people were repenting and capable of faithful service, even though institutional Judaism was unwilling to reinstate them. He would establish a new faith community as a spiritual home for them. The Story of the Marriage Feast eloquently depicts this change of agenda: "'The wedding is ready, but those invited were not worthy. Go therefore into the main streets, and invite everyone you find to the wedding banquet.' Those slaves went out into the streets and gathered all whom they found, both good and bad; so the wedding hall was filled with guests" (Matt 22:8–10). Matthew's wording—especially "both good and bad"—implies that some of those accepting the invitation would be folk whom "respectable Jews" regarded as *persona non grata*.

Evidence of Jesus' change of agenda is plain in the synoptics and present, although less obvious, in the Fourth Gospel. All three synoptics record the episode immediately following the healing of the paralytic as Jesus' call to discipleship of the tax collector named Matthew or Levi.[46] That no evangelist has attempted to insert material between these two episodes may be because it was remembered not only that they happened one soon after the other but also that their juxtaposition marked a significant turning point. The second is an indirect consequence of the first: it was the attitude of the officials at the healing of the paralytic that led Jesus to abandon his attempted reform of Pharisaic Judaism and immediately begin building his new community in which "sinners," including even tax collectors, would be welcome.

To his disciples it must have seemed remarkable that Jesus should call a tax collector since until then he had disparaged their kind (Matt 5:46). But while the call of Matthew/Levi was completely sincere, it was also a highly symbolic action: Jesus was in effect making a public statement: "Even tax collectors, dismissed by so many as the scum of the earth, are now welcome as my disciples, for I see worth in them." When the tax collector held a dinner—presumably so that his friends and former colleagues could meet this teacher who so unusually was willing to spend time with their kind—the synoptists report that "the Pharisees" criticized Jesus for dining with "sinners." That they do not explain the presence of these Pharisees is perhaps evidence that they expected their readers to recognize them as the same

---

45. For further see The *"Sinners"* on page 8 and *Excommunication: a Hypothesis* on page 10.

46. Matt 9:9–13; Mark 2:13–17; Luke 5:27–32.

officials[47] who had made their first appearance in the previous episode, the healing of the paralytic.[48] This was, of course, because they were the surveillance team continuing its observation. They were present for the rest of Jesus' public ministry.[49]

Change of Methods

The constant presence of the surveillance team caused Jesus to change his *modus operandi*. Aware that "anything he said might be given in evidence," he ceased teaching in plain language and instead used mainly parable. This change was so significant that it was remembered many years later when Mark wrote or compiled his gospel:

> When he was alone, those who were around him along with the twelve asked him about the parables. And he said to them, "To you has been given the secret of the kingdom of God, but for those outside, everything comes in parables; in order that 'they may indeed

47. One commentator who comes close to making that connection is Nolland who claims that the Pharisees "belong in a natural pairing" with the scribes of the previous episode" (*Matthew*, 386). But he stops short of concluding that they were the same individuals. On the Lucan parallel he claims that the presence of the Pharisees is "unexplained" (*Luke*, 1:245).

48. Horsley's objection that it is not credible that Pharisees "just happened" to see Jesus dining in Levi's house (see fn 36 on page 125) is absolutely correct, but not because the dinner did not happen. No Pharisee would set foot inside the home of a tax collector and even the mental picture of the Pharisees standing outside and watching the festivities inside through the windows, though appealing, is most unlikely: large Palestinian houses at that time were built around an inner courtyard, the only windows opening on to this. So the Pharisees could not have literally seen Jesus and his disciples dining in Levi's house with tax collectors and sinners. Although the NRSV renders *idontes hoi Pharisaioi* as "When the Pharisees saw this" (Matt 9:11; Mark 2:16 is similar), *eidō* has a broad spectrum of meaning which includes "know" and "hear about." If they were following Jesus in order to maintain their surveillance, presumably they would have seen him and his disciples and the tax collectors and sinners entering Levi's house at the customary hour for dinner and drawn the obvious conclusion. Another possibility is that they heard about the dinner afterwards from someone who had been present.

49. To some extent it is on account of this hypothesized surveillance that so much of Jesus' ministry has been documented. The mere fact that these learned officials had been dispatched from Jerusalem to observe him must have indicated to the Galilean populace that Jesus was an extraordinary person, someone in whom the authorities were taking a special interest. The team's debates with Jesus provided ordinary Jews with first-rate entertainment; that they were witnessed by large crowds ensured that these episodes would be remembered and later committed to writing.

> look, but not perceive, and may indeed listen, but not understand; so that they may not turn again and be forgiven.'" . . . With many such parables he spoke the word to them, as they were able to hear it; he did not speak to them except in parables, but he explained everything in private to his disciples. (Mark 4:10–12, 33f)

Parable, a traditional teaching medium in Pharisaic circles, offered two advantages. Firstly, its content was innocuous; the surveillance team would find no incriminating material in it. Secondly, it was both easily memorable and accessible; even hearers who had received little or no previous religious instruction might, upon subsequent reflection, discern the spiritual truths underlying the familiar elements in the story. These features made it an eminently suitable medium when addressing the marginalised people whom Jesus now sought as disciples.

This mid-ministry change in Jesus' methods and target people is reflected in the Fourth Gospel. John 10:16 records Jesus as telling "the Jews,"[50] "I have other sheep that do not belong to this fold. I must bring them also, and they will listen to my voice. So there will be one flock, one shepherd." Beasley-Murray considers these "other sheep" to denote Gentiles,[51] but this is unlikely as there is no record elsewhere in the gospels of Jesus deliberately targeting Gentiles. But if they were Jews, they were clearly Jews outside the regular "fold," such as the "sinners" whom the Pharisees had excommunicated.

That Jesus was now envisaging a new faith community rather than attempting to reform an existing one is confirmed by his conversation with Peter as recorded in Matt 16:16–18. When Jesus said, "I tell you, you are Peter, and on this rock I will build my church," the meaning is surely that Jesus was creating a new movement in which Peter was to be the prototype member, analogous to a foundation stone. This significant pronouncement was precipitated by Peter's confession: "You are the Messiah, the Son of the living God." According to Jesus, this confession was possible only because "flesh and blood has not revealed this to you, but my Father in heaven." So this new community was to be based upon not membership of a particular race or nationality (as Judaism was), but upon faith in Jesus as Messiah and/or Son of God and that faith could be awakened only by God himself. Moreover, those in whom God awakened faith in Jesus might be of any race or nationality, so that the new movement would be open to all, although

---

50. This probably means a deputation of Pharisees; see fn 8 on page 116.
51. Beasley-Murray, *John*, 171.

the evangelists seem reluctant to mention this.[52] As this awakening pro-cess became attributed to the Holy Spirit (1 Cor 12:3), the new community fulfilled Joel's end-time prophecy that God would pour out His Spirit on all flesh (Joel 2:28f).

Jesus' deliberate targeting of "sinners" did not escape the crowds, who dubbed him "friend of tax collectors and sinners."[53] Jesus' concern for these outcasts was so unexpected in a respected teacher whom some regarded as a prophet that it was remembered decades later and incorporated into the gospels.

THE CLIMAX

The narrative of the synoptic gospels builds to a climax when Jesus and his followers journey to Jerusalem to celebrate the Passover. Horsley points out that centuries earlier this celebration of the people's liberation from bondage in Egypt had been observed by families in their home communi-ties, but now it had become centralized in the Temple, presumably to bring more revenue into the hands of the Jerusalem elite. Roman rule in Judea, however, gave this celebration of the people's liberation a new significance, becoming a trigger for protest against Roman domination. In an attempt to suppress this the Roman governors would bring a company of soldiers into Jerusalem at Passover tide and station them "on the porticoes of the Temple so as to quell any uprising that might occur" (Josephus, *Ant.* 20:106).[54]

That all four canonical gospels recount the story of Jesus' triumphal entry to Jerusalem[55] prior to his last week of earthly ministry indicates that the evangelists regarded it as significant. Similarly the three synoptics record the cleansing of the temple as happening soon after the triumphal

---

52. Surely the most explicit exception to this is the Great Commission at the end of Matthew's Gospel: "Go therefore and make disciples of all nations" (Matt 28:19). But perhaps the reason that the brief Parable of the Mustard Seed appears in all three synop-tics (Matt 13:31f; Mark 4:31f; Luke 13:19) is that it held special significance for the early Christian communities: it depicted their new global movement as growing from small beginnings by welcoming Gentiles. This interpretation assumes that the "greatest of all shrubs" symbolizes the Christian movement and that the "birds of the air" who find shelter within its shade represent Gentiles, as do such scholars as Dodd, *Parables*, 190; Cranfield, *St Mark*, 169; France, *Matthew*, 526 and Nolland, *Luke*, 2:729.

53. Matt 11:19; Luke 7:34; 15:2.

54. Horsley, *Prophet*, 89.

55. Matt 21:1–11, Mark 11:1–11, Luke 19:29–40, and John 12:12–19.

entry,[56] while the Fourth Gospel places this in Jesus' early Judean ministry (John 2:13–22). Although Sanders regards the cleansing as symbolizing the temple's destruction,[57] it is possible that its primary purpose was to secure a confrontation with the Jewish authorities. As a Galilean and, moreover, as one known to the hierarchy as a troublemaker, Jesus recognised that a request for a private audience with the chief priests through the regular channels would probably result in his arrest. So now he sought that audience in an unorthodox manner. Moreover, that audience would take a form that the religious hierarchy would find even less welcome—a public confrontation in the temple while it was crowded with Passover pilgrims to act as witnesses.

All three synoptists record the occasion on which a delegation of Jewish officials challenges Jesus' authority to do "these things,"[58] referring presumably to the cleansing of the temple. Jesus responds to the officials' question by asking one of his own which also concerns authority, but that of John the Baptist. When the officials decline to answer Jesus' question, he refuses to answer theirs. Indirectly, however, Jesus' question itself had answered theirs. If Jesus' protagonists in the delegation had believed John, they would have understood the meaning of the cleansing. They were, however, bound to reject John since to accept him would have required them to acknowledge that their own positions in the Jewish hierarchy were meaningless; John—and Jesus—believed the temple to be an outmoded institution.[59] The Jewish hierarchy, in contrast, had a vested interest in maintaining the temple and its cultus since not only their livelihood, but also their status depended upon it. As for Jesus' authority, that—like John's—was gifted directly by God, bypassing the regular structures and processes of obsolete institutional Judaism.

Matthew alone at this point inserts the brief Parable of the Two Sons (Matt 21:28–32). This develops the discussion concerning authority. Perhaps Jesus' reference to the ministry of John the Baptist prompted this simple but hard-hitting illustration. When Jesus forces his hearers to think about the parable by asking them a question about it, they give the correct answer, although the question was hardly difficult. It was the first son who,

---

56. Matt 21:12–17, Mark 11:15–19, and Luke 19:45–48.

57. Sanders, *Jesus and Judaism*, 69f.

58. Matt 21:23–27, Mark 11:27–33, and Luke 20:1–8.

59. See *Repudiation of Institutional Judaism* on page 71 and *Repudiation of the Religious Establishment* on page 90.

despite initial protestations, did what was asked of him, and not the second who, after saying all the right words, did nothing. But although they give the right answer, his hearers fail to recognize the awful significance of the parable, namely, that it is about *them—they are* that second son who failed to obey his father. Unusually in this parable the shock element comes not in the story itself, but in the interpretation that follows.

While his audience of distinguished religious leaders is congratulating itself on answering correctly—that is, while it is off its guard—Jesus plunges the knife in. In what is surely the most audacious statement of his ministry, he confronts them with the devastating meaning of the parable: "the tax collectors and the prostitutes"—that is, the most despised[60] kinds of "sinner" represented by the first son—"are going into the kingdom of God ahead of you"—that is, the elite of Judaism, represented by the second son. Contrary to popular belief, the supposedly accursed underclass of the "sinners" is closer to the Kingdom than the nation's spiritual leaders. To explain this statement Jesus returns to the subject of the Baptist: "For John came to you in the way of righteousness and you did not believe him, but the tax collectors and the prostitutes believed him; and even after you saw it, you did not change your minds and believe him." That the tax collectors and the prostitutes had "believed" the Baptist means, presumably, that they had responded to his preaching through repentance and baptism; they recognised a genuine prophet of God when they saw one. In contrast, Israel's spiritual leaders were unwilling even to answer Jesus' question about John's authority.

Next Jesus told the story that sealed his fate.

The Story of the Tenants

It is not surprising that traditionally the Story of the Tenants[61] has been interpreted allegorically: its introduction, widely believed to be based upon Isa 5:1f, uses typical Jewish symbolism. The reader is therefore tempted to assume that—as in the Two Sons which immediately precedes it in Matthew—the vineyard represents Israel and its owner and builder is God, so the tenants become the Jewish leaders and the slaves sent to collect the produce are the prophets. The refusal of the tenants to hand over the agreed

60. Apart from the unsavory aspects of their occupations, both tax collectors and prostitutes worked ultimately for the Romans and so were despised by Jews as traitors.

61. Matt 21:33–46; Mark 12:1–12; Luke 20:9–19.

proportion of the harvest to the landowner represents the Jewish leaders' failure to serve God. The sending of the son and his murder by the tenants symbolize the incarnation and crucifixion of Jesus. The final suggestion that the owner will come in person is a warning of impending divine judgment upon the corrupt Jewish leaders.

But although this interpretation has been accepted by scholars and expositors since apostolic times,[62] it does not fit the story perfectly. For example, this particular landowner seems unscrupulous: his lack of concern for the welfare of his slaves and even his own son is evident in his insistence upon sending them to collect the agreed proportion of the harvest despite the tenants' history of assault and murder. This hardly accords with the God that Jesus portrayed as a loving Father.

Recent[63] scholarship, as surveyed by Stephen Wright,[64] has suggested that underlying the Tenants in its present form is a realistic story which Jesus told reflecting the harsh socio-economic conditions in Roman-controlled Palestine, especially Galilee, that were identified in chapter 3. The allegorical interpretation, however, has become so influential—indeed normative—that it has effectively eclipsed the original realistic story. Present-day readers, for example, are so accustomed to the landowner figure in Jesus' parables representing God,[65] that they assume that this applies also in this story. But, when Jesus told this story in the temple that Passover-tide the first mention of the landowner would have aroused the suspicion of the peasantry who probably formed most of the crowd of listening pilgrims, because it was the landowners who charged them extortionate rents and, when they could not pay, evicted them from the land. Landowners were people to be feared and distrusted.

To understand this story we need to know *why* the tenants not only refused to hand over the agreed share of the harvest, but also resorted to

---

62. That Matthew, for example, has amended the Marcan version so that the death of the landowner's son more closely resembles the death of Jesus shows that he understood the story allegorically.

63. As early as 1961 C. H. Dodd wrote that the Story of the Tenants had suffered some expansion, but otherwise is natural and realistic (*Parables*, 93). In fact Dodd's original book was published in 1935, based on lectures given at the Divinity School, Yale University, in that year.

64. Wright, *Storyteller*, 149–162.

65. As he does, for example, in the Sower (Mark 4:2–9and parallels), the Tares (Matt 13:24–30), the Workers in the Vineyard (Matt 20:1–16) and the Two Sons (Matt 21:28–32).

seemingly pointless violence and murder. The story itself does not give the reason; this may be because Jesus considered that the reason was obvious or perhaps he *did* originally give the reason, but when the allegorical interpretation became normative, the reason no longer fitted the story and so scribes omitted it. Although it could be that the harvest had failed or the vines had not yet reached maturity, a more likely scenario is that this was a deliberate "rent strike" in protest at the landowning elites' exploitation of the peasantry. The tenants might even have been the original owners of the land, which had been forcibly expropriated from them to create the vineyard.[66] Although as peasant farmers they were unlikely to be familiar with the fine detail of the law, as Jews they would surely have believed that the land belonged ultimately to Yahweh, who had apportioned it between the various tribes and clans to remain in their stewardship in perpetuity. If so, they might have reckoned that this overruled any agreement that they had made with the new landowner and so they refused to recognize his claim on the land and entitlement to a share of the harvest.[67] Discontent had been simmering for years; this might be the spark needed to ignite a full-blown peasants' revolt. In such revolutionary circumstances the murders of the landowner's slaves and son no longer seem the excessive acts that they appear to be in an uncritical reading of the story; as Stephen Wright comments, "To think of this action as unrealistic folly is to underestimate the despair of those who saw their very livelihood threatened by the expropriation of their land by powerful elites."[68] Indeed, H. D. Hester even suggests that in the eyes of the peasantry those tenants were not evil murderers, but heroes in their quest for justice.[69]

On the face of it, this story is an unmitigated tragedy: the landowner never receives his rent, his slaves and son are assaulted or killed, and the tenants in the end are subjected to a miserable death. There are no winners,

66. As Luisa Schottroff (*Parables*, 16) points out, it is possible that the tenants are the previous owners of the land. It must often have happened that through crop failure or excessive taxation peasant farmers were compelled to sell their land; it made sense for new landowners to retain the former owners as tenants since they were familiar with the peculiarities of the local soil and climatic conditions.

67. The tenants' suggestion in Mark 12:7 and parallels, "This is the heir; come, let us kill him, and the inheritance will be ours," is farfetched under most systems of law. But if the land had originally belonged to the tenants and had been expropriated from them by dubious means, the removal of other claimants might open a route for them to regain their former possession. Even so, of course, it would not sanction murder.

68. Wright, *Storyteller*, 153.

69. Hester, "Socio-Rhetorical Criticism," 51.

only losers; every action in the story is futile. So why did Jesus tell it? In fact it is wholly explicable when we recognize that its telling took place when a number of key factors combined to offer an unique opportunity. The first such factor is Jesus' original intention to strike a blow for justice for his fellow Galilean Jews, as identified in chapter 3; he had never abandoned that ambition. The second is that Jesus now had the attention of a deputation of high-ranking Jewish officials, most of them probably landowners themselves, who represented the elite classes exploiting the peasantry. The third was that this confrontation took place within the temple at Passover-tide, so that it was witnessed by crowds of pilgrims, many of whom would have been peasantry who identified with the tenants in the story. Concisely and yet vividly the story informed those officials of the plight of the Galilean agricultural community—and also, to some extent, that in Judea—to which they had long turned a blind eye. It was a warning to them that discontent had reached that critical pitch at which violent insurrection was likely—emphasized perhaps by a cheer from the crowd when the withholding of the rent was mentioned! It depicted the kind of violence that would surely become commonplace unless the authorities intervened, ideally persuading Caesar through Pilate to remove Antipas and his Herodian cronies from the governorship of Galilee.

Although the story failed to unseat Antipas, it did cause the deputation of leaders considerable embarrassment. With characteristic terseness Mark states, "When they realized that he had told this parable against them, they wanted to arrest him, but they feared the crowd" (Mark 12:12). Although this might seem a trivial detail, that Matthew (21:45f) and Luke (20:19) copied it suggests that at the end of the century the telling of this story and its impact on the Jewish authorities were still remembered as a significant occasion. On account of its repercussions this was one of the most important turning-points in the gospel narrative: surely it was the telling of this story more than any other action or saying of Jesus that sealed his fate. The leaders could not allow Jesus to continue stirring the populace by proclaiming the awful truth. Although the presence of the crowds made the leaders afraid to arrest Jesus there and then, a few days later, under the cover of darkness and with the connivance of a treacherous disciple they arrested him in the seclusion of Gethsemane.

CONCLUSION

This reconstruction of part of Jesus' earthly ministry is based upon the testimony of ancient documentation (mostly the New Testament) and hypotheses concerning the "sinners," the socio-economic conditions in Galilee, the authority's mistaken belief that Jesus was an insurgent and its placing of Jesus under surveillance. What is apparent is that the story fits together seamlessly, the hypotheses filling the gaps in the gospel narrative. That does not mean that the story as told above is correct in every detail— sadly in this world there are few such certainties. But this reconstruction is offered as a plausible interpretation of the documentary evidence.

7

CONCLUSION

A PhD THESIS—and this book began life as one, albeit one that was never completely finished and not submitted—is required to make an original contribution to knowledge. In historical research an original contribution may be a new interpretation of established facts; inevitably this will be, to some extent, hypothesis. Ben Meyer acknowledges the dependence of historical research on hypothesis in his statement: "History is reconstruction through hypothesis and verification."[1] Ideally to verify a historical hypothesis would involve time travel to visit the period of interest in order to ascertain that the real world was as conjectured. As technology does not at present allow this, reconstruction provides the best alternative. To use the jigsaw puzzle analogy, if the established facts and the hypotheses are the pieces of the puzzle, can we fit them together to form a picture that is not only coherent but also plausible? The last chapter shows that it is possible to reconstruct the career of Jesus taking into account the various hypotheses made in this study and that the resulting reconstruction is self-coherent and accords with what is generally accepted. If this helps us to understand matters that previously were obscure, that is an indication that the hypotheses are possibly correct.

Standing in the tradition of the Third Quest,[2] this study's primary research question was, "Precisely what outcome did Jesus hope to achieve from his earthly ministry?" Its point of departure from other attempted

1. Meyer, *Aims*, 19.
2. For further see *Introduction to the Quest* on page 145.

reconstructions lies in its assumption that Jesus' ministry was a response to one or more needs in his society. This allowed us to formulate a secondary research question to identify those needs: "What motivated a thirty-year-old carpenter from an obscure village in Galilee to abandon his trade and become the itinerant preacher, teacher, and healer described in the gospels?" The answers to this question should provide pointers to the aims of Jesus' ministry and therefore to the outcome that he hoped to achieve.

WHAT MOTIVATED THE CARPENTER TO CHANGE HIS TRADE?

This study agrees with those scholars who consider that Jesus' public ministry began as a quest for justice for the indigenous Jews in Galilee, who were suffering severe economic hardship under Herod Antipas's regime.[3] An original element in this study is its conjecture that there was a schism in Galilee's indigenous Jewish community between those who were willing to have dealings with the Hellenistic Jews whom Antipas had encouraged to settle and those who were not.[4] The seriousness of this assumed collaboration with Antipas's pro-Roman regime was exacerbated by the ritual purity movement.[5] Jesus possibly fell victim to this, experiencing hostility from his neighbors in Nazareth because he worked on the reconstruction of nearby Sepphoris. This hostility may have been a contributory factor in his relocation to Capernaum.[6] There he befriended some local fishermen who, it is conjectured, had themselves experienced hostility for similar reasons and who shared his desire to campaign for justice, that is, for work providing a livable wage for all Jews. Lacking the skills required for such political action, they sought a mentor and found one in John the Baptist.[7]

Since it was after his period with the Baptist that Jesus began his public ministry, this study agrees with those scholars who have concluded that John became his mentor.[8] John had had considerable success leading "sinners," such as tax collectors and prostitutes (Matt 21:32), to repentance. This study argues that the "sinners" mentioned in the gospels were Jews

3. See under *Galilee's Socio-economic Conditions* on page 27.

4. See under *Social Divisions between Jewish Groups in Galilee* on page 29.

5. See *Purity* on page 6.

6. See under *Capernaum* on page 43.

7. See under *John the Baptist* on page 46.

8. For details see under *The Relationship between John and Jesus* on page 83.

who had been excluded from observant Jewish society for various breaches of Torah.[9] A whole underclass had been formed as a consequence of Pharisaism's emphasis on the observance of both written Torah and its own oral law, intensified by the purity movement's demands for ritual cleanliness. Exclusion was used in place of Torah's death sentences, which the Romans had outlawed. But these "sinners" were also victims of injustice because they remained excluded even after demonstrating repentance.[10] It was the Baptist who revealed to Jesus that the injustice suffered by the "sinners" and that experienced by Galilean Jews were symptoms of the same spiritual malaise. Under John's tutelage Jesus' mission broadened from local political activism to nationwide prophetic ministry. After his baptism and the period in the "wilderness" he toured Judea[11] and Galilee,[12] preaching that Jews should radically rededicate their lives to God's service. This would lead to a more just and compassionate society.

But Jesus had not forgotten his original concern for the suffering Galilean Jews. This study hypothesizes that one of his early schemes on their behalf—perhaps the recruitment of unemployed agricultural workers to join a "hunger march" to Jerusalem[13]—so alarmed Galilee's community leaders that they notified the Sanhedrin, which feared that it was a rebel army that Jesus was planning to march into Jerusalem. This led it to send a surveillance team to Galilee to gather intelligence about his activities and intentions.[14] His interactions with this team account for the fourteen episodes recorded in the synoptic gospels in which Jesus encounters scribes or Pharisees or both in Galilee, even though at that time such officials rarely ventured there.[15] One scholar[16] has published the suggestion that the Pharisees kept Jesus under surveillance, although not their reason for

9. For details see under *The "Sinners"* on page 8 and *Excommunication: a Hypothesis* on page 10. The author has published this suggestion previously (Amos, *Hypocrites*, 155–159).

10. This, surely, is the meaning of the final clause in Matt 23:13 and the attitude of the elder brother (representing the Jewish leadership) in the Prodigal Son (Luke 15:11–32).

11. See under *The Early Judean Ministry* on page 113.

12. See under *The Galilean Period* on page 118.

13. For the evidence for this see fn 70 on page 44.

14. For details see under *Justice for the Galilean Jews* on page 120 and *Under Surveillance* on page 123.

15. Many scholars argue convincingly that scribes and Pharisees rarely visited Galilee at the time of Jesus. For details see fn 66 on page 42.

16. See fn 38 on page 126.

plotting against him. When Jesus found himself under surveillance, he abandoned the proposed hunger march, recognizing that to proceed with it might endanger the deprived men whom he was trying to help.

Perhaps the second most important contribution to knowledge made by this project is its assertion that Jesus' public ministry divides into two distinct phases in which he used different methods to reach different target groups.[17] It was the arrival and continuing presence of the surveillance team that led him to make these changes. Before their arrival he targeted observant Jews, preaching in plain language in his attempt to reform Judaism, making it more compassionate towards those whom it had marginalized. After the surveillance team's arrival he changed his primary target to the marginalized underclass of "sinners." He ceased teaching in plain language and used mainly parable (Mark 4:33f), which was easily understood by those who had received little previous religious instruction and whose content was so innocuous that the listening surveillance team would find in it no grounds to arrest him.

Since his target "sinners" were excluded from synagogues, for their benefit Jesus created the new community that evolved into the church universal, open to all on the basis of faith alone. His saying to Peter, "I tell you, you are Peter, and on this rock I will build my church" (Matt 16:18), implies a new movement with Peter as its prototype member. Built by the agency of the Holy Spirit (Matt 16:17), the new movement fulfilled the end-time prophecy that "I will pour out my spirit on all flesh" (Joel 2:28), welcoming Gentiles as well as Jews.[18] Unlike other religious institutions, it would have no hierarchy: under Jesus all members would be equal, serving one another as in a co-operative,[19] and the distinctions which commonly divide humanity into categories would be abolished (Gal 3:28). Within this new movement all would access God as a loving Father[20] and all sins would be forgiven.[21]

---

17. For further see under *Jesus' Change of Agenda* on page 127. The author has previously published this suggestion (Amos, *Hypocrites*, 173–193).

18. This is explicit in the Great Commission (Matt 28:19) and implicit in, for example, the Mustard Seed (Matt 13:31f) where the "birds of the air," representing Gentiles, find a home in the new community, and the Yeast (Matt 13:33) where the "three measures of flour" transformed by the yeast represent the whole of humanity.

19. See under *Jesus' New Egalitarian Community* on page 93.

20. See under *Personal Relationship with God* on page 88.

21. See under *Forgiveness of Sins* on page 102.

The long-sought opportunity to strike a blow for Galilee's beleaguered indigenous Jews came when Jesus and his disciples traveled to Jerusalem for the Passover. Scholars have attached symbolic meaning to his cleansing of the temple, but surely its main purpose was to force a confrontation with the Jewish hierarchy. When a deputation from the Sanhedrin approached Jesus in the temple demanding to know what authority he claimed for his actions, he told them the Story of the Tenants. Although this has widely been treated as allegory, recent scholarship recognizes an underlying realistic story. This depicts the frustration of the exploited agricultural community and the violence that was likely to erupt between peasantry and landowners unless there was sweeping reform. The officials listening were probably landowners themselves and it is likely that many of the pilgrims in the wider audience were suffering peasants. All three synoptists record the embarrassment of the officials when they recognized themselves as the villain of the story. They would have arrested him there and then, but for the surrounding peasant crowds who regarded Jesus as their champion. A few days later, under the cover of darkness they arrested him in Gethsemane. It was this story that cost Jesus his life.[22]

SO WHAT WAS JESUS HOPING TO ACHIEVE?

In view of the above it is tempting to answer "social justice," but that is a broad category which requires nuancing. Although social justice was arguably the overarching aim of his entire ministry, that largely unrecognized mid-ministry change of target people and methods has historically complicated the task of identifying Jesus' intention. The picture painted by the gospels presents a paradox of almost poetic symmetry: first Jesus attempts to reform institutional Judaism; when that attempt is frustrated he founds a new faith community as a spiritual home for the very people whom institutional Judaism had rejected.

A second paradox complicates the picture: from its inception that new faith community welcomed people of all races who sought to worship the one true God through Jesus. Jesus' teaching had hinted that this would happen, even though there is no evidence that he deliberately targeted Gentiles during his earthly ministry. In retrospect it appears that the principal intention of Jesus' earthly ministry was the creation of this new global community that would serve God in a radical manner.

22. For further see under *The Story of the Tenants* on page 133.

The pieces of the jigsaw, both hypothesis and established fact, fit together to form a coherent and plausible picture, the first step towards verification. If "history is reconstruction through hypothesis and verification," this study has made several original contributions to our knowledge of the historical Jesus.

EPILOGUE

Of course, for Christian believers Jesus' crucifixion and subsequent resurrection achieved more than his earthly ministry did; it is through these that Jesus saved them. Deliberately this study has not mentioned this because its focus has been on the factors that led Jesus to begin his ministry; while Jesus might have had his atoning death in mind from the start, it is impossible to prove this from the NT or other sources.

Perhaps this is why the intention underlying Jesus' ministry has been neglected. Since scholars began studying Jesus there has been a tension between the historical Jesus and the Christ of faith.[23] This study has been concerned only with the historical Jesus. The salvific benefits of Jesus' passion and resurrection are a property of the Christ of faith and therefore beyond the scope of this study. But although it may seem that this tension threatens to split the person of Jesus in two, that is not so. It is surely essential that the person central to Christian worship should have a sound historical basis. And no less surely it is the epic growth of the global community worshipping the transcendent Christ that inspires researchers to discover more of the historical person who founded it.

---

23. For further on this distinction see page 145.

Appendix 1

The Quest for the Historical Jesus

INTRODUCTION TO THE QUEST

As early as the second century Bible scholars began creating harmonies of the gospels in an attempt to provide a coherent reconstruction of the Jesus that they portrayed; arguably these were early quests for the historical Jesus. It was, however, the eighteenth-century Enlightenment, which brought scientific enquiry to bear on a broad spectrum of subjects, that is generally regarded as stimulating modern scholarly research into the historical Jesus. This, as Helen Bond observes, allowed distinctions to be made between the "Christ of faith" and the "Jesus of history."[1] As the mystical, omnipresent person who has traditionally been the focus of Christian worship, at one time piety considered that the "Christ of faith" was sacrosanct and that "faith should not seek security in historical data."[2] In contrast, the "Jesus of history" is the historical person whose life and crucifixion in first-century Palestine is described in the gospels, the initiator of the Christian movement. Recently historical Jesus research has flourished, perhaps because the Christian community has recognized that the integrity of faith and worship is compromised unless it is grounded in historical reality.

The modern Quest is commonly divided into four phases, although the boundaries between them are sometimes tenuous. (i) The Old Quest is

1. Bond, *Historical*, 7.
2. Sanders, *Jesus and Judaism*, 1.

generally considered to have begun with G. E. Lessing's posthumous publication in 1778 of Hermann Reimarus's *On the Intentions of Jesus and His Disciples* and to have ended in 1906 with Albert Schweizer's *The Quest for the Historical Jesus*. (ii) There followed a period of "No Quest" as critiques of the Old Quest led scholars to debate whether reconstruction of the historical Jesus was possible, the Christ of faith assuming greater importance. Perhaps the most influential scholar of this period is Rudolf Bultmann. (iii) The "New Quest" began in 1953 when Ernst Käsemann gave a lecture entitled "The Problem of the Historical Jesus" to a group of Bultmann's students. Attempting to establish links between the Christ of faith and the historical Jesus, its participants were mainly Protestants in German academic institutions. It sought to recover the actual words of Jesus and developed various criteria of authenticity,[3] including those of dissimilarity and multiple attestation, as tools for this purpose. (iv) The "Third Quest" is regarded as having begun in the mid 1980s. Although E. P. Sanders's *Jesus and Judaism* (1985) is sometimes claimed as initiating it, that was only one of several developments around that time that stimulated a new wave of research into the historical Jesus; others were the publication of the Dead Sea Scrolls, new discoveries from archaeology and important new studies of Josephus, the Rabbinic literature, and Hellenism. The Third Quest is characterized by an emphasis on the Jewishness of Jesus and on establishing the broader picture rather than individual sayings. The participants are mainly from the English-speaking world, but are remarkably diverse, including Protestants, Catholics, Jews, and non-believers. Moreover, they practice a multiplicity of disciplines, including sociology and anthropology.[4]

ALBERT SCHWEITZER

Albert Schweitzer's *The Quest for the Historical Jesus* (1911) marks the culmination of what some scholars term the "Old Quest." This is generally considered to have begun with Hermann Reimarus who published two treatises on Jesus in 1777 and 1778. Schweitzer's ground-breaking book summarizes the course of the Old Quest, which was conducted largely by German scholarship, and it is not until the penultimate chapter that the author's own hypothesis is revealed. He considered that the liberal Protestantism that had dominated German scholarship had ignored the eschatological

3. For further on these see Appendix 2 on page 166.
4. Bond, *Historical*, 7–22.

elements which he regarded as an important feature of Jesus' ministry. Schweitzer's historical Jesus initially heralded God's imminent ending of the world through the intervention of a separate person, the Son of man. When this and other predicted events failed to happen, Jesus became the suffering Son of man himself in an attempt to force God's hand. Although Schweitzer viewed the historical Jesus as a failed prophet, he nevertheless retained faith in the "Spiritual Jesus" whom he regarded as more important than the historical figure.

BEN F. MEYER

Ben F. Meyer's *The Aims of Jesus* was first published in 1977, before E. P. Sanders's alleged initiation of the "Third Quest," but a new edition was launched by Pickwick in 2002 with a specially commissioned introduction by N. T. Wright. He describes it as a "masterpiece": "To be frank, if Meyer's arguments had been taken seriously in the academy, much of the nonsense that has been written about Jesus in the last twenty years, not least by the so-called 'Jesus Seminar,' could have been avoided."[5]

In the brief Introduction Meyer describes what he considers to be the cause of past mistakes. These concern not only the reliability of sources, but also "a dilemma formulated by Van Austin Harvey as the incompatibility between intellectual honesty and traditional Christian belief."[6] The "old" mistake was in historians' presuppositions. History is the asking and answering of certain kinds of question; the known facts in the question that specify it form one set of presuppositions. Answering is by formulation of hypotheses, possible answers, limited by what the historian conceives as possible, that forming another set of presuppositions. These presuppositions reflect culture and there is a cultural continuum from Reimarus to the post-Bultmannians. "The immediate aim of the present work . . . is to understand the Jesus of ancient Palestine. It is remarkable that such key figures in the history of the question as Strauss, Wrede, and Bultmann were not deeply interested in this aim. . . . History is reconstruction through hypothesis and verification. Its topic is 'aims and consequences . . . '"[7]

5. Meyer, *Aims*, 9a.

6. Meyer, *Aims*, 14.

7. Meyer, *Aims*, 19.

Part One, entitled "Hermeneutical Issues," is concerned with "confronting the log-jam of conflicting interpretations."[8] Chapter 2, "A Review of the Quest," surveys two centuries of the Quest from Reimarus and Strauss to Bultmann and Jeremias and concludes by considering "The Quest as a Historical Phenomenon." A gulf exists between the gospels and the literature of explanation, due to a "hermeneutical law": "Before data can generate new knowledge they must be understood in their own terms. The gospels, designed to evoke a faith-response, could present evidence serviceable to historical explanation only on condition that they were already understood in their own right. But to men who instinctively found religious dogma alien, New Testament perspectives were not easily identifiable."[9] Chapter 3, "The Gospel Literature: Data on Jesus?" is intended to challenge the proposition that the gospels do not supply data on Jesus. If true, this would thwart the project of defining Jesus' aims. The proposition is that the gospels are confessional, a product of the faith community and not necessarily based on historical data. In chapter 4, "Jesus and Critical History," Meyer asserts that "understanding of history as a mode of knowledge is relevant to the history of Jesus."[10] He distinguishes between interpretation, which is the grasp and mediation of meaning, and explanation. "Historical criticism was born of the realization that even pure exegesis required that the historical context of the work to be interpreted be defined . . . the aim of criticism is arrival at interpretation and explanation . . . "[11] Chapter 5, "History and Faith," explores the implications that "From the beginning Christian faith has been a confession of events in human history."[12] We understand words by understanding the things they refer to; we understand things by understanding the words that refer to them. So the understanding of any communication presupposes a pre-understanding of the things communicated. In the Enlightenment Europe abandoned its traditional authority of scripture and Christian interpretation. By the inter-war years of the 20th century such authority had disappeared and empty liberalism prevailed.

In Part 2, entitled "The Aims of Jesus," Meyer presents his reconstruction of the historical Jesus. Chapter 6, "The Judgment and Salvation of Israel," is concerned with John the Baptist. He sees significance in John's

8. Meyer, *Aims*, 23.

9. Meyer, *Aims*, 55.

10. Meyer, *Aims*, 76.

11. Meyer, *Aims*, 78.

12. Meyer, *Aims*, 95.

self-identification as a prophet and in his confinement of his ministry to the wilderness. Chapter 7 is entitled "Public Proclamation and Career"; interestingly Meyer distinguishes between Jesus' public sayings and his "esoteric" ones, that is, those to his disciples. It is in the former that Meyer's quest for Jesus' aims focuses. Meyer reckons that after John's arrest Jesus ceased baptizing and understood his new career as proclamation, teaching, and healing. The reign of God replaced the wrath to come as his main theme.[13] In chapter 8, "The Secret of the Reign of God," Meyer deals with "esoteric traditions," dealing with Jesus when he was alone or with his disciples. His teaching to his disciples, Meyer claims, "presented the full scheme of meaning, the interpretive and explanatory perspective."[14] Most fundamental is Jesus' identity, *c.f.* Peter's confession which triggers the passion predictions. Although "the goal of Jesus' career was the messianic restoration of Israel,"[15] it is unclear how he hoped to achieve this. Meyer's final chapter is entitled "Confirmation and Reflection." He surmises that "The sea-change in the history of ancient Israel was, in fact, the evolution from ethnic to religious community."[16]

Meyer is a challenging author to read. His delight in technical terminology sometimes compels the reader to analyze a sentence for several minutes before it reluctantly yields its meaning. But the effort is rewarded by the sagacity of his insight. Moreover, there is genuine entertainment in the enthusiasm with which he heaps scorn on scholarship that he considers guilty of misleading our understanding of Jesus.

E. P. SANDERS

A remarkably erudite scholar, E. P. Sanders regards himself primarily as "a historian and an exegete"[17] and admits, "I am no theologian."[18] His frequent citation of other writers, drawing attention either to their errors or to their astuteness and often building upon the latter, make his works effectively guides to relevant scholarship and invaluable aids to students and researchers. Perhaps the most relevant of his books to our present quest is *Jesus and*

13. Meyer, *Aims*, 129.
14. Meyer, *Aims*, 174.
15. Meyer, *Aims*, 202.
16. Meyer, *Aims*, 223.
17. *Jesus and Judaism*, 334.
18. *Jesus and Judaism*, 331.

Judaism (1985), but *Judaism: Practice and Belief 63 BCE–66 CE* (1992) and *The Historical Figure of Jesus* (1993) are also significant works.

In *Jesus and Judaism* Sanders approaches the study of Jesus in a scientific and, indeed, a clinical manner. Much of the content of the gospels he dismisses as the creation of the early Christian communities and therefore not a reliable source of information on Jesus himself. So he works with a small canon, a number of "almost indisputable facts" about Jesus. These include his baptism by John the Baptist, that he was a Galilean who preached and healed; he called disciples (the Twelve), he confined his activity to Israel, he engaged in a controversy about the Temple, he was crucified by the Roman authorities, and after his death his followers continued as an identifiable movement. Sanders chooses the temple controversy as the most secure of these on which to base his reconstruction.[19]

After an Introduction which includes an extensive literature survey, Sanders devotes Part One to the restoration of Israel. This includes the Temple controversy which embraces Jesus' cleansing of the temple and his prediction of its destruction and rebuilding. Sanders concludes that the cleansing was a symbolised destruction, which prefigured destruction and points on to a restoration.[20] After a chapter on the new Temple and restoration in Jewish literature, he surveys other indications of restoration eschatology in the teaching of Jesus. Interestingly in view of what comes later, he finds plenty of references to forgiveness, but few to repentance.

Part Two concerns the Kingdom with chapters on the sayings, miracles and crowds, the sinners and the gentiles. Perhaps most significant is that the kingdom would include the sinners.[21] But despite incorporating a section attempting to distinguish between the sinners, the wicked, the poor, and the *'amme ha-aretz*[22] and another devoted to the terminology involved,[23] Sanders like many other scholars concludes his chapter on "sinners" without any firm indication as to precisely who these people were whom Jesus befriended. This chapter includes Sanders's most controversial statement: attempting to discover which aspect of Jesus' ministry so offended his peers that they sought his death, he decides that it was his proclamation of the

19. *Jesus and Judaism*, 11.

20. *Jesus and Judaism*, 69–71.

21. *Jesus and Judaism*, 174.

22. *Jesus and Judaism*, 176f.

23. *Jesus and Judaism*, 177–186.

inclusion of the wicked in the kingdom without requiring repentance, a sin offering or restitution.[24]

Part Three includes chapters on the law, opposition and opponents and the death of Jesus. Perhaps here Sanders is at his least controversial. He concludes that in general Jesus upheld the law, a notable exception being his demand to the man whose father had died. It may be significant that after his death his disciples continued to worship in the temple. The chapter on opposition and opponents concludes that there was no substantial conflict between Jesus and the Pharisees, but Jesus was executed by the Romans and the only Jews with access to the Romans were the chief priests.[25] The chapter on the death of Jesus seeks to establish the precise reason that Jesus was executed. Here Sanders raises a significant point that few scholars admit, namely that we do not know what happened when the high priest questioned Jesus.[26] Sanders believes that it was Jesus' action against the temple that led to his death.

Sanders concludes that the restoration of Israel is the thread that connects Jesus' agenda, his death, and the rise of the movement. Jesus fits into the general context of renewal movements at the time of the Roman occupation. He relied on his predecessor the Baptist for the message of repentance and taught that the wicked would be included in the coming kingdom. The great symbolic acts of his life stayed within the framework of Jewish restoration eschatology.

Sanders is a skilful writer: his style commands attention and his arguments are persuasive. They tempt the reader to accept as beyond question his conclusions that Jesus was a Jewish restoration eschatological prophet and that he did not seek death although neither did he attempt to escape it. (The doctrine that he died *for* sinners Sanders regards as having originated with Paul.[27]) Pretentiously Sanders even describes the process whereby the church will accommodate itself to his findings.[28]

But Sanders's conclusions are not indisputable. For example, his proposal that Jesus accepted sinners without repentance[29] has been ably

---

24. *Jesus and Judaism*, 207.

25. *Jesus and Judaism*, 291–293.

26. *Jesus and Judaism*, 299.

27. *Jesus and Judaism*, 331.

28. *Jesus and Judaism*, 333–335.

29. *Jesus and Judaism*, 207f.

refuted.[30] Even when his conclusions are undeniably true, they are not the *whole* truth. His entire reconstruction is based upon the limited canon of material that passes the "test of double dissimilarity" and Sanders himself admits that this is too meager to allow a coherent reconstruction of Jesus or his ministry.[31]

And it is not hard to find flaws in that test. For the "test of double dissimilarity" makes some dubious assumptions. Why should not Jesus reiterate some Jewish sayings? And surely we should expect the early church to treasure and reproduce genuine sayings of Jesus? Yet the test dismisses both sorts of material as inauthentic and unreliable. Most damning is the implication that the early church deliberately falsified or corrupted its teaching about Jesus. How likely is that? The early Christians believed themselves answerable to Jesus, moreover that Jesus was about to come again in judgment—they certainly did not wish to be caught misrepresenting him. Bauckham's argument that the gospels are based upon generally reliable reminiscences seems more plausible.[32]

All this by no means belittles the importance of *Jesus and Judaism*. It has, after all, been credited with initiating the "Third Quest."[33] Its comprehensiveness and scholarship are second to none. Undoubtedly Sanders's findings contain significant truth, but that truth applies to Jesus only insofar as he is represented in the limited tranche of tradition that survives the "test of double dissimilarity." Surely the historical person of Jesus is in reality rather more multi-faceted than Sanders's portrayal of him.

J. D. CROSSAN

J. D. Crossan is the most prominent member of the Jesus Seminar, a group of largely US academics which analyzed Jesus' sayings and actions as recorded in the canonical and some deuterocanonical gospels using an ingenious voting procedure to evaluate their authenticity. In *The Historical Jesus: The Life of a Mediterranean Jewish Peasant* (1991) Crossan depicts Jesus as an illiterate peasant adopting ideas from the Cynics; originally a disciple of John the Baptist, he rejected his asceticism and his understanding of the kingdom.

---

30. Chilton, "Jesus and Repentance," 3f.
31. Sanders, *Jesus and Judaism*, 16.
32. Bauckham, *Eyewitnesses*, 341–346.
33. Bond, *Historical*, 19.

Crossan employs a rather different approach to Sanders in assessing the authenticity of scripture passages. He insists upon *multiple attestation,* that is the tradition must be present in at least two *independent* sources in order to be accepted as authentic. This allows him a broader canon of source material than Sanders used, all the more so since he uses a number of deuterocanonical sources.

He opens his work with the perceptive observation that our knowledge of the first century is obscured by three filters: (i) records of the past are concerned almost exclusively with that minority of the population that was wealthy, powerful, and educated; (ii) those records are themselves filtered by later elites and by chance; and (iii) our present interpretation of the surviving ancient records is colored by our own experiences of today's very different world.[34] How, then, can today's researchers learn about the peasants, the regular uneducated folk of that period? Crossan suggests three sources: (i) anthropological and sociological studies, especially those using cross-cultural disciplines; (ii) archaeology; and (iii) papyrus documents and archives, such as the Oxyrhynchus finds in Egypt which allow glimpses into the lives of individual peasants.[35]

Crossan's work takes a diametrically opposite approach to that of Sanders in *Jesus and Judaism.* Whereas Sanders attempts to reconstruct Jesus from the limited tranche of the gospels whose authenticity he recognizes, Crossan begins with a comprehensive survey of the world into which Jesus was born. He analyses the class structure of ancient cultures and covers the two prevalent philosophical systems, Cynicism and Stoicism. He devotes a chapter to Flavius Josephus and points out the need for a critical approach to his writings. A series of chapters surveys various "types" of remarkable person: visionaries and teachers, magicians and prophets, bandits (including the Zealots and Messianic claimants) and rebels and revolutionaries. Appendix 2 appears to show a special concentration of such folk emerging in Palestine in the first century CE, but without comparable figures for other centuries or regions it is impossible to determine whether those figures are significant.

Not until chapter 11 do we meet John and Jesus. Crossan notes Josephus's observation that John's baptism presupposes repentance and Morton Smith's view that John's success stemmed from his offering a cheaper absolution than was available through the temple cultus. He sees significance in

34. Crossan, *Historical*, 3.
35. Crossan, *Historical*, 20–30.

Judeans being baptized in the Jordan before returning home, that is, a symbolic reconquest of the Promised Land, and notes the theological problems concerning the baptism of Jesus, which make it "one of the surest things we know about them both." He surveys John's eschatological preaching and Jesus' Son of Man sayings.

In chapter 12 on "Kingdom and Wisdom" Crossan considers some of Jesus' "kingdom" sayings including those about children (a kingdom of nobodies), the poor, the rich (their difficulty in entering the kingdom) and the undesirables. The widely used expressions "kingdom of God," "kingdom of heaven" and "kingdom" are analyzed in detail, particular attention being given to their apocalyptic, sapiential, and liturgical uses. Chapter 13, "Magic and Meal," draws together four strands: (i) the miracle workers characteristic of religion; (ii) the tension in the first century between wealthy respectable folk and counter-cultural poor folk such as wandering Cynics; (iii) turmoil among first-century Palestinian peasantry and (iv) Jesus' invocation of the kingdom of God as a present mode of life.

Crossan opens chapter 14, "Death and Burial," by referring to Jonathan Smith's observation that from the second century BCE onwards access to the divine shifted from a sacred place, often a temple, to a specially gifted man, a magician. That role is filled by John the Baptist and, even more adequately, by Jesus. So did Jesus in any way damage the Temple and, if so, did that lead to his crucifixion? Crossan analyses Jesus' sayings concerning the Temple, the memorial meal and the passion narrative. In chapter 15, "Resurrection and Authority," he turns to the contrasting tradition concerning Jesus' resurrection and post-resurrection appearances. These show remarkable diversity in contrast with the near unanimity of the passion narrative. Crossan believes that Mark retrojected some post-resurrection appearances into the earthly ministry of Jesus: the transfiguration, miraculous feeding, fishing for men and walking on water; these were originally intended to show Jesus' leadership of the church.

In his Epilogue Crossan draws together the findings in the earlier chapters, concluding that the historical Jesus must be understood within his contemporary Judaism.[36] Three moot questions: (i) Left to itself, what would have happened to the dialectic of exclusive and inclusive Judaism? (ii) Left to itself, would Judaism have been willing to compromise on, say, circumcision, in order to gain missionary possibilities among Greco-Roman pagans? (iii) Left to itself, could Judaism have converted the Roman

36. Crossan, *Historical*, 417.

empire? But Judaism was not left to itself. Jesus was a peasant Jewish Cynic who worked among the farms and villages of Lower Galilee. His strategy: free healing and common eating, a religious and economic egalitarianism that negated the hierarchical and patronal normalcies of Jewish and Roman power.

While many scholars are critical of Crossan's methods, especially his readiness to use deuterocanonical sources, he offers some interesting insights and raises some significant questions that all Jesus researchers need to consider.

GERD THEISSEN AND DAGMAR WINTER

Readers hoping to find in Gerd Theissen and Dagmar Winter's *The Quest for the Plausible Jesus: The Question of Criteria* (as translated by M. Eugene Boring and published in 2002) a description of "the plausible Jesus" will be disappointed. The book is more about the quest than its object. It considers the history of the quest, the techniques it uses, and the pitfalls that those undertaking it must avoid. As such it is valuable preparatory reading for a study such as this. But it is principally a critique of the test of dissimilarity favored by Sanders and others; moreover it proposes an alternative test of historical plausibility. The book consists of four long chapters and a comprehensive appendix.

The first chapter, "The Quest for Criteria in Jesus Research," concentrates on the shortcomings of the criterion of dissimilarity. The authors prefer the criterion of *coherence*, which increases the amount of authenticated Jesus material available by declaring material authentic if it coheres with material authenticated by the test of dissimilarity.[37] The authors point out that the criterion of dissimilarity comprises two distinct criteria—one oriented to the early Christian community and the other to the Jewish community—and these must be legitimized in two different ways. The chapter analyses in depth the problems raised by the criterion of dissimilarity.

The second chapter, written by Dagmar Winter, is entitled, "The Criterion of Dissimilarity in the History of Jesus Research" and subtitled "Aspects of the Quest for Criteria." As its title suggests, it is effectively a history of Jesus research showing the stages through which the criterion of

---

37. Theissen and Winter, *Plausible Jesus*, 17.

dissimilarity evolved. The section on the "Third Quest" overviews some of the authors covered in this Survey, such as Sanders, Crossan, and Meyer.[38]

In the third chapter, "The Criterion of Historical Plausibility as a Correction of the Criterion of Dissimilarity: Methodological Aspects of the Quest for Criteria" the authors expound their ideas concerning coherence and plausibility. Separate treatment is applied to the plausibility of historical effects and the criterion of dissimilarity vis-à-vis Christianity and the plausibility of historical context and the criterion of dissimilarity vis-à-vis Judaism. The problems of historical authenticity and historical plausibility are surveyed, leading to a historically plausible comprehensive picture.[39]

Chapter 4 is entitled "Criteria in Jesus Research and the 'Wide Ugly Ditch' of History: Hermeneutical Aspects of the Criteria Issue." It begins by considering "Lessing's Problem: Faith and History." The "wide ugly ditch" of Lessing's problem is the gap between conditional historical knowledge and the unconditional certainty of faith. The rest of the chapter is concerned with the problems of historical source criticism, of historical relativism, and of historical strangeness. Its concluding section, "A Paradoxical Resolution: Coming to Terms with the Hypothetical in Life and Thought," offers four reasons for coming to terms with the fact that "Everything in Jesus research is more or less hypothetical."

The book ends with an Appendix consisting of a comprehensive collection of formulations and commentaries on the general theme of the criterion of dissimilarity. Arranged in chronological order its 118 citations span history from Martin Luther in 1521 to Jürgen Becker in 1996. The collection concentrates on German scholarship.

This book stands in sharp contrast with those reviewed so far, being concerned only with the methodologies by which reconstructions of Jesus are made; as its title suggests, it is more to do with the quest than with Jesus himself. Nevertheless, the authors' real Christian faith and reverence for the Bible shine through its pages, perhaps most clearly in the closing paragraph of chapter 4.

SEÁN FREYNE

Seán Freyne's *Jesus: a Jewish Galilean*, published in 2004, offers a different perspective on Jesus. Freyne is perhaps best known for his *Galilee from*

---

38. Theissen and Winter, 144–152.

39. Theissen and Winter, 209.

Alexander the Great to Hadrian, a Study of Second Temple Judaism, first published in 1980. His focus on Jesus as a Galilean stands in contrast with Sanders's as a restoration prophet and Crossan's as a peasant Cynic. His specialized knowledge of Galilee allows insights into the way in which Jesus' Galilean environment might have impacted him. In regard to the gospels as sources Freyne takes a more liberal approach than Sanders or Crossan. He considers that Crossan's insistence upon double attestation may lead to the rejection of good historical information that appears in only one source. His approach is to be a critical, but not too suspicious reader of texts; he also draws upon the social sciences.[40]

Freyne observes that other historians of Jesus have concentrated on the Jewish literature of the period as a sociological/religious influence, neglecting the canonical Old Testament which a practicing Jew would surely revere. Moreover, he observes in those Hebrew scriptures an emphasis on humanity's task of caring for the environment. Accordingly he focuses upon ecology, chapter 2 being entitled, "Jesus and the ecology of Galilee," a somewhat neglected topic. Scholarship has so far ignored Jesus' respect for the natural environment, a consequence of his understanding of the earth as God's creation. Some of Freyne's example texts, however, seem somewhat imaginative.[41]

Jesus' move from the wilderness to Galilee Freyne explains in terms of the ways in which human life was lived and had adapted to the different habitats.[42] But even in urbanized Galilee Jesus maintained a nomadic lifestyle. His sayings assume familiarity with agriculture. Rome and Herod made heavy demands upon peasant farmers, whose existence was precarious. Sepphoris's sophisticated water system probably deprived local villagers, those whom Jesus addressed. The land God had given to his chosen people was now being given to Herodian favorites. Jesus' move to Capernaum may have been for a number of reasons. The fishing industry was important, as was farming on the fertile soil. Freyne considers links between landscape and religion, even Judaism via Stoicism.

"Stories of Conquest and Settlement" is the title of a chapter concerned with the manner in which Jesus related to the special election of Israel as this had expressed itself in the stories of conquest and occupation of the land. Albrecht Alt traced Galilee's population from the 8th century to

40. Freyne, *Jesus*, 3, 17.

41. Freyne, *Jesus*, 26.

42. Freyne, *Jesus*, 42.

Roman times. The canonical OT as a post-exilic production colors its narratives; we cannot be certain that there was any Israelite presence in Galilee
until after the exile. The chapter evaluates the OT records of the tribal al-
locations with special reference to the northern tribes whose settlements
formed Galilee. In "Zion Beckons" Freyne examines Isaiah's theology of
Zion and Jesus' use of this. Isaiah based in Jerusalem after the separation of
the two kingdoms predicted a restoration of Israel.

In "Confronting the Challenges of Empire" Freyne traces the transformation of Yahweh from national deity to cosmic Lord. Mighty empires,
at first from the east but, from Alexander onwards, from the west "glo-
balize" the world, Alexander and his successors introducing Greek-style
cities. Freyne retells the story of Antiochus Epiphanes and the emergence
of the Pharisees, Sadducees, and Essenes. Galilee was less Romanized than
Judea, as the disciples' amazement at the grandeur of the temple reveals
(Mark 13:2). Roman rule depleted Galilee's resources, the retainer classes
replacing the old Hasmoneans. The new cities, though populated mainly by
Jews, were parasitic on the neighboring territory and increased taxes on the
peasantry. Jesus appears to have avoided the two Herodian foundations in
Galilee while ministering in the surrounding villages. Freyne considers that
Jesus was critical of urban life. But he was also critical of Herodian rule. His
apocalypticism shows he regarded all earthly rulers as transient.

In the closing chapter, "Death in Jerusalem," Freyne points to Jerusalem as the symbolic centre of Judaism despite its exploitation of the
peasantry, such as Galileans. Jesus' Galilean sayings reveal no animosity
towards the temple and its institutions. How might his Galilean origin have
affected his understanding of the place of Gentiles in the eschatological
community inaugurated by his ministry? Jesus was familiar with Isaiah,
both in his understanding of God and his adoption of Isaiah's servant figure. But Isaiah envisaged Gentiles performing priestly functions (Isa 56:7;
66:21). The historical questions surrounding Jesus' death are fraught with
questions. That he died on a Roman cross is clear, although its full implications are rarely explored. The book concludes with an "Epilogue: Return to
Galilee." The instruction that the disciples should return to Galilee (Mark
16:7) indicates that Galilee still held special significance for Jesus' followers.

Freyne's style is easy to read and his knowledge of the primary and
secondary sources is extensive. Nevertheless one might take issue with
some of his exegesis. For example, he mentions the scribes who according to Mark had come from Jerusalem to discredit Jesus' healing ministry

in Galilee (Mark 3:31; 7:1).[43] Although both verses refer to scribes who had come from Jerusalem, neither gives any indication of the reason that they had undertaken that journey. Moreover, for a work allegedly having a Galilean emphasis, the references to Galilee were few in some chapters. Perhaps this is an indication that Jesus' Galilean heritage turned out to be less significant than he was expecting to find.

RICHARD HORSLEY

Published in 2012, Richard Horsley's *The Prophet Jesus and the Renewal of Israel* is subtitled "Moving Beyond a Diversionary Debate." It is a response to two major problems which the author identified in discussions of the historical Jesus. The first, a legacy of Albert Schweizer, concerns the prominence of "apocalypticism" at the time of Jesus. The second is the focus of most investigations of the historical Jesus on individual sayings, which taken out of context can be used as "proof texts" for almost any theory.[44] The two parts of this short book deal respectively with these two problems.

Horsley begins the first part of the book by considering the apocalyptic scenario proposed by Schweizer and Bultmann. Both insisted that Jesus' message of the kingdom should be understood in the context of Jewish expectations about the end of the world.[45] A difficulty is that if that end is imminent, the rest of Jesus' teaching becomes largely irrelevant, mere "interim ethics."[46] But the end of the world did not come and in the twentieth century the apocalyptic scenario lost popularity. In particular the "Jesus Seminar" doubted that Jesus had proclaimed the imminent end of the world.[47] Focusing on individual sayings of Jesus isolated from their context, they claim that Jesus was a teacher of wisdom. Crossan sees John the Baptist as an apocalyptic counterpart to wisdom-teacher Jesus. But the Baptist's preaching is not particularly apocalyptic, more renewal of Israel.[48] Horsley is critical of form criticism, which is more often content criticism. He draws parallels between Jesus of Nazareth and Jesus ben Sira.[49] In recent debate

43. Freyne, *Jesus*, 82f. Surely by Mark 3:31 he means Mark 3:22.
44. Horsley, *Prophet*, 1.
45. Horsley, *Prophet*, 11.
46. Horsley, *Prophet*, 12.
47. Horsley, *Prophet*, 16.
48. Horsley, *Prophet*, 19.
49. Horsley, *Prophet*, 24.

both sides agree that the Baptist, Jesus, and Paul shared the apocalyptic worldview with its central end of the world scenario. But did or did not Jesus believe and preach this eschatology?[50] The debate proves to be about a modern scholarly construct. Apocalyptic texts are important sources for the historical context in which Jesus lived and worked. The scribal visions and interpretations show that the overarching reality in late second-temple Judea was Hellenistic and then Roman imperial rule.[51]

In Part 2 Horsley focuses on the historical Jesus. He begins by pointing out that studies of Jesus as presented in the NT need to allow for layers of theological reflection in the texts. Historians must evaluate the sources to show how they can be used. Enlightenment made scholars aware of irrationalities in the gospel narratives, leading to a skeptical attitude to their historicity. The difficulty is that sayings need a context to give them meaning.[52] But the gospels as a whole tell a story consisting of related incidents in which Jesus communicates with real people; he was a historical person. Moreover western culture projects its own dominant individualism on to Jesus, distorting our understanding of him. Christological concerns exacerbate this. Traditional Christian teaching depicts Jesus calling individual disciples who after his death formed communities which coalesced into the church; he did not catalyze a movement during his lifetime. But surely he became a significant historical figure only because he interacted with others in the real world.

Chapter 7 gives a useful summary of the history of Israel from 168 BCE to the time of Jesus to show the devastating effects of successive conquests by various empires.[53] Apocalyptic texts offered some hope of restoration of Israel; the Qumran community regarded itself as working towards such an aim.[54] Lack of literacy makes it difficult to determine the behavior of ordinary people in ancient time, including popular movements. The only documentation is from the state sources against which they rebelled and this gives a one-sided account. Many mid-century movements were led by prophets.[55] In chapter 8 Horsley reassesses the gospels as sources of data for reconstructing the historical Jesus, emphasizing their integrity as whole

50. Horsley, *Prophet*, 53.

51. Horsley, *Prophet*, 62.

52. Horsley, *Prophet*, 70.

53. Horsley, *Prophet*, 79–83.

54. Horsley, *Prophet*, 85.

55. Horsley, *Prophet*, 92–94.

stories with overall plots; he concentrates on Mark and "Q." Most notable is his identification of several conflicts running through the Marcan narrative.[56] Mark presents Jesus as a prophet engaged in the renewal of Israel, a new Moses, and a new Elijah. Similarly Q is now recognized as a series of speeches rather than a collection of separate sayings.[57] The speeches follow an intelligible sequence of topics, presenting John the Baptist and Jesus in the role of prophet and engaged in the renewal of Israel.

Chapter 9 considers Jesus leading the renewal of Israel, based upon the whole gospels as sustained stories. The stories were adapted to suit various communities and evidence of adaptation is apparent in places.[58] The gospels show Jesus in the role of a prophet generating a movement for the renewal of Israel, healings and exorcisms in Mark pointing to his role as the coming one announced by the Baptist. These inspired trust, the basis of a movement. His disciples are also key, the twelve symbolizing Israel.[59] Chapter 10 focuses on Jesus' opponents, the rulers of Israel. A detailed consideration of the scribes and Pharisees concludes that Jesus' denunciation of then was typically prophetic. Next he surveys Jesus' prophetic pronouncements against the Temple and the High Priests. Jesus prophesied destruction of the temple and building of a new one without hands, *i.e.*, a new people of God, renewed Israel.[60]

Horsley writes clearly and succinctly; this book has the merit of brevity; he offers some fresh insights and some useful critiques of other scholarship, especially the "Jesus Seminar."

JAMES G. CROSSLEY

James G. Crossley's *Why Christianity Happened: A Sociohistorical Account of Christian Origins (26–50 CE)*, published in 2006, is unusual in that it takes a secular approach to Christian origins. Believing that biblical scholars who have religious beliefs are often tempted towards conclusions that conform with their personal beliefs, Crossley offers a different approach. His primary question is, "How did . . . a law-observant Jewish movement turn into a Jewish and Gentile movement with notable numbers no longer

56. Horsley, *Prophet*, 98.

57. Horsley, *Prophet*, 103.

58. Horsley, *Prophet*, 111–114.

59. Horsley, *Prophet*, 115–122.

60. Horsley, *Prophet*, 143.

observing key aspects of the law?"[61] In chapter 1 he argues that research into Christian origins benefits from approaches by a diversity of interest groups. Next he surveys scholarly literature which pursues a non-theological approach to Jesus and Christian origins, including such authors as Geza Vermes and E. P. Sanders.

Chapter 2 locates the origins of Jesus' ministry in peasant unrest. While rejecting much of Crossan's portrait of Jesus, he nevertheless applauds Crossan's location of the origins of the Jesus movement in a precise social context.[62] But while the agrarian society in which Jesus lived was likely to have been highly exploitative, it had been so for centuries; something different needed to have occurred to spark the movement.[63] Commercialization—encouraged by Rome—exacerbated peasant exploitation. Peasants need leadership if they are to rise up in rebellion; past peasant revolts have involved the assistance of intellectuals. A vision of a better world—Jesus' presentation of the kingdom of God?—also encouraged revolt. Many passages in Josephus's *Life* testify to Galilean hatred of Sepphoris and Tiberias because of their loyalty to Rome.[64] The gospels and archaeology both demonstrate the exploitation of Galilean peasantry at the time of Jesus.[65] Banditry was also common, some "social bandits" being connected with the peasantry as a kind of protest against exploitation.

Chapter 3 surveys Jesus' dealings with the "sinners." He begins with a detailed survey of sinners in Jewish literature.[66] Then he surveys sinners in the gospel tradition, especially their association with tax collectors. Chapter 4 is entitled "From Jewish Sinners to Gentile Sinners" and subtitled "The Beginnings of the Spread of Earliest Christianity." Crossley considers that Jesus' identification of Jewish sinners with the oppressive rich is the key to understanding his attitude to Gentile sinners who show similar traits. In the 30s Gentile Christians were expected to observe the Jewish law; only in the 40s does this change. Conditions favored travel and the spread of ideas; old local religions seemed outdated in a global society; first Buddhism, then Christianity and then Islam claimed to be universal faiths. Monotheism was probably more widespread than is commonly believed. At length

61. Crossley, *Christianity*, 1f.
62. Crossley, *Christianity*, 36.
63. Crossley, *Christianity*, 39.
64. Crossley, *Christianity*, 46f.
65. Crossley, *Christianity*, 47–49.
66. Crossley, *Christianity*, 76–87.

Crossley examines the "Q" traditions showing that they support observance of the law and proceeds to study the extent to which people observed
"expanded non-Temple purity laws." He then considers in detail Mark 6–8
and its implications for the earliest Christians; Crossley has argued elsewhere that this gospel must be dated before the early 40s, at a time when
Christianity was largely law observant. This leads him to a radical reading
of Mark 7:1–23 about the "tradition of the elders."[67] Crossley concludes that
the earliest Gentile Christians were expected to uphold Jewish morality,
although not to the extent that Pharisees are caricatured of doing in "Q."

Chapter 5 concerns the origins of the Pauline mission and is entitled
"Recruitment, Conversion and Key shifts in Law Observance." Although
the Christian movement began with a stress on biblical law, by the mid-
40s many Gentile Christians no longer observed these. What caused this
change? Social science suggests that social networks are important in conversion. Early Christianity opened its activities to non-members and this
attracted new members through existing social networks.

In his conclusion Crossley draws attention to the huge diversity of
people who entered the Jesus movement, poor and rich,"[68] and law-observant Jews besides Gentiles. He suggests that the deification of Jesus resulted
from the perceived need for a new global monotheistic faith.

While Crossley's scholarship and attention are beyond question, it is
tempting to ask whether his avowedly secular approach has achieved anything new: his conclusions mostly accord with those of other scholars. This
suggests that sectarian allegiance—or its absence—need not hinder historical Jesus research.

67. Crossley, *Christianity*, 127.
68. Crossley, *Christianity*, 173.

Appendix 2

CRITERIA OF AUTHENTICITY

INEVITABLY THE PRIMARY SOURCE for this study is the New Testament, especially the gospels. Other ancient sources such as Josephus are useful for background information. Secondary sources, that is, recent scholarship, are also valuable in helping to avoid the futile duplication of other researchers' work and allowing some building upon the foundations that established scholarship has laid.

In recent years many scholars have become cautious regarding the use of the New Testament as a basis for historical research, especially in regard to Jesus. The principal reason for this is a widespread suspicion that much of the material in the gospels was created by the early Christian communities and so reflects their interests rather than those of Jesus himself. Sanders, for example, claims that rarely can a saying be attributed to Jesus with absolute certainty, but after careful testing it might be assigned tentatively to an author.[1] The "double dissimilarity" test by which he and some other scholars assess the authenticity of sayings works as follows: the only material which can be safely attributed to Jesus is that which can be accounted for neither as traditional Jewish material nor as later church material. Sanders himself acknowledges the likelihood that this will eliminate so much material that it will be possible to create only an incomplete and misleading picture: the material that remains after the test is applied tends to enhance the uniqueness of Jesus.[2] As a consequence of his dependence on this test

1. Sanders, *Jesus and Judaism*, 13.
2. Sanders, *Jesus and Judaism*, 16.

Sanders works with a limited canon of "almost indisputable facts" about Jesus.[3]

Among those who have critiqued the test of double dissimilarity are Gerd Theissen and Dagmar Winter. In their 2002 book, *The Quest for the Plausible Jesus*, they argue that because Jesus had continuity with both Judaism and the early Christian community, it is to be expected that he sometimes used traditional Jewish material in his teaching and that some church material originated with him. But since most Jesus tradition originated within the Christian communities, it is important to eliminate material showing obviously later Christian perspectives from any reconstruction of the historical Jesus.[4]

Theissen and Winter emphasize the distinction between *contextual* plausibility (Jesus among Jews) and plausibility of *effects* (Jesus and Christians). They accept that word-for-word reconstruction of Jesus' preaching is not possible—all we can obtain is the essential content of what Jesus wanted to communicate.[5] So they agree with Sanders that an accurate reconstruction of the person and teaching of Jesus is simply not possible. But instead of the criterion of dissimilarity favored by Sanders and others they use the "criterion of coherence" which declares material authentic if it coheres with material authenticated by the test of dissimilarity. This yields a more plentiful supply of authenticated material. Their intention to reconstruct a *plausible* Jesus, rather than a strictly historical one, uses a process like that described by Helen Bond which emphasises major trajectories and overarching themes, rather than minutiae.[6]

But while this focus on "major trajectories and overarching themes" as the basis of Jesus research may seem commendably sensible, it nevertheless harbors a danger. Whence do researchers obtain those trajectories and themes if not from the gospels? But these are the same gospels whose content is widely suspected to be the product of the early Christian communities and therefore unreliable as sources of information on Jesus. Presumably the researchers compile the "trajectories and themes" themselves by selecting mutually consistent items from the gospel tradition. Surely, however, this selection process itself introduces the risk that, consciously or otherwise, by including items which conform to the researcher's presuppositions about

3. Sanders, *Jesus and Judaism*, 11.

4. Theissen and Winter, *Plausible Jesus*, 173.

5. Theissen and Winter, *Plausible Jesus*, 210.

6. Bond, *Historical*, 21.

Jesus and excluding those which do not, the resultant "trajectories and themes" are themselves flawed.

Other more sophisticated tests of authenticity have been used. That used by Crossan, for example, involves three stages: (i) a declaration of sources, canonical and deuterocanonical; (ii) stratification, which is the positioning of each item in a chronological timeline; and (iii) independent attestation, which indicates the number of independent witnesses recording the event or saying. This latter, nevertheless, introduces limitations; Crossan himself admits that this entails the elimination of any material found only in single attestation.[7] Although this allows Crossan a greater canon of authenticated source material than Sanders used, there is still the risk of potentially useful authentic material being discarded as unreliable if it was recorded by only one writer.

But surely it is reasonable to suppose that the writers of the New Testament exercised prudence—they would not wish to misrepresent Jesus, whom they revered as Lord and whose imminent return in judgment many of them expected! If so, they probably had good reason for every item they recorded about him. While it is undeniable that the gospels contain contradictions and inconsistencies and that some passages in the gospels appear to reflect early church practice,[8] Richard Bauckham argues persuasively that the gospels were written within living memory of the events they recount.[9] Concerning the reliability of the reminiscences of Jesus from which the evangelists compiled their gospels Bauckham describes nine factors identified in psychological studies that make an event so memorable that the recollection of it is likely to be accurate; examples from the gospels show that these factors applied to the ministry of Jesus as the evangelists recorded it.[10]

It is difficult not to applaud Bauckham's eloquent attempt to reintroduce into the Jesus tradition the authenticity that had been eroded by various aspects of recent scholarship. But Jens Schröter identifies three shortcomings in Bauckham's work: (i) that the gospels are the product of theological reflection; (ii) oral tradition is liable to change over time under the influence of theological reflection; and (iii) Bauckham encourages an uncritical view that trusts the gospels rather than subjecting them to

7. Crossan, *Historical*, xxxii–xxxiii.

8. For example, Matt 18:15–17 appears to reflect ecclesiastical disciplinary procedure.

9. Bauckham, *Eyewitnesses*, 7.

10. Bauckham, *Eyewitnesses*, 341–346.

detailed scrutiny.[11] Schröter's balance of the value on the one hand of "eye-witness testimony" and on the other of historical-critical analysis is surely astute, reconciling elements of Bauckham's emphasis that the gospels contain accurate reminiscences of Jesus' ministry with recognition that they are also the product of theological reflection upon the meaning of that ministry.

Criteria Used in This Study

This study assumes, with Bauckham, that in general the gospel texts are based upon genuine reminiscences of Jesus, but also recognizes, with Schröter, that they have been interpreted through the theological understanding of the early Christian communities. For this reason they must be subjected to critical scrutiny; sometimes the truth they express may be metaphorical rather than literal. Crossan's criterion of multiple attestation is also sometimes useful. While single attestation need not necessarily indicate that the tradition is inauthentic, multiple attestation suggests that a tradition was widely known in the early Christian communities, allowing greater confidence in its authenticity.

11. Schröter, "Gospels," 207f.

Appendix 3

Literature on John the Baptist

While one might expect there to be rather less literature concerning John than concerning Jesus, the comparative lack of literature on John is remarkable; arguably he has been somewhat neglected by scholarship. A search of Google Books in December 2015 found only two scholarly books devoted to the Baptist published since 2000, although in that period numerous papers about him had been published as had scholarly books containing sections devoted to him. This survey will examine first the Qumran controversy, then the person of John and finally his relationship with Jesus. In each section the literature will be considered in roughly chronological order so that developments of thought may be traced.

The Qumran Controversy

Following the discovery of the Dead Sea Scrolls and the publication of some of their content in the 1940s and 1950s there was a revival of interest in John the Baptist as various scholars conjectured that John had been associated with the Qumran community, perhaps as a member or even a leader. At the time the arguments seemed convincing, attracting considerable attention. Three papers supporting this theory are the following:

John A. T. Robinson: "The Baptism of John and the Qumran Community: Testing a Hypothesis" in *The Harvard Theological Review*, Vol. 50, No. 3 (Jul., 1957), pp. 175–191.

W. H. Brownlee: "John the Baptist in the New Light of Ancient Scrolls" in *The Scrolls and the New Testament* ed. Krister Stendahl, New York: Crossroad (1992). This paper was originally published in 1955 and substantially revised for its later republication.

Otto Betz: "Was John the Baptist an Essene?" in *Understanding the Dead Sea Scrolls* ed. Hershel Shanks, New York: Vintage Books (1993).

Robinson's paper differs from the other two in that it is more concerned with John's baptism than his person, but all three explore the similarities between John's ministry and Qumran practice and inevitably consider whether John was impacted by Qumran and, if so, to what extent. While Robinson judiciously emphasizes that John's connection with the Qumran Community remains a hypothesis, Betz openly confesses his view that the Baptist was raised in the community and strongly influenced by it, but later left it to preach to a wider community of Jews.[1] Brownlee cautiously admits his conviction that John had some Essene connections.

All three papers suggest that as a child John may have been sent to Qumran, perhaps because his elderly parents had died; all cite Josephus's observation that the Essenes adopted children and raised them in their discipline. Betz and Robinson point out that Qumran was close to both Jericho, John's possible childhood home, and the Judean wilderness which was one traditional site of his later ministry. Robinson and Brownlee both mention that the Qumran Community Rule (1QS, sometimes called the Manual of Discipline) divides the community into units of ten men, one being a priest. Robinson alone expresses the significant implication that Qumran must have had a considerable following among priestly families.[2]

Among many correspondences noted between John and Qumran, not least is the prophecy of Isa 40:3, "A voice cries out: 'In the wilderness prepare the way of the Lord, make straight in the desert a highway for our God,'" which in the Community Rule forms a kind of "mission statement" for the community and which all four canonical gospels associate with the Baptist. Brownlee suggests as a likely explanation for this fact that in his later ministry John appears to be not associated with Qumran or any other group; he postulates that John was dissatisfied with the way in which the Community members were seeking to fulfill Isa 40:3: they were preparing only themselves, not the nation. Eventually he went out alone to become

---

1. Betz, "John," 206.
2. Robinson, "Baptism," 176.

that voice. He soon established a reputation as a prophet so that people sought him out.[3] Robinson, however, offers an alternative reason for John's departure from Qumran: believing that the eschatological moment was nearer than they believed, John went out to announce the imminent coming of the Prophet and to gather the faithful by summoning the people to the baptism of repentance that earned him his epithet.[4]

The scholars disagree on the origin of John's baptism. Brownlee is convinced that it derives from Jewish proselyte baptism, its originality being John's insistence that the rite be applied to persons born Jews. This implied that the whole nation was apostate and if it was to become the people of God it must enter the society of God's people through repentance and baptism.[5] This radical view, reflected in John's language in the gospel accounts, accords with Essene beliefs. Robinson, however, claims that attempts to link John's baptism to proselyte baptism or regular Jewish ablutions do not allow for the distinction between ritual impurity and sin. He refers to J. Thomas who in *Le mouvement Baptiste en Palestine et Syrie* (Gembloux, 1935) claimed that in the baptist sects baptism was taking the place of sacrifice which dealt with sin, offering a possible origin for baptism for the remission of sins. The hypothesis that John was adapting Qumran ideas to his own mission would explain his own activity, although the Qumran scrolls themselves do not mention a baptism of repentance for the remission of sins. John called people to an act quite unlike any in Qumran. He did not summon people to a community life, but the nation to purify itself in preparation for the coming mighty one.[6]

All three scholars agree that John's baptism was effective only for those who repented.[7] Robinson alone, however, makes the significant observation that John's baptism differs from the Christian initiatory rite of baptism in that it was not a once-for-all event, but might be repeated, like other Jewish and Essene purificatory washings.[8]

John's baptism was linked intimately with his proclamation of the coming mightier one who would baptize with the Holy Spirit and fire. All three scholars find close parallels in Essene thought. Betz claims that

3. Brownlee, "John," 35f.
4. Robinson, "Baptism," 179.
5. Brownlee, "John," 36f.
6. Robinson, "Baptism," 180f.
7. Brownlee, "John," 40; Betz, "John," 209; Robinson, "Baptism," 183.
8. Robinson, "Baptism," 182.

Qumran expected its ritual washings to be superseded by a purification by the Holy Spirit at the end of time.[9] According to Brownlee, the Community Rule mentions a man upon whom God will sprinkle the Spirit as purifying water, *c.f.* Mark 1:8, and in the complete Isaiah scroll from Qumran there is a Messianic reading of Isa 52:14f which pictures an anointing which qualifies the Lord's servant to sprinkle others—the Messiah is so described in the Damascus Document.[10] Robinson finds evidence that Qumran believed that the dispensation of water was provisional until the Messianic age when it would be superseded by a dispensation of the Holy Spirit.[11]

Brownlee and Robinson both observe that the Dead Sea Scrolls have caused a major re-estimation of the historical value of the Fourth Gospel, especially in regard to John the Baptist.[12] According to Brownlee the Fourth Gospel portrays John and Jesus differently from the synoptics, its language and ideas showing connections with those of the Community Rule. And John 1:23 supports the picture of John's leaving the Essenes to take on the role of the "voice."[13]

Despite his conviction, mentioned earlier, that John was raised in Qumran, Betz alone balances his argument with evidence that John was *not* an Essene: he is not mentioned in any of the DSS found so far and neither the NT nor Josephus associates him thus although Josephus seems to have had a partiality for the sect. Moreover, John was critical of civil government which is untypical of the Essenes. John's concern for the salvation of his fellow Jews is also untypical. The Essenes never engaged in outreach, but waited for God to send people to them. John, however, dared to address the whole nation, becoming the voice in the wilderness. He did not incorporate his candidates into a community, but sent them home to live out the fruits of their repentance. This is very unlike an Essene.[14]

Although the three papers differ in various ways, at the time of publication each argued that the hypothesis that John the Baptist was impacted by the Qumran community is plausible. That all three scholars express this opinion may make the hypothesis seem more likely to be correct.

9. Betz, "John," 209f.

10. Brownlee, "John," 43f.

11. Robinson, "Baptism," 184.

12. Robinson, "Baptism," 190.

13. Brownlee, "John," 45–47.

14. Betz, "John," 212f.

Hutchinson, John C., "Was John the Baptist an Essene from Qumran?" *Bibliotheca Sacra*, 159 (Apr–June 2002), 187–200.

Hutchinson presents what is perhaps the clearest and most compelling argument *against* a connection between John the Baptist and Qumran. His reasoning is based principally upon disparities between John's teaching and methods and those of Qumran. The perceived connections he regards as due partly to misinterpretations of such texts as Luke 1:80, but mainly to a failure to perceive the differences (i) between the types of separation from mainstream Judaism exhibited by John and by the Qumran Community, (ii) between the kinds of preparation for the coming Messiah practiced by John and by Qumran, and (iii) between their respective water rituals.[15] Hutchinson relies heavily upon traditional understandings of the NT, especially concerning the Baptist's understanding of the Messiah—although he is reported as having used the word "Messiah" only in John 1:20 where he denies being the Messiah—but this need not detract from the overall soundness of his arguments.

The Person of John

Robert L. Webb's book *John the Baptizer and Prophet: A Socio-historical Study* is based upon his PhD dissertation submitted to the University of Sheffield in 1990; first published by Sheffield Academic Press in 1991, it was republished by Wipf & Stock in 2006. A monumentally comprehensive study, Webb includes sections on the traditions concerning John in Christian and non-Christian literature, ablutions in the OT, second-Temple Jewish literature, and the DSS, the administration and functions of John's baptism, judgment/restoration figures in the OT and second-Temple Jewish literature, John's proclamation of an expected figure, prophetic figures in late second-temple Judaism and the socio-political orientation of John's prophetic ministry. He seems to anticipate the writing, 15 years later, of Daniel Dapaah's work (see below) since he specifically excludes John's relationship with Jesus: "Our concern in this book is with John the Baptist himself—the quest for the 'historical John' as it were—but it is helpful to begin by placing this concern in the larger context of historical Jesus research, for it is in this context that John is usually discussed."[16]

---

15. Hutchinson, "John the Baptist," 198–200.
16. Webb, *John the Baptizer*, 19.

Webb focuses on John's role as baptizer and prophet, highlighting both the similarities between his baptism and Jewish proselyte baptism and the distinctive differences. His chapter on the expected figure whom John proclaims interestingly concludes that Yahweh himself is the most likely identity,[17] but he also points out that "a person in that period could expect God to be coming to judge and restore in theological/celestial terms and at the same time expect an agent to execute the judgment and restoration in historical/terrestrial terms."[18] Webb attaches special importance to his conclusion that John's ministry produced a Jewish sectarian movement. Interestingly he found also that "John did not expect the 'end of the world' but a radical reorientation of the concrete, socio-historical situation in which the Jewish people in Palestine found themselves."[19] Webb rarely enters the realms of speculation, offering only a limited interpretation of his sources. For example, he relegates the debate concerning John's connection with the Qumran community to a single footnote: "concrete evidence is lacking, and even if John had been a member at one time, the certain elements of his public ministry are sufficiently different from the ideology of the Qumran community to indicate that he must have broken with them."[20] One might conclude that Webb is more interested in cataloguing what is definitely known about the Baptist than in offering speculative interpretations of the known facts.

Joan Taylor's book *John the Baptist within Second Temple Judaism: a Historical Study*, published in 1997, resembles Webb's work in its comprehensiveness. However, while Webb's analysis of his sources is limited, Taylor adopts a thematic approach to the Baptist's person and ministry, exegeting the sources as necessary. For example, in contrast with Webb's solitary footnote, she devotes a whole chapter to the controversy concerning the Baptist's connection with Qumran. She reaches the same conclusion as Webb, but usefully provides comprehensive reasons for her conclusions. Other chapters are concerned with immersion and purity, teaching and predictions, John and the Pharisees, opposition and death, and, finally, John and Jesus. Taylor is a cautious scholar, reluctant to entertain any possibility where the evidence is less than indisputable. For example, she regards John's priesthood as provisional depending upon the historicity of Luke

17. Webb, *John the Baptizer*, 283.
18. Webb, *John the Baptizer*, 380.
19. Webb, *John the Baptizer*, 381.
20. Webb, *John the Baptizer*, 213 fn 137.

1:5, but fascinatingly she finds the links between John's disciples and the Pharisees more substantial, although it cannot be assumed that John was a Pharisee himself.[21] She stands at variance with Webb and Dapaah in denying that John started a significant movement.[22] She accepts that Jesus was a disciple of John, but this was a matter of convenience, considered necessary prior to immersion; it did not initiate him into John's disciples.[23] So Jesus went through John's "baptismal preparation classes," but not any further training for a ministry comparable to John's.

Taylor has made a useful contribution to the literature on the Baptist. Situated midway between Webb's reluctance to build upon the sources and Murphy O'Connor's profusion of new theories (see below), she offers a common-sense analysis of her subject.

Published in 2018, **Joel Marcus's** book *John the Baptist in History and Theology* swims against the tide of recent scholarly thought concerning the Baptist in several respects. After an introductory consideration of criteria for historicity and sources, Marcus introduces his "key thesis," that serious competition between followers of the Baptist and followers of Jesus from the first century onwards affected the presentation of John in the Gospels.[24] Marcus devotes chapter 1 to it. In chapter 2 Marcus expounds his belief that the Baptist had formerly belonged to the Qumran sect.[25] Although he admits that the evidence for this is circumstantial, he lists no fewer than twelve fundamental similarities between John and Qumran.[26] In fairness he also lists five differences.[27] It is interesting that Marcus does not allude to Hutchinson's paper arguing against John's connection with Qumran. He adds three more reasons to those that Brownlee suggested for John's break with Qumran; one involves Qumran's attitude to Gentiles; he cites Matt 3:7–10 as evidence that John had greater sympathy for Gentiles than Qumran had.[28] He explores at length the OT plant imagery underlying this

---

21. Taylor, *John*, 319.
22. Taylor, *John*, 320.
23. Taylor, *John*, 321.
24. Marcus, *John*, 9.
25. Marcus, *John*, 27.
26. Marcus, *John*, 28–33.
27. Marcus, *John*, 33f.
28. Marcus, *John*, 38.

passage. Another factor was his dawning consciousness of his own eschatological role.[29]

In chapter 3 Marcus argues that John claimed to be the eschatological Elijah and forerunner as reflected in the synoptics; his denial of that identity in John 1:19–21 is the product of Johannine theology.[30] The description of John's clothing in Mark and Matthew reflects a historical memory of John deliberately dressing like Elijah. Marcus also sees further similarities with Elijah in John's settling of disputes and in his association with the Jordan. Baptism is the subject of Marcus's fourth chapter. He discusses the connections between baptism, repentance, and the forgiveness of sins, including Josephus's version and the Qumran Community Rule. All four gospels contrast John's water baptism with a coming baptism in the Holy Spirit and (in Q) fire. This may be a tendency of Christians to claim sole possession of the Spirit, to the detriment of John.[31] Did John's baptism cleanse ritual impurity (so Joan Taylor) or bring forgiveness of sins (so Jonathan Klawans)?[32] Was John's baptism a once-for-all experience or repeated?

Chapter 5 considers the relationship between John and Jesus. All four Gospels have a saying in which John contrasts his baptism in water with the baptism of a superior "coming one" whom the writers understand to be Jesus.[33] But it is not certain that he talking about Jesus; his words are typical of prophecy. "The one coming after me" (John 1:15) could refer to Jesus as a disciple of John.[34] Marcus finds evidence for the competition theory in John 4:2 where we see attempts to suppress the memory that Jesus himself baptized, because this makes him too like John.[35] Nevertheless Jesus did baptize, first as John's emissary and later independently. If John thought of himself as Elijah, he may have thought of Jesus as Elisha, his protégé. But was Jesus John's successor or did rivalry develop between them? Jesus' saying in Matt 11:7–11 and Luke 7:24–28 is ambivalent: John is more than a prophet and one of the greatest men of all time but less than the least of Jesus' own disciples.[36] Marcus explores parallels in other religions.

29. Marcus, *John*, 45.

30. Marcus, *John*, 47–49.

31. Marcus, *John*, 66.

32. Marcus, *John*, 74.

33. Marcus, *John*, 81f.

34. Marcus, *John*, 85.

35. Marcus, *John*, 86.

36. Marcus, *John*, 90.

In chapter 6 Marcus explores relations between John and Herod Antipas. The synoptics and Josephus both describe Antipas's execution of John. He sees parallels with Pilate's execution of Jesus.[37] Josephus is probably right that Antipas had good cause to fear the revolutionary tendencies of the movement that the Baptist spawned. Marcus draws parallels from medieval history. Next he explores Antipas's Jewish identity, pointing out that he probably would not have lasted as tetrarch for forty-three years if he had outraged public opinion.[38] He gives examples of Antipas's piety. Next he explores the principle that an attack on a ruler's marriage may be a veiled threat; he provides examples from subsequent history. He considers the Q saying in Matt 11:12f which may associate the Baptist with militant tendencies. But there is also evidence that John was a pacifist.

A comprehensive assemblage of appendices covers: (i) the chronology of John's life, (ii) the possibility that Josephus's account of John is a Christian interpolation, (iii) a database of source information, (iv) whether John was from a priestly background, (v) the identity of the "others" in Josephus's account of John, (vi) Knut Backhaus's alternative interpretation of Acts 19:1–7 (in which Paul in Ephesus preaches to followers of John who are ignorant of Jesus), (vii) the "Day Baptists" (a description applied to John in the Pseudo-Clementine *Homilies*), (viii) John the Baptist's use of Isa 40:3, (ix) John the Baptist in the Slavonic version of Josephus's *Jewish War*, (x) apocalyptic belief and perfectionism, and (xi) the meaning of "purification" in John 3:25.

Professor Marcus is to be commended on producing a book about the Baptist that is not over-long or over-technical and that is not afraid to run counter to the main stream of contemporary thought. It explores details that other authors have (perhaps deliberately) neglected. As such it is a valuable reference tool for researchers.

John's Relationship with Jesus

Jerome Murphy-O'Connor's paper *John the Baptist and Jesus: History and Hypotheses* was originally delivered at the 44th General Meeting of the Society for New Testament Scholars held in Dublin in 1989 and subsequently published in *New Testament Studies*, 36 (1990), 359–374. It draws heavily on Josef Ernst's *Johannes der Taufer, Interpretation – Geschichte*

---

37. Marcus, *John*, 99.
38. Marcus, *John*, 103.

– *Wirkungsgeschichte,*[39] which Murphy-O'Connor considered thorough, but with some blind spots.

The paper explores John's relationship with Jesus, raising more questions than it answers, all inviting further investigation. Murphy-O'Connor follows much of recent scholarship in accepting that Jesus' career began as a disciple of the Baptist.[40] Furthermore, he treats the Fourth Gospel as a historical account rather than theological reflection, although at times his interpretations are perhaps more literal than the evangelist intended. More plausible is his suggestion that John was arrested in Galilee and Jesus left Judea for Galilee not for fear of the Pharisees (as John 4:1–3 implies) but to continue John's unfinished ministry there.

This paper is unlikely to suggest answers to questions that the reader had been considering. It is more likely to make the reader question what previously seemed well established; it is a fertile seed bed for further studies. As its title includes the word *Hypotheses*, it is reasonable for it to include the hypothetical: it is, after all, "doing what it says on the box."

Daniel S. Dapaah's book *The Relationship between John the Baptist and Jesus of Nazareth: A Critical Study*, published in 2005, appears to be the only scholarly book devoted to this relationship. After the customary introductory material including an analysis of the gospel traditions and the historical Jesus quest, Dapaah first considers John's origins in the light of the Qumran Community and then moves on to the relationship that is the subject of the work. He devotes a chapter each to the proclamation of John, John and Jesus as the two Baptists, and Jesus' tribute to John. Like Webb, Dapaah concludes that John began a significant movement; moreover, he postulates that rivalry between the early church and John's followers, who of course regarded Jesus as subservient to John, was responsible for the NT writers' tendency to emphasize Jesus' independence of John and minimize the continuity between them.[41]

The work is briefer than Webb's, but this is not surprising as it is a more specialized study. It is difficult to avoid the conclusion that Dapaah is more interested in baptism—and in particular the connection between the baptism practiced by John and Jesus and Christian initiation—than in the relationship between the two "Baptists," even though that is the work's title.

---

39. BZNW 53; Berlin/New York: De Gruyter, 1989.

40. Murphy-O'Connor, *John*, 362.

41. Dapaah, *Relationship*, 143.

Bibliography

Amos, Roger. *Hypocrites or Heroes? The Paradoxical Portrayal of the Pharisees in the New Testament*, Eugene: Wipf and Stock, 2015.

Arndt, William F. and F. Wilbur Gingrich. *A Greek-English Lexicon of the New Testament and Other Early Christian Literature* (Second Edition Revised and Augmented by F. Wilbur Gingrich and Frederick W. Danker from Walter Bauer's Fifth Edition, 1958), Chicago: University of Chicago Press, 1979.

Badham, Paul. "The Contemporary Relevance of the Just War Tradition in Christianity," *Modern Believing* 48 No 2 (2007) 25–33.

Baird, William. *History of New Testament Research*, Minneapolis: Fortress, 2003.

Barrett, C. K. *The Gospel According to St John*, London: Society for Promoting Christian Knowledge, 1978.

Barth, G. "Matthew's Understanding of the Law." In *Tradition and Interpretation in Matthew*, edited by G. Bornkamm, G. Barth, and H. J. Held, 58–164. Philadelphia: Westminster, 1963.

Bauckham, Richard, *Jesus and the Eyewitnesses: The Gospels as Eyewitness Testimony*, Grand Rapids: Eerdmans, 2006.

Beasley-Murray, G. R. *Word Biblical Commentary: John*, Nashville: Thomas Nelson, 1999.

Betz, Otto. "Was John the Baptist an Essene?" in Shanks, H. (ed), *Understanding the Dead Sea Scrolls*, New York: Vintage, 1993.

Blomberg, Craig L. *Neither Poverty nor Riches*, Nottingham: Apollos, 1999.

Bond, Helen K. *The Historical Jesus: A Guide for the Perplexed*, London: Bloomsbury T. & T. Clark, 2012.

Brown, Colin. "What Was John the Baptist Doing?", *Bulletin for Biblical Research*, 7 (1997), 37–50.

Brown, Raymond E. *The Birth of the Messiah*, New York: Bantam Doubleday Dell, 1993.

Brownlee, W. H. "John the Baptist in the New Light of Ancient Scrolls." In *The Scrolls and the New Testament*, edited by Krister Stendahl, 33–53. New York: Crossroad, 1992.

Bultmann, Rudolf. *The History of the Synoptic Tradition* (English translation by Marsh, John), Oxford: Basil Blackwell, 1972.

Caird, G. B. *The Gospel of St Luke*, Harmondsworth: Penguin, 1963.

Charlesworth, James H. "The Historical Jesus in the Fourth Gospel: A Paradigm Shift?," *Journal for the Study of the Historical Jesus,* 8 (2010), 3–46.

———. "The Temple, Purity, and the Background to Jesus' Death," in *Revista Catalana De Teologia*, 33 No 2 (2008), 395–442.

Charlesworth, James H. and Mordechai Aviam. "Reconstructing First-Century Galilee: Reflections on Ten Major Problems." In *Jesus Research: New Methodologies and Perceptions – The Second Princeton-Prague Symposium on Jesus Research, Princeton 2007*, edited by James H. Charlesworth, 103–137. Grand Rapids: Eerdmans, 2013.

Chilton, Bruce D. "Jesus and the Repentance of E. P. Sanders," *Tyndale Bulletin*, 39 (1988), 1–19.

Cranfield, C. E. B. *The Gospel according to St Mark*, Cambridge: Cambridge University Press, 1966.

Crenshaw, James L. *Education in Ancient Israel: Across the Deadening Silence*, New York: Doubleday, 1998.

Crossan, J. D. *The Historical Jesus: The Life of a Mediterranean Jewish Peasant*, New York: HarperCollins, 1991.

Crossley, James G. *Why Christianity Happened: A Sociohistorical Account of Christian Origins (26–50CE)*, Louisville: Westminster John Knox, 2006.

Culpepper, R. A. "Education." In *International Standard Bible Encyclopedia (Revised Edition)* as packaged in *PC Study Bible version 5*, Seattle: Biblesoft, 2008.

Dapaah, D. S. *The Relationship between John the Baptist and Jesus of Nazareth: A Critical Study*, Lanham: University Press of America, 2005.

Davies, W. D. and D. C. Allison, *A Critical and Exegetical Commentary on the Gospel According to Saint Matthew*, London: T. & T. Clark, 1988, 1991 and 1997.

Deines, R. "The Pharisees Between 'Judaisms' and 'Common Judaism.'" In *Justification and Variegated Nomism: Vol 1: The Complexities of Second Temple Judaism*, edited by D. A. Carson, P. T. O'Brien, and M. A. Seifrid, 443–504. Tübingen: Mohr Siebeck/ Grand Rapids: Baker Academic, 2001.

Dodd, C. H. *The Parables of the Kingdom* (Revised Edition), London: Collins, 1961.

Donaldson, T. L. "Zealot." In *International Standard Bible Encyclopedia (Revised Edition)* as packaged in *PC Study Bible version 5*, Seattle: Biblesoft, 2008.

Downing, F. Gerald. "Deeper Reflections on the Jewish Cynic Jesus," *Journal of Biblical Literature*, 117 (1998), 97–104.

Dunn, J. D. G. *Jesus' Call to Discipleship*, Cambridge: Cambridge University Press, 1992.

Eddy, Paul Rhodes. "Jesus as Diogenes? Reflections on the Cynic Jesus Thesis," *Journal of Biblical Literature*, 115 (1996), 449–469.

Edwards, Douglas R. "First Century Urban/Rural Relations in Lower Galilee; Exploring the Archeological and Literary Evidence." In *Society of Biblical Literature Seminar Papers*, edited by David J. Lull, 169–182. Atlanta: Scholars, 1988.

France, R. T. *The Gospel of Matthew, The New International Commentary on the New Testament*, Grand Rapids: Eerdmans, 2007.

Freyne, Seán. *Galilee from Alexander the Great to Hadrian: A Study of Second Temple Judaism*, Wilmington: Michael Glazier, 1980.

———. *Jesus, a Jewish Galilean; a new reading of the Jesus-story*, London: T. & T. Clark International, 2004.

Goodman, Martin. *Mission and Conversion: Proselytizing in the Religious History of the Roman Empire*, Oxford: Clarendon, 1994.

Glancy, Jennifer. *Slavery in Early Christianity*, Minneapolis: Fortress, 2006.

Gray, Ilka Knüppel. "What can the Archaeology of Sepphoris Reveal about the Historical Jesus?" Paper presented in "Archaeology of the New Testament," Hebrew University, Jerusalem, 2015. Available from the website Academia.edu.

Hagner, D. A. *Word Biblical Commentary: Matthew*, Dallas: Word, 1995.

Harrison, John, "Weeds: Jesus' Parable and Economic and Political Threats to the Poor in Roman Galilee," *Stone-Campbell Journal*, 18 (Spring 2015), 73–88.

Heitmüller, Wilhelm. *Taufe und Abendmahl bei Paulus: Darstellung und Religionsgeschichliche Beleuchtung* (Gottingen: Vandenhoeck & Ruprecht, 1903).

Hengel, Martin. *Judaism and Hellenism*, London: SCM, 1974.

Hester, H. D. "Socio-Rhetorical Criticism and the Parable of the Tenants," *Journal for the Study of the New Testament*, 45 (1992), 27–57.

Horsley, Richard. *Jesus and the Politics of Roman Palestine*, Columbia: University of South Carolina Press, 2014.

———. *The Prophet Jesus and the Renewal of Israel*, Grand Rapids: Eerdmans, 2012.

Hutchinson, John C. "Was John the Baptist an Essene from Qumran?" *Bibliotheca Sacra*, 159 (Apr–June 2002), 187–200.

Isbouts, Jean-Pierre. *In the Footsteps of Jesus: A Chronicle of His Life and the Origins of Christianity* (Second Edition), Washington DC: National Geographic, 2017.

Jensen, Morten Hørning. *Herod Antipas in Galilee* (WUNT 2:215), Tübingen: Mohr Siebeck, 2010.

———. "Herod Antipas in Galilee: Friend or Foe of the Historical Jesus?", *Journal for the Study of the Historical Jesus*, 5 (2007), 7–32.

———. "Purity and Politics in Herod Antipas's Galilee: The Case for Religious Motivation," *Journal for the Study of the Historical Jesus*, 11 (2013), 3–34.

Jeremias, J. *New Testament Theology: Part One: The Proclamation of Jesus*, London: SCM, 1971.

Johansson, Daniel. "The Dichotomy of Judaism and Hellenism Revisited: Roots and Reception of the Gospel," *Concordia Theological Quarterly*, 80 (2016), 101–112.

Jossa, Giorgio. *Jews or Christians?* (WUNT 202), Tübingen: Mohr Siebeck, 2006.

Keener, Craig S. *A Commentary on the Gospel of Matthew*, Grand Rapids: Eerdmans, 1999.

———. *The Gospel of John: A Commentary*, Peabody: Henrickson, 2003.

Kuhn, Karl Georg. "The Two Messiahs of Aaron and Israel." In *The Scrolls and the New Testament*, edited by Krister Stendahl, 54–64. New York: Crossroad, 1992.

Levine, Lee (Ed.). *Ancient Synagogues Revealed*, Jerusalem: Israel Exploration Society, 1981.

Liddell, Henry George, and Robert Scott. *A Greek-English Lexicon*, Oxford: Clarendon, 1996.

Maccoby, H. *Jesus the Pharisee*, London: SCM, 2003.

Manson, T. W. *The Sayings of Jesus*, London: SCM, 1949.

Marcus, Joel. *John the Baptist in History and Theology*, Columbia: University of South Carolina Press, 2018

Meier, John P. "The Historical Jesus and the Historical Herodians," *Journal of Biblical Literature*, 119 No 4 (Winter 2000), 740–746.

Meyer, Ben F. *The Aims of Jesus*, Eugene: Pickwick, 2002.

Mézange, Christophe. "Simon le Zélote Était-il un Révolutionnaire?," *Biblica*, 81 (2000), 489–506.

Morris, N. *The Jewish School: An Introduction to the History of Jewish Education*, London: Eyre and Spottiswoode, 1937.

Motyer, Alec. *The Prophecy of Isaiah*, Leicester: Inter-Varsity, 1993.

Murphy-O'Connor, Jerome. "John the Baptist and Jesus: History and Hypotheses," *New Testament Studies*, 36 (1990), 359–374.

Nolland, John. *The New International Greek Testament Commentary: The Gospel of Matthew*, Grand Rapids: Wm B. Eerdmans and Bletchley: The Paternoster Press, 2005.

———. *Word Biblical Commentary: Luke*, Nashville: Thomas Nelson, 2000.

Overman, J. A. "Who Were the First Urban Christians? Urbanization in Galilee in the First Century." In *Society of Biblical Literature Seminar Papers*, edited by David J. Lull, 160–168. Atlanta: Scholars, 1988.

Philo. *De Vita Contemplativa* (English text). Available on the website: http://www.earlychristianwritings.com/yonge/book34.html.

Przybylski, Benno. *Righteousness in Matthew and his World of Thought*, Cambridge: Cambridge University Press, 1980.

Ramelli, Ilaria. "Origen, Patristic Philosophy and Christian Platonism: Rethinking the Christianisation of Hellenism," *Vigiliae Christianae*, 63 (2009), 217–263.

Reed, Jonathan. *Archaeology and the Galilean Jesus*, Harrisburg: Trinity, 2000.

Rivkin, E. *A Hidden Revolution*, Nashville: Abingdon, 1978.

Robinson, J. A. T. "The Baptism of John and the Qumran Community: Testing a Hypothesis," *Harvard Theological Review*, Vol. 50, No. 3 (July 1957), pp. 175–191.

Saldarini, A. J. *Pharisees, Scribes and Sadducees in Palestinian Society*, Wilmington: Michael Glazier, Inc, 1988. Republished by Grand Rapids: Eerdmans, 2001.

Sanders, E. P. *The Historical Figure of Jesus*, New York: Penguin, 1993.

———. *Jesus and Judaism*, London: SCM, 1985.

———. *Judaism: Practice and Belief 63 BCE–66 CE*, London: SCM, 1992.

Schäfer, Peter. *Jesus in the Talmud*, Princeton: Princeton University Press, 2007.

Schottroff, Luise. *The Parables of Jesus*, Minneapolis: Fortress, 2006.

Schröter, Jens. "The Gospels as Eyewitness Testimony? A Critical Examination of Richard Bauckham's *Jesus and the Eyewitnesses*," *Journal for the Study of the New Testament*, 31 (2008), 195–209.

Schumer, Nathan. "The Population Size of Sepphoris: Rethinking Urbanization in Early and Middle Roman Galilee." Undated paper available from the website Academia. edu.

Schweitzer, Albert. *The Quest of the Historical Jesus* (English translation by Montgomery, W.), London: Adam and Charles Black, 1911.

Smith, Morton. *Clement of Alexandria and a Secret Gospel of Mark*, Cambridge MA: Harvard University Press, 1973.

———. "The Dead Sea Sect in Relation to Ancient Judaism," *New Testament Studies* 7, 1960–61, 347–60.

Stoddart, Eric. "(In)visibility, Surveillance, and Privacy," *Cosmologics Magazine* (a project of the Science, Religion, and Culture program at Harvard Divinity School). Posted November 2014. Available on http://cosmologicsmagazine.com/eric-stoddart-invisibility-surveillance-and-privacy/

Storkey, Alan. *Jesus and Politics*, Grand Rapids: Baker Academic, 2005.

Strange, J. F. "Nazareth." In *ABD* 4:1050–51.

———. "Recent discoveries at Sepphoris and their relevance for biblical research," *Neotestamentica*, 34 No.1 (2000), 125–141.

Taylor, Joan. *John the Baptist within Second Temple Judaism: a Historical Study*, London: Society for Promoting Christian Knowledge, 1997.

———. "Scrolls and Hellenistic Jewish Literature." In *T&T Clark Companion to the Dead Sea Scrolls*, edited by George J. Brooke and Charlotte Hempel, 139–155. London: T. & T. Clark, 2019.

Theissen, Gerd, and Dagmar Winter. *The Quest for the Plausible Jesus* (English translation by Boring, M. Eugene), Louisville: Westminster John Knox, 2002.

Vermes, Geza. *The Authentic Gospel of Jesus*, London: Penguin, 2004.

———. *Jesus the Jew*, London: SCM, 1973.

Wassên, Cecilia. "Daily Life." In *T&T Clark Companion to the Dead Sea Scrolls*, edited by George J. Brooke and Charlotte Hempel, 547–558. London: T. & T. Clark, 2019.

———. 'The Jewishness of Jesus and ritual purity,' *Scripta Instituti Donneriani Aboensis*, 27 (2016), 11–36.

Webb, Robert L. *John the Baptizer and Prophet: A Socio-Historical Study*, Eugene: Wipf & Stock, 2006.

Weiss, Zeev. *The Sepphoris Synagogue; Deciphering an Ancient Message through Its Archaeological and Socio-Historical Context*, Jerusalem: Israel Exploration Society, 2005.

Westermann, Claus. *Isaiah 40–66*, London: SCM, 1969.

Wright, N. T. *Jesus and the Victory of God*, London: Society for Promoting Christian Knowledge, 1996.

Wright, Stephen I. *Jesus the Storyteller*, London: Society for Promoting Christian Knowledge, 2014.